CAMPBELL'S POTPOURRI II OF QUIZ BOWL QUESTIONS

REVISED EDITION

By John P. Campbell

Campbell's High School/College Quiz Book

Campbell's Potpourri I of Quiz Bowl Questions

Campbell's Potpourri II of Quiz Bowl Questions

Campbell's Middle School Quiz Book #1

Campbell's Potpourri III of Quiz Bowl Questions

Campbell's Middle School Quiz Book #2

Campbell's Elementary School Quiz Book #1

Campbell's 2001 Quiz Questions

Campbell's Potpourri IV of Quiz Bowl Questions

Campbell's Middle School Quiz Book #3

The 500 Famous Quotations Quiz Book

CAMPBELL'S POTPOURRI II OF QUIZ BOWL QUESTIONS

by John P. Campbell

Revised Edition

PATRICK'S PRESS
Columbus, Georgia

Printed in the United States of America

Campbell, John P., 1942-
Campbell's Potpourri II of quiz bowl questions.

Rev. ed.

   Includes index.
   Summary: Questions and answers on a wide-range of topics, such as history, literature, geography, sports, the Bible, science, art, mythology, and religion, are arranged into twenty-five "rounds" and assigned points.
   1. Questions and answers. [1. Questions and answers]
I. Title II. Title: Campbell's Potpourri 2 of quiz bowl questions.
III. Title: Potpourri II of quiz bowl questions.
IV. Title: Potpourri two of quiz bowl questions.
AG195.C289a   1991   O31'.02

   ISBN (International Standard Book Number): 0-944322-04-2

First Edition, First Printing, October 1984
Revised Edition, First Printing, March 1991

ACKNOWLEDGMENTS

I am once again very indebted to Rinda Brewbaker for taking my material and turning it into readable prose.

I want to thank Keith Abney, Emory University senior and member of his school's College Bowl Team, for his fine research in verifying most of the questions and answers.

I am also thankful to Dr. Jay Cliett, Department of Mathematics Coordinator at Georgia Southwestern College and GSW's High School Academic Bowl and Mathematic's Coordinator and College Bowl Coach, for his help in reading most of the material and making valuable suggestions.

I appreciate the help of Mona Crawford, Columbus College student, for her help in proofreading most of the material. I also thank Ruth Lieberman for her proofreading assistance.

I want to thank my mother, Mrs. John Campbell, for her support.

I thank the following for their corrections and suggestions: *American Literature*: Jack Norton, Georgia Southwestern College; *Ancient* and *European History*: Richard L. Baringer, Georgia Southwestern College; and Dr. Hugh I. Rodgers, Columbus College; *Art* and *Architecture*: Dr. Ben Paskus, Georgia Southwestern College; *Astronomy*: Dr. Phil Manker, Georgia Southwestern College; *Bible* and *Religion*: Charles W. Blaker, Brookstone School; and Father Donal Keohane, Pacelli High School; *Biology*: Dr. Jack Carter, Georgia Southwestern College; *Chemistry*: Dr. Wayne Counts, Georgia Southwestern College; *English Grammar*: Rinda Brewbaker; *English* and *World Literature*: Dr. Allen D. Towery, Georgia Southwestern College; *Mathematics*: Dr. Jay Cliett; and Pamela Coffield, Brookstone School; *Music"* Dr. Duke Jackson, Georgia Southwestern College; *Physics*: Dr. Frank B. Jones, Georgia Southwestern College; *Political Science*: Dr. William L. Chappell, Jr., Columbus College; and Kent M. Sole, Georgia Southwestern College; *U.S. History*: Dr. Frank M. Lowrey, Georgia Southwestern College; and Dr. John S. Murzyn, Columbus College.

I also thank Jen Stewart of Central High School, Mary Starke of Chavala High School, Helen Johnson of Smiths Station High School, and their quiz bowl team members for the help they provided.

I would also like to thank Eileen Offley for her typing and Kim Baxley for the book's indexing. I also thank Cornerstone Images for their typesetting services.

To

Sequels,

II's,

Follow-ups,

Second Tries,

Continuations,

Second Volumes,

Successors,

And Other Close Encounters of the Second Kind.

PREFACE

This book is intended as quiz bowl material not only for the coach of an Academic Bowl team to use in conducting practices but also for individual team members to use as study material. The complete index complements this intention as the users of this book are able to find quickly material they wish to review.

This book was revised primarily because of the difficult and sometimes obscure nature of some of the questions that were intended to reach a college quiz group. In revising this work for the high school level, the questions were changed to a toss-up/bonus format like that of *Potpourri III* and *Potpourri IV*.

Your suggestions and comments will be appreciated. Please send them to me care of PATRICK'S PRESS, Box 5189, Columbus, Georgia, 31906.

John Campbell

CONTENTS

ROUND ONE

1) TOSS-UP. 10 points.

What name is given to a literary work complete in itself but one that continues a story line begun in an earlier work, or what *Campbell's Potpourri II* could be considered?

Answer: A sequel.

1) BONUS. 20 points. 5 points each.

Identify the following groups, each of which begins with the word *Black*.

1) The Serbian nationalist society that assassinated Francis Ferdinand in 1914, or the lawless secret society organized by Sicilians and Italian-Americans in the United States (especially in New York) in the early 20th century (from the Italian for *La Mano Nera*)

2) The members of a militant religious organization of American blacks advocating the teachings of Islam, especially self-discipline, self-denial, and racial separation

3) The members of a militant American black organization advocating black nationalism

4) The members of a Fascist organization, especially the Italian Fascist militia, so called from an item of clothing they wore

Answer: 1) **Black Hand**
2) **Black Muslims**
3) **Black Panthers (accept Black Nationalists)**
4) **Black Shirts (Blackshirts).**

2) TOSS-UP. 10 points.

What was the name of the little girl born to Ananias and Ellinor (or Eleanor) on August 18, 1587, on Roanoke Island, in what was then Virginia? She was the first English child to be born in America.

Answer: Virginia Dare.

2) BONUS. 20 points. 5 points each.

Identify each American from the following nicknames and biographical data.
1) He lived from 1801 to 1872, was sometimes called "Uncle Billy," and served as Secretary of State under Presidents Lincoln and Johnson.
2) He lived from 1837 to 1876 and was known as "Wild Bill."
3) He lived from 1846 to 1917 and was called "Buffalo Bill."
4) He lived from 1859 to 1881 and was known as "Billy the Kid."

Answer: 1) William Henry Seward
2) James Butler Hickok
3) William Frederick Cody
4) William H. Bonney (real name was Henry McCarty / McCarthy; also called Kid Antrim).

3) TOSS-UP. 10 points.

The French influence on the American language has been significant, *n'est-ce pas?* Give the French phrase that in English means "isn't that so."

Answer: *N'est-ce pas?* (literally, is it not?).

3) BONUS. 20 points. All or nothing.

Identify each of the following as animal, vegetable, or mineral: gold, frankincense, and myrrh.

Answer: Gold is a mineral, frankincense is vegetable, and myrrh is vegetable.

4) TOSS-UP. 10 points.

In which U.S. capital city is the arena known as the Omni located?

Answer: Atlanta.

4) BONUS. 20 points. 5 points each.

Identify the U.S. city in which each of the following arenas is located.
1) Pauley Pavilion
2) Madison Square Garden
3) The Spectrum
4) The Forum

Answer: 1) Los Angeles (California, on the campus of UCLA)
2) New York (New York)

    3) **Philadelphia (Pennsylvania)**
    4) **Inglewood (accept Los Angeles; California).**

5) TOSS-UP. 10 points.

To which knight of the Round Table did Alfred, Lord Tennyson ascribe these lines, "My good blade carves the casques of men, / My tough lance thrusteth sure, / My strength is as the strength of ten / Because my heart is pure"?

Answer: Sir Galahad.

5) BONUS. 20 points. 5 points each.

Complete each of the following taken from a Lewis Carroll work.
1) The title *The Hunting of the* _____
2) "What's the good of _____'s North Poles and Equators, / Tropics, Zones, and _____ Lines? / So the _____ would cry: and the crew would reply, / "They are merely conventional signs!"

Answer: 1) *Snark*
          2) "Mercator" / "Meridian" / "bellman."

6) TOSS-UP. 10 points.

Identify the astronomical phenomenon first noticed in 1836 and named after a British astronomer. This phenomenon is defined as "brilliant spots of sunlight shining through valleys on the rim of the moon just after a total eclipse of the sun."

Answer: Baily's Beads (after Francis Baily).

6) BONUS. 20 points. 5 points each.

Answer each of the following.
1) Who said and in which book, "And Oh, Aunt Em! I'm so glad to be at home again!"
2) To which land did this speaker travel and from which state was she transported?

Answer: 1) **Dorothy in** *The Wizard of Oz* **(by L. Frank Baum)**
          2) **Land of the Munchkins and Kansas.**

7) TOSS-UP. 10 points.

What is the mathematical name for a path traced out by a pebble caught in the tread of a bicycle wheel tire if the cycle is ridden in a straight line on a level surface?

Answer: Cycloid.

7) BONUS. 20 points. 10 points each.

Identify each of the following.
1) The name of the German parliament building whose burning on February 27, 1933, was blamed on the Communists but probably carried out by the Nazis
2) The name for the "empire" the Nazis established on March 23, 1933, known as the "National Government of the Third_____"

Answer: 1) *Reichstag*
            2) *Reich.*

8) TOSS-UP. 10 points.

The teaching of Charles Darwin's theory of evolution in a high school classroom in 1925 was a cause célèbre. In which state did a trial over this matter take place in the town of Dayton?

Answer: Tennessee.

8) BONUS. 20 points. 5 points each.

Identify each of the following concerning the 1925 trial.
1) The high school teacher who taught this theory
2) The name of the orator and statesman, a believer in religious fundamentalism, who assisted the prosecuting attorney
3) The name of the defense attorney who defended the teacher
4) The nickname including an animal's name by which this trial was known

Answer: 1) John Thomas Scopes (Scopes lost and was fined $100, but the law was repealed about 30 years later)
            2) William Jennings Bryan (he died in Dayton five days after the trial)
            3) Clarence Seward Darrow
            4) "Monkey Trial."

9) TOSS-UP. 10 points.

American Archibald McNeal Willard painted the rather famous and much imitated *The Spirit of '76*, a painting of 3 people marching across a field. What 2 musical instruments are featured in this painting?

Answer: Drum and fife (2 drummers and a fifer).

9) **BONUS.** 20 points. 5 points each.

Identify each of the following concerning Greek mythology.
1) The character who killed his father and married his mother
2) The name of his father and his mother
3) The city of which this character was king

Answer: 1) Oedipus
           2) King Laius and Queen Jocasta
           3) Thebes.

10) **TOSS-UP.** 10 points.

The symbols for this Canadian city, nicknamed the "Foothills City," are the Rockies, a buffalo, a horse, and a steer. Name this largest city in Alberta, famous for its Exhibition and Stampede.

Answer: Calgary.

10) **BONUS.** 30 points. 10 points each.

Name the 3 counties in Delaware.

Answer: Kent, New Castle, and Sussex.

11) **TOSS-UP.** 10 points.

Which character in which novel by Charles Dickens is an eccentric lady who, having been stood up on the morning of her wedding day, often wears her wedding dress in a gloomy, locked house with all the clocks still set on the day her bridegroom failed to appear?

Answer: Miss Havisham in *Great Expectations*.

11) **BONUS.** 30 points. 5 points each.

Identify the character described, the novel, and the author for each of the following.
1) The poor peasant who is imprisoned for 19 years for stealing a loaf of bread and who after his escape is relentlessly pursued by police officer Javert
2) The shy, sensitive youth with a clubfoot, who has an unhappy love affair with Mildred Rogers, a waitress, but studies medicine and

settles down as a married country doctor

Answer: 1) Jean Valjean in *Les Misérables* by Victor Hugo
2) Philip Carey in *Of Human Bondage* by W. Somerset Maugham.

12) TOSS-UP. 10 points.

Although he crashed on his first solo flight, he became the squadron leader of a combat group known as the "Flying Circus." By what nickname was German aviator and World War I ace Manfred von Richthofen known?

Answer: The Red Baron.

12) BONUS. 20 points. 5 points each.

Identify each of the following concerning the Heisman Memorial Trophy.
1) The club in New York City which presents this trophy to the nation's outstanding college football player
2) The 1945 winner from Army or the 1946 winner from Army
3) The 1958 winner from Army
4) The 1960 winner from Navy or the 1963 winner from Navy

Answer: 1) Downtown Athletic Club
2) Felix Blanchard or Glenn Davis
3) Pete Dawkins
4) Joe Bellino or Roger Staubach.

13) TOSS-UP. 10 points.

Name either the early 20th century U.S. President whose policies were referred to as "cowboy diplomacy" or his successor, whose policies were known as "Dollar Diplomacy."

Answer: (Theodore) Roosevelt's or (William H.) Taft's.

13) BONUS. 20 points. 5 points each.

Identify each of the following concerning Halley's comet.
1) The famous American author and humorist who was born during the year of Halley's comet in the 19th century and died (as he predicted) during the year of its reappearance in the 20th century
2) The years of the humorist's birth and death
3) The first name of Halley, the English scientist who first predicted the 76-year cycle of the comet

Answer: 1) Mark Twain (Samuel Clemens)
2) 1835 and 1910
3) Edmond.

14) TOSS-UP. 10 points.

Which novel by which author is subtitled *Life in the Woods*?

Answer: *Walden* by Henry David Thoreau.

14) BONUS. 20 points. 5 points each.

Identify not only the title but also the author of the novels with the following subtitles.
1) *A Tale of the Christ*
2) *The Children's Crusade*
3) *Life Among the Lowly*
4) *The Silver Skates*

Answer: 1) *Ben Hur* by Lewis Wallace
2) *Slaughterhouse-Five* by Kurt Vonnegut
3) *Uncle Tom's Cabin* by Harriet Beecher Stowe
4) *Hans Brinker* by Mary Elizabeth Mapes Dodge.

15) TOSS-UP. 10 points.

Who was the Spanish dictator from 1936 to 1975?

Answer: Francisco Franco.

15) BONUS. 20 points. 5 points each.

Identify each of the following world leaders.
1) The queen who ruled the United Kingdom of Great Britain and Ireland from 1837 to 1901
2) The leader of Yugoslavia from 1945 to 1980
3) The emperor of Ethiopia from 1930 to 1974
4) The king of France from 1643 to 1715

Answer: 1) Queen Victoria
2) Tito (Josip Broz)
3) Haile Selassie I
4) Louis XIV.

16) TOSS-UP. 10 points.

Name not only the hunchback who is the bellringer of Notre Dame in Victor Hugo's *The Hunchback of Notre Dame* (*Notre Dame de Paris*) but also the Gypsy girl who befriends him.

Answer: Quasimodo and Esmerelda.

16) BONUS. 30 points. 10 points each.

Name the following principal characters in the *Divine Comedy*.
1) The one who is given a tour
2) This person's guide
3) The soul of the beloved of the person on tour

Answer: 1) Dante
     2) Virgil
     3) Beatrice.

17) TOSS-UP. 10 points.

What is the name of the sacred tree of Apollo, the leaves of which he wore for a crown and the leaves of which were woven in wreaths and used by the ancient Greeks to crown contest victors?

Answer: Laurel.

17) BONUS. 20 points. 5 points each.

Identify each of the following concerning plants.
1) The plant whose name means "noble white" in German
2) The 3 most important plant nutrients commonly provided by fertilizers

Answer: 1) Edelweiss
     2) Nitrogen, phosphorus, and potassium, usually expressed in terms of Nitrogen (N), phosphorus pentoxide (P_2O_5), and potash (K_2O).

18) TOSS-UP. 10 points.

In which palace in which city in The Netherlands is the World Court located?

Answer: Peace Palace (*Vredespaleis*) in The Hague.

18) BONUS. 20 points. 5 points each.

In which country is or was each of the following famous structures located?
1) Escorial

2) Hagia Sophia (Sancta Sophia)
3) Pitti Palace
4) Tuileries

Answer: 1) **Spain (about 30 miles, or 48 kilometers, from Madrid)**
2) **Turkey (Istanbul; formerly Constantinople)**
3) **Italy (Florence)**
4) **France (Paris).**

19) TOSS-UP. 10 points.

What is the grammatical term for "a word that expresses emotion and has no grammatical relation to other words in the sentence"?

Answer: Interjection.

19) BONUS. 20 points. 10 points each.

Name both the part of speech about which he was talking and the person who said that a rule about it "leads us to the kind of nonsense (impertinence) up with which we should not put."

Answer: Preposition/Winston Churchill (at least attributed to him).

20) TOSS-UP. 10 points.

His slogans in the 1930 campaign were "Share the Wealth" and "Every Man a King." He served as governor from 1928 to 1932 and as U.S. senator from 1932 to 1935. Name this Louisiana man who was nicknamed the "Kingfish."

Answer: Huey Pierce Long (He was elected senator in 1930, but did not take his seat until 1932 because he did not want the Lieutenant Governor to succeed him.)

20) BONUS. 20 points. 5 points each.

Identify each of the following concerned with 20th century spying in the U.S.
1) The State Department official (1936 to 1947) who was accused of being a Communist agent and found guilty on January 21, 1950
2) The confessed former Communist spy who in 1948 accused the State Department official of having passed him military secrets during the 1930's

3) The object in which confidential government "papers" (filmstrips of official government documents) were supposedly hidden on a farm and the state in which this farm was located

Answer: 1) Alger Hiss
2) Whittaker Chambers
3) In a pumpkin (known as the "Pumpkin Papers")/ in Maryland.

21) TOSS-UP. 10 points.

Name the first century Christian "Apostle to the Gentiles," who wrote, "And unto the Jews, I became a Jew, that I might gain the Jews" (I Corinthians 9:20).

Answer: Saint Paul.

21) BONUS. 20 points. 5 points each.

Identify each of the following.
1) The 4 U.S. Presidents whose names have just 4 letters
2) The 4 C's that denote the value of a diamond
3) The 4 writers of the New Testament Gospels
4) The (first) 4 dimensions

Answer: 1) Ford, Polk, Taft, and Bush
2) Cut, carat, clarity, and color
3) Matthew, Mark, Luke, and John
4) Length, width, depth, and time.

22) TOSS-UP. 10 points.

What is the name of what has been called the "greatest manuscript discovery of modern times"? These manuscripts were found by a Bedouin shepherd boy in the Wadi Qûmran (Qumran Valley) in 1947 in caves near the Dead Sea.

Answer: Dead Sea Scrolls.

22) BONUS. 20 points. 5 points each.

Give 4 of the 5 months of the year named after gods and name these gods.

Answer: 1) January for Janus (god of beginnings and endings who had two faces looking in opposite

directions, symbolizing his knowledge of the past and future)
2) March for Mars (god of war for the opening of military campaigns; or for Martius, possibly the god of fecundity as March is the month of the awakening of nature)
3) April for Aphro, short for Aphrodite (goddess of love)
4) May for Jupiter Mayo (god of growth; or for Maiia or Maiius, "big," since plants grow during this time)
5) June for Juno (goddess of marriage, childbirth, and adult life).

23) TOSS-UP. 10 points.

George Cornwallis's surrender at Yorktown and Robert E. Lee's surrender at Appomattox Court House both occurred in which state?

Answer: Virginia.

23) BONUS. 20 points. 5 points each.

Identify each of the following.
1) The beginning date (month, day, and year) of the American Civil War
2) The fort and the South Carolina city where it started
3) The 2 leaders who signed the terms of surrender in the farmhouse of Wilmer McLean at Appomattox Court House in Virginia
4) The date (month, day, and year) the terms of surrender were signed

Answer: 1) April 12, 1861
2) Fort Sumter in Charleston
3) Ulysses S. Grant and Robert E. Lee
4) April 9, 1865.

24) TOSS-UP. 10 points.

What phrase from Revelation 1:8 means "the beginning and the end" and consists of the first and last letters of the Greek alphabet?

Answer: Alpha and Omega.

24) BONUS. 20 points. 5 points each.

Identify the following by spelling each one correctly.
1) The name by which George, John, Paul, and Ringo are known
2) The name of the order of insects which contains the most species
3) The former name for a minor parish officer who kept order in the church of England
4) The last name of American geneticist George Wells _____, who shared with Edward L. Tatum and Joshua Lederberg the 1958 Nobel Prize for physiology or medicine for their discovery that genes act by regulating specific chemical processes

Answer: 1) Beatles
2) beetles
3) beadle
4) Beadle.

25) TOSS-UP. 10 points.

In which cities are the Silverdome and Superdome?

Answer: Pontiac (accept Detroit; Michigan) and New Orleans (Louisiana).

25) BONUS. 20 points. 5 points each.

Identify the city in which each of the following domed stadiums is located.
1) Astrodome
2) Hoosierdome
3) Metrodome (Hubert H. Humphrey Metrodome)
4) Kingdome

Answer: 1) Houston (Texas)
2) Indianapolis (Indiana)
3) Minneapolis (Minnesota)
4) Seattle (Washington).

CATEGORY TOSS-UP. 100 points. 10 points each.

Identify each of the following concerning the Statue of Liberty.
1) The country which gave the 151-foot copper statue to the U.S. in commemoration of the centennial of American independence
2) The designer and sculptor of the statue (from a suggestion by French historian Edouard de Laboulaye)
3) The French or English proper or original name for the statue

4) The person who constructed the supporting iron framework of the statue
5) The U.S. President who dedicated the monument, or the year in which it was dedicated
6) The former name of Liberty Island in New York Harbor on which the statue is located
7) The name of the poem located on a tablet within the pedestal
8) The name of the poet who composed the poem
9) The completion of the poem's well-known lines, "Give me your _____, your_____, / Your _____ yearning to breathe free . . ."
10) The date inscribed on the tablet or on the lawbook held in the statue's left arm

Answer: 1) **France (A model of this statue stands on a bridge over the Seine River in Paris)**
2) **Frédéric Auguste Bartholdi**
3) *La Liberté Éclairant le Monde* **or** *Liberty Enlightening the World*
4) **Alexandre Gustave Eiffel**
5) **Grover Cleveland on October 28, 1886 (the Statue of Liberty was presented to the Minister of the U.S. in Paris, on July 4, 1884, and shipped to the U.S. in May 1885 aboard the French ship *Isère*).**
6) **Bedloe's Island**
7) **"The New Colossus"**
8) **Emma Lazarus**
9) **tired / poor / huddled masses**
10) **July 4, 1776 (the date of the Declaration of Independence).**

ROUND TWO

1) TOSS-UP. 10 points.

What is the astronomical term for "the distance that light traverses in a vacuum in one year at the speed of approximately 299,793 km/sec.," or approximately 6 trillion miles?

Answer: Light-year.

1) BONUS. 20 points. 5 points each.

With which instrument is each of the following musicians most closely identified?
1) Benny Goodman
2) William "Count" Basie
3) Glenn Miller
4) Lawrence Welk

Answer: 1) Clarinet
2) Piano
3) Trombone
4) Accordion.

2) TOSS-UP. 10 points.

Identify the real number indicated by the cube root of –125 (negative 125).

Answer: –5 (negative 5).

2) BONUS. 20 points. 5 points each.

Identify the real number indicated by each of the following.
1) The cube root of 8
2) The cube root of 27
3) The cube root of 64
4) The cube root of 1728

Answer: 1) 2
2) 3

3) 4
4) 12.

3) TOSS-UP. 10 points.

At what location did Franklin Roosevelt meet with Winston Churchill in 1943, Dwight Eisenhower meet with Nikita Khrushchev in 1959, and Jimmy Carter host peace talks with President Anwar al-Sadat of Egypt and Prime Minister Menachem Begin of Israel in 1978?

Answer: Camp David (Maryland; accept Shangri-La, the former name; changed in 1953).

3) BONUS. 20 points. 5 points each.

Identify each of the following U.S. Presidents associated with Buffalo, New York.
1) The one who lived there as a young man and who, after his presidency, returned and was buried there in 1874.
2) The one who was Mayor of the town in 1881.
3) The one who was assassinated there.
4) The one who took the oath of office there in the Ensley Wilcox House.

Answer: 1) Millard Fillmore
2) Grover Cleveland
3) William McKinley
4) Theodore Roosevelt.

4) TOSS-UP. 30 points after the first clue. 20 after the second. 10 after the third.

Who am I?
1) I was born Anna Mary Robertson in Greenwich, Washington County, New York, in 1860.
2) My autobiography, published in 1952, is entitled *My Life's History*.
3) I started painting when I was 76 years old and continued painting until I died in 1961. I was known as "Grandma."

Answer: Grandma Moses.

4) BONUS. 20 points. 5 points each.

Identify each of the following "apple"-related people.
1) The scientist who said he discovered the principle of gravity by

watching an apple fall to the ground
2) The legendary archer who shot an apple off the top of his son's head, and the nationality of this archer
3) The cultivator, John _____, whose name identifies a red apple and in a variant spelling an Apple computer

Answer: 1) **Isaac Newton**
              2) **William Tell / Swiss**
              3) **McIntosh (not Macintosh).**

5) TOSS-UP. 10 points.

What is the name of the strait joining the Aegean Sea with the Sea of Marmara (Marmora) and formerly called the *Hellespont* by the ancient Greeks?

Answer: Dardanelles.

5) BONUS. 20 points. 5 points each.

Identify the body of water between each of the following pairs of cities.
1) Calais and Dover
2) Liverpool and Dublin
3) Tangier and Tarifa
4) Rochester and Toronto

Answer: 1) **Strait of Dover (English Channel)**
              2) **Irish Sea**
              3) **Strait of Gibraltar**
              4) **Lake Ontario.**

6) TOSS-UP. 30 points after the first clue. 20 after the second. 10 after the third.

What's my name?
1) Many people attributed my mental breakdown to my dog Diamond, who knocked over a lighted candle and destroyed several years of accumulated research; but I don't remember owning a dog.
2) I am nicknamed the "Priest of Nature," and I am considered to have ushered in the Age of Reason.
3) In 1687 I published the *Principia* or *Principia Mathematica*.

Answer: Sir Isaac Newton.

6) BONUS. 20 points. 5 points each.

Name any 4 of the 10 novels by Sinclair Lewis in which the leading character's name is used as the title of the book.

Answer: *Babbitt, Dodsworth, Arrowsmith, Elmer Gantry, Cass Timberlane, Ann Vickers, Gideon Planish, Kingsblood Royal, Our Mr. Wrenn,* and *Bethel Merriday.*

7) TOSS-UP. 10 points.

With which country are Leprechauns ("The Little People") and Banshees associated?

Answer: Ireland.

7) BONUS. 20 points. 5 points each.

With which country are the following sets of fairies associated?
1) Korrigans, Courils, and Lutins
2) Trolls and Gnomes
3) Brownies, Silkies, and Pixies
4) Kobolds, Nixies, and Dwarfs

Answer: 1) France
          2) Denmark, Norway, or Sweden
          3) England
          4) Germany.

8) TOSS-UP. 10 points.

Name not only the man in the Bible who was ordered by the Roman guards to carry Jesus' cross to the place of crucifixion but also the town from which he came (Matthew 27:32; Mark 15:21; Luke 23:26).

Answer: Simon of Cyrene.

8) BONUS. 20 points. 10 points each.

For Jews, Christians, and Muslims, Jerusalem is a very holy city; but which 2 cities in Saudi Arabia are more sacred to the Muslims?

Answer: Mecca and Medina (Mecca is the site of the Kaaba, and Medina is the city to which Mohammed fled in 622. His flight is called the Hegira, *(Hijra)*, and Medina was his residence until his death in 632.)

9) TOSS-UP. 10 points.

According to Greek legend, who was the last king of Troy?

Answer: Priam.

9) BONUS. 20 points. All or nothing.

Give the word for "emperor" in each of the following: in ancient Rome, in pre-revolutionary Russia, and in imperial Germany through WWI.

Answer: Caesar / Czar (Tsar) / Kaiser.

10) TOSS-UP. 10 points.

Presidents are called "Accidental Presidents" if they become President upon the death of the person in that office. There have been several "Accidental Presidents," but which of these was the first to serve a second term?

Answer: Theodore Roosevelt.

10) BONUS. 20 points. 5 points each.

Identify each of the following concerned with the 20th century Alger Hiss spy case in the U.S.
1) The U.S. Congressman from California who gained national prominence for his pursuit of a conviction in this case, especially for his investigation into the use of a typewriter
2) The U.S. Senator who gained national prominence in 1950 by charging that Communists had infiltrated the government
3) The state represented by this senator who was "condemned" by the senate in 1954
4) The U.S. President during the late 40's who established a federal board to investigate the loyalty of government employees

Answer: 1) Richard M. Nixon
2) Joseph Raymond McCarthy
3) Wisconsin
4) Harry S Truman.

11) TOSS-UP. 10 points.

What is the name of the area in southwestern South Dakota and in northwestern Nebraska called *les mauvaises terres* by French explorers who found the land bumpy, difficult to travel across, and unfit for cultivation?

Answer: Badlands.

11) **BONUS. 20 points. 5 points each.**

Identify each of the following.
1) The name of the highway that when opened in 1965 became the longest national highway in the world
2) The two Canadian provinces connected by this 5,000-mile highway (8,000 kilometers)
3) The Atlantic Ocean capital in which it begins or the Pacific Ocean capital in which it ends

Answer: 1) Trans-Canada Highway
2) Newfoundland and (Vancouver Island) British Columbia
3) St. John's or Victoria.

12) **TOSS-UP. 10 points.**

Give the month, date, and year that President Roosevelt called the "Day of Infamy," the day Pearl Harbor was attacked by the Japanese.

Answer: December 7, 1941.

12) **BONUS. 20 points. 5 points each.**

Identify each of the following concerning the settlement of Jamestown, Virginia.
1) The English captain who helped establish the first permanent English colony at Jamestown in 1607
2) The Indian chief, the head of a confederacy of tribes in Tidewater Virginia, whose followers supposedly captured this English captain
3) The daughter of the Indian chief who supposedly intervened to save the captain from a ritual execution
4) The man who married this Indian "princess" in 1614 and took her and their son, Thomas, to England in 1615

Answer: 1) Captain John Smith
2) Chief Powhatan (real name was Wahunsonacock)
3) Pocahontas (her name in translation is "The Playful One," her real Indian name is Matoaka, and her Christian name is Rebecca)

4) **John Rolfe (she became known as Lady Rebecca Rolfe).**

13) TOSS-UP. 10 points.

What is the name of the character described as "a fat, merry, ribald knight, bold in talk but cowardly," who appears in Shakespeare's *Henry IV*: Parts I and II and in *The Merry Wives of Windsor*?

Answer: (Sir John) Falstaff.

13) BONUS. 20 points. 10 points each.

Name the 2 planets of our solar system which have no natural satellites.

Answer: Mercury and Venus.

14) TOSS-UP. 10 points.

Identify the Russian Czar who served from 1533-1584 and who in 1547 had himself crowned czar of all Russia.

Answer: Ivan IV (the Terrible).

14) BONUS. 20 points. 5 points each.

Identify the Russian Czar or Empress for each of the following dates.
1) 1682-1725
2) 1762-1796
3) 1825-1855
4) 1894-1917

Answer: 1) Peter I (the Great)
2) Catherine II (the Great)
3) Nicholas I
4) Nicholas II.

15) TOSS-UP. 10 points.

Name the Canadian province or provinces bordering on 4 of the 5 Great Lakes.

Answer: Ontario.

15) BONUS. 20 points. 10 points each.

Complete the following lines from *De Gustibus* with the name of a European country, and identify the author: "Open my heart, and you will see / Graved inside of it, '_____.' "

Answer: "Italy" / Robert Browning.

16) TOSS-UP. 10 points.

What is the name of the hardest tissue in the human body?

Answer: Enamel.

16) BONUS. 20 points. 10 points each.

Name both an electrolytic cell's positively charged electrode toward which current flows and its negatively charged electrode from which current flows.

Answer: Anode and cathode.

17) TOSS-UP. 10 points.

By which amendment to the U.S. Constitution are the courts prohibited from requiring excessive bail or excessive fines and from inflicting cruel and unusual punishment?

Answer: 8th Amendment.

17) BONUS. 20 points. All or nothing.

Name in chronological order the last 3 contiguous U.S. territories to become U.S. states.

Answer: Oklahoma (11/16/1907), New Mexico (1/6/1912), and Arizona (2/14/1912).

18) TOSS-UP. 10 points.

Students at this California college are nicknamed the "Poets" and the college was named (along with the town) after the "American Quaker Poet." Name the college.

Answer: Whittier College (after John Greenleaf Whittier).

18) BONUS. 20 points. 10 points each.

Identify each of the following.
1) The author of *Prometheus Bound* (c. 465 B.C.)
2) The author of *Prometheus Unbound* (1820)

**Answer: 1) Aeschylus
2) Percy Bysshe Shelley.**

19) TOSS-UP. 10 points.

What percent of the Earth's surface is water—50, 60, 70 or 90%?

Answer: 70%.

19) BONUS. 20 points. 10 points each.

Name the verb form used as an adjective and the part of speech used to modify a verb, an adjective, or another adverb.

Answer: Participle (or infinitive) and adverb.

20) TOSS-UP. 10 points.

In which city are both the Corcoran Gallery of Art and the Freer Gallery of Art?

Answer: Washington, D.C.

20) BONUS. 20 points. 5 points each.

In which city is each of the following art galleries located?
1) State Hermitage Museum
2) El Prado (Museo del Prado)
3) Le Louvre (Musée du Louvre)
4) Rijksmuseum

Answer: 1) Leningrad, Soviet Union
2) Madrid, Spain
3) Paris, France
4) Amsterdam, The Netherlands.

21) TOSS-UP. 10 points.

Name the railroad that when completed in 1916 became the longest rail line in the world. It extended more than 5,700 miles (9,200 kilometers) from Yekaterinburg in the Ural Mountains to Vladivostok on the Sea of Japan.

Answer: Trans-Siberian Railroad.

21) BONUS. 20 points. 5 points each.

Give the general location of each of the following Capes.
1) Cape Horn
2) Cape of Good Hope (also called Cape Province or Kaapland)
3) Cape Agulhas
4) Cape Verde (Peninsula or Islands)

Answer: 1) **Tip of South America**
2) **Near the tip of South Africa**
3) **Tip of South Africa**
4) **Coast of Senegal, West Africa, or islands off the coast.**

22) TOSS-UP. 10 points.

Identify Bram Stoker's 1897 literary character whose name today designates any person who like a vampire saps the physical or emotional strength of another person.

Answer: Dracula.

22) BONUS. 20 points. 5 points each.

Identify the following words or phrases, each of which includes the word *saw*.
1) The slang term for a doctor
2) The slang term for a ten-dollar bill
3) A rack used to support a piece of wood being sawed
4) Having notches along the edge like the teeth of a saw; serrate

Answer: 1) **sawbones**
2) **sawbuck**
3) **sawhorse**
4) **saw-toothed (saw-tooth).**

23) TOSS-UP. 10 points.

About which Civil War general did President Abraham Lincoln say: "Only _____ could have managed such a coup, wringing one last spectacular defeat from the jaws of victory"? This general sent his troops to slaughter in Antietam, succeeded General McClellan as commander of the Army of the Potomac, suffered a terrible defeat at Fredericksburg, and then sent his troops to slaughter again in the crater at Petersburg.

Answer: Ambrose Everett Burnside.

23) BONUS. 20 points. 10 points each.

Name the University for which the Seven Mules played and the University for which the Seven Blocks of Granite played. These Catholic colleges are located in Indiana and New York respectively.

Answer: Notre Dame and Fordham.

24) TOSS-UP. 20 points after the first clue. 10 after the second.

What is my name?
1) I received the Nobel Prize in 1904 in medicine or physiology for my work on digestion and the nervous system.
2) My later and more important work developed the concept of a conditioned reflex and involved the ringing of a bell and the salivating of a dog.

Answer: Ivan Petrovich Pavlov.

24) BONUS. 20 points. 5 points each.

Identify each of the following concerning Norse mythology.
1) The god of light, beauty, wisdom, and goodness
2) The plant that killed this god
3) The evil god who was jealous of the other god's beauty
4) The blind man who was tricked by the evil god into killing his brother with the plant

Answer: 1) Balder (or Baldur or Baldr)
          2) Mistletoe
          3) Loki
          4) Hoth.

25) TOSS-UP. 10 points.

In which work by which author is the slogan, "All animals are equal, but some animals are more equal than others"?

Answer: *Animal Farm* by George Orwell.

25) BONUS. 20 points. 5 points each.

Identify each of the following concerning George Orwell's *Animal Farm*.
1) The name of the pig who represents Stalin
2) The pig who represents Trotsky and is banished
3) The pig who represents Lenin and expounds a Marxian thesis
4) The draft horse who represents the working class and is taken to the glue factory by the other pigs

Answer: 1) Napoleon
          2) Snowball
          3) Major
          4) Boxer.

CATEGORY TOSS-UP. 100 points. 10 points each. 10 points deducted for an incorrect answer.

Ludwig Feuerbach, a German philosopher, wrote, "Man is what he eats." Who wrote each of the following citations that begin with the word "man"?

1) The French-Swiss philosopher who wrote in *The Social Contract*: "Man is born free, and everywhere he is in chains."

2) The Greek philosopher who wrote in *Politics*: "Man is by nature a political animal."

3) The German monk who wrote in *The Imitation of Christ*: "Man proposes, but God disposes."

4) The New Testament author who recorded Jesus' words in chapter 4 verse 4: "Man shall not live by bread alone, but by every word that proceedeth out of the mouth of God."

5) The French scientist and religious philosopher who wrote in *Pensées*: "Man is but a reed, the weakest in nature, but he is a thinking reed."

6) The Scottish poet who wrote in *Man Was Made to Mourn*: "Man's inhumanity to man / Makes countless thousands mourn."

7) The American humorist who wrote in *Pudd'nhead Wilson*: "Man is the only animal that blushes. Or needs to."

8) The French existentialist who wrote in *Being and Nothingness*: "Man can will nothing unless he has first understood that he must count on no one but himself."

9) The English romantic poet who wrote in *Don Juan*: "Man's love is of man's life a thing apart; / 'Tis woman's whole existence."

10) The German philosopher who wrote in *Thus Spake Zarathustra*: "Man is something to be surpassed."

Answer: 1) **Jean Jacques Rousseau**
2) **Aristotle**
3) **Thomas à Kempis**
4) **Matthew**
5) **Blaise Pascal**
6) **Robert Burns**
7) **Mark Twain (or Samuel Langhorne Clemens)**
8) **Jean Paul Sartre**
9) **Lord Byron**
10) **Friedrich Nietzsche.**

Round Three

1) TOSS-UP. 10 points.

Identify the U.S. fortress bearing the following inscription: "Thermopylae had its messengers of defeat. The _____ had none."

Answer: Alamo.

1) BONUS. 20 points. 10 points each.

For the first time a cabinet officer testified before a congressional panel chaired by her husband when the Secretary of Transportation of the Reagan administration appeared before the Senate Finance Committee in February 1984. Give the first and last names of this pair.

Answer: Elizabeth Dole and Robert Dole.

2) TOSS-UP. 10 points.

What is the name of "a book of alphabetically arranged terms and their meanings used in any science, art, or other branch of knowledge or work"?

Answer: Dictionary.

2) BONUS. 20 points. 10 points each.

Name the nominator and the nominee in the following speech: "We offer one who has the will to win—who not only deserves success but commands it. Victory is his habit—the Happy Warrior—_____!" This nomination speech took place at the 1928 Democratic Convention.

Answer: Franklin Roosevelt nominated Alfred E. Smith.

3) TOSS-UP. 10 points.

If a student makes a 90, an 88, an 86, and an 86 on his first four math tests, what must he make on the next test to have a 90 average?

Answer: 100.

3) BONUS. 30 points. 10 points each.

Name Sophocles' 3 extant plays about Oedipus and his family.

Answer: *Oedipus the King (Oedipus Rex* or *Oedipus Tyrannus), Oedipus at Colonus (Oedipus Coloneus),* and *Antigone.*

4) TOSS-UP. 10 points.

Identify the French-Swiss architect who said, *"Une maison est une machine-à-habiter"* ("A house is a machine for living in").

Answer: Le Corbusier (or Charles Édouard Jeanneret).

4) BONUS. 20 points. 10 points each.

Name the wars of 1668 and 1740-1748 that were concluded with the Treaty of Aix-la-Chapelle.

Answer: War of Devolution and the War of the Austrian Succession (King George's War).

5) TOSS-UP. 30 points after the first clue. 20 after the second. 10 after the third.

What's my name?
1) I was a ziggurat in Shinar near Babylon in Mesopotamia.
2) My name means "gate of God" in Assyrian or "to confuse" in Hebrew.
3) I was built by the descendants of Noah after the Deluge because they wanted to reach heaven. They were prevented from completing me by a confusion of tongues (Genesis 11:1-9).

Answer: Tower of Babel.

5) BONUS. 20 points. 5 points each.

Identify each of the following German words or phrases connected with Adolf Hitler.
1) The name for a "rebellion" such as the unsuccessful one on November 8, 1923, in a Munich Beer Hall known as the *Beer Hall* _____
2) The name of the two-volume work Hitler wrote while in prison

(translated as *My Struggle*) that became the "bible" of the Nazi party
3) The name of the policy of territorial aggrandizement used by Hitler and the German government after 1933, translated as "living space"
4) The name of the title meaning "leader" which Hitler conferred upon himself

Answer: 1) *Putsch*
       2) *Mein Kampf*
       3) *Lebensraum*
       4) *Führer.*

6) TOSS-UP. 10 points.

What's my name? Georg Stahl, a German chemist, isolated me from vinegar in 1700, and my name comes from the Latin word for "vinegar" or "sour wine."

Answer: Acetic acid.

6) BONUS. 30 points. 10 points each.

Identify each of the following architectural terms from the definition.
1) A semicircular projection of a building, especially one at the east end of a church where the main altar is located
2) A support, generally of brick or stone, built against an outside wall to reinforce it
3) The upper part of an entablature, or the horizontal molding projecting along the top of a building

Answer: 1) Apse
       2) Buttress
       3) Cornice.

7) TOSS-UP. 10 points.

Name the locomotive built by Matthias William Baldwin in the early 1830's and now located in Philadelphia's Franklin Institute museum. This locomotive shares its name with the nickname of the U.S.S. *Constitution* now located in the Boston harbor.

Answer: *Old Ironsides.*

7) BONUS. 20 points. 5 points each.

Identify the following U.S. ships from the given nicknames.
1) "Big E" or "The Old Lady"
2) "Mighty Mo"
3) "Big Ben"
4) "The Fighting Lady"

Answer: 1) U.S.S. *Enterprise*
2) U.S.S. *Missouri*
3) U.S.S. *Ben Franklin*
4) U.S.S. *Yorktown* (formerly the *Bon Homme Richard*)

8) TOSS-UP. 10 points.

Name the Strait between Iran and North Trucial Oman connecting the Persian Gulf and the Gulf of Oman.

Answer: Strait of Hormuz (or Ormuz).

8) BONUS. 20 points. All or nothing.

Name the ancient region of Southwest Asia called the "Cradle of Civilization," and the 2 rivers between which this region is located.

Answer: Mesopotamia and the Tigris and the Euphrates.

9) TOSS-UP. 10 points.

Which word derived from Greek mythology today means "protection, sponsorship, or auspices"? This word originally identified the shield of Zeus and later the shield of Athena and the sun god Apollo.

Answer: Aegis.

9) BONUS. 30 points. 10 points each.

Answer each of the following questions concerning a 1960 spy plane incident.
1) What was the letter and number of the U.S. reconnaissance plane that was shot down?
2) What was the name of the American pilot?
3) For which Russian spy was the American pilot exchanged?

Answer: 1) *U-2*
2) **Francis Gary Powers**
3) **Colonel Rudolph Ivanovich Abel.**

10) TOSS-UP. 30 points after the first clue. 20 after the second. 10 after the third.

What is my name?
1) In 1649 and 1650, I was a philosopher at the court of Swedish ruler Queen Christina. I instructed her 3 times a week at 5:00 a.m., caught pneumonia because of the cold, and died. My body minus my head was returned to France for burial.
2) I wrote *Discours de la Méthode* (*Discourse on Method*; 1637).
3) I am sometimes called the "Father of Modern Philosophy."

Answer: René Descartes.

10) BONUS. 20 points. 5 points each.

Identify each of the following.
1) The 2 countries whose names are missing in the last 2 lines of the following stanza: "On desperate seas long wont to roam, / Thy hyacinth hair, thy classic face, / Thy Naiad airs, have brought me home / To the glory that was _____ / And the grandeur that was _____ "
2) The author of these lines and the poem from which they are taken

Answer: 1) "Greece" / "Rome"
2) Edgar Allan Poe and "To Helen."

11) TOSS-UP. 10 points.

Name the 2 American lithographers of the 19th century whose work comprises a pictorial history of American life and whose first names were Nathaniel and James Merritt.

Answer: Currier and Ives.

11) BONUS. 20 points. 10 points each.

Identify each of the following.
1) The woman nominated by the Equal Rights Party in 1872 as the first female candidate for President of the U.S.
2) The woman chosen by Walter Mondale in 1984 as the first female candidate for Vice President on a major party ticket

Answer: 1) Victoria Claflin Woodhull
2) Geraldine Ferraro.

12) TOSS-UP. 10 points.

What is the last name of the following father and 2 sons? The father,

Samuel, was a minister of the Church of England; his youngest son, Charles, became a famous Methodist hymn writer; and his other son, John, founded the Methodist Church.

Answer: Wesley.

12) **BONUS. 30 points. 10 points each.**

Identify the following sites in Jerusalem.
1) The site that is believed to be the remaining portion of the wall of the courtyard of the Temple of Solomon
2) The building on the hill believed to be Calvary or Golgotha, the traditional location of Christ's crucifixion and resurrection
3) The building over the rock, from which, according to Muslim belief, Mohammed rose to be with the angel Gabriel

Answer: 1) Wailing Wall, or Western Wall, or Happiness Wall
2) Church of the Holy Sepulcher
3) Dome of the Rock, or the Mosque of Omar (or Umar).

13) **TOSS-UP. 30 points after the first clue. 20 after the second. 10 after the third.**

1) I am called by my medieval name Aix-la-Chapelle by the French.
2) I am a West German city that was the home of Charlemagne and the northern capital of the Carolingian civilization. Charlemagne's chair and tomb are here in the cathedral.
3) I was the site for the coronation of 28 Holy Roman Emperors and for international peace conferences in 1668 and 1748.

Answer: Aachen (or Bad Aachen).

13) **BONUS. 20 points. 5 points each.**

Name the first 4 Soviet leaders designated by *Time* magazine as "Man of the Year."

Answer: Joseph Stalin (1939 and 1942) / Nikita Khrushchev (1957) / Yuri Andropov (1984; shared with Ronald Reagan) / Mikhail Gorbachev (1987 and 1990, as the "Man of the Decade").

14) **TOSS-UP. 10 points.**

Which word means "a short, fictitious story illustrating a moral or religious truth"? The Biblical stories of the prodigal son and the good Samaritan are examples.

Answer: Parable.

14) BONUS. 30 points. 10 points each.

Answer each of the following.
1) What is the translation of the following line from a French philosophical novel, ". . . *mais il faut cultiver notre jardin*"?
2) From which work is this line taken?
3) Who is the author of this line?

Answer: 1) *". . . but we must cultivate our garden"*
2) *Candide*
3) **Voltaire.**

15) TOSS-UP. 10 points.

Name the distant galaxy that is nearest to our own.

Answer: Andromeda.

15) BONUS. 20 points. 5 points each.

Identify the 4 U.S. state capitals whose names include the word "city," and give the state in which each is located.

Answer: Jefferson City, Missouri; Carson City, Nevada; Oklahoma City, Oklahoma; and Salt Lake City, Utah.

16) TOSS-UP. 10 points.

Which sportswriter said: "For when the One Great Scorer comes to mark (write) against your name, he marks (writes)—not that you won or lost—but how you played the game"?

Answer: Grantland Rice.

16) BONUS. 30 points. 10 points each.

Identify the person who killed each of the following.
1) Jesse James
2) James Butler "Wild Bill" Hickok
3) Billy the Kid (or William H. Bonney, Henry McCarty/McCarthy, or Kid Antrim)

Answer: 1) Bob Ford

>   2) Jack McCall
>   3) (Sheriff) Pat Garrett.

17) TOSS-UP. 10 points.

How many distinct ways are there to arrange 5 people around a circular table?

Answer: 24 ways.

17) BONUS. 20 points. 5 points each.

Identify each of the following metaphorical phrases from its definition and its literary derivation.

1) "very uncomfortable, uneasy, nervous" (from the 1955 title of a play by Tennessee Williams)
2) "burden, weight, any hindrance; a reminder of one's transgressions" (from *The Rime of the Ancient Mariner* by Samuel Taylor Coleridge in which the killer of the bird of good omen was punished by having the dead bird hung around his neck)
3) "to attempt a dangerous job, especially for the good of others" (from an Aesop Fable about a group of mice who want to place a noisemaker on a certain animal to warn them of its approach. The mice are enthusiastic about the idea until one of them asks, "But who's _____?")
4) "to pay the cost of one's pleasures or bear the consequences of one's actions or decisions" (probably from the legend of the magician and flute player who upon being refused the payment from the residents of Hamelin, Germany, for ridding the town of its rats, led the children of the town away to the mountains by playing his pipe)

Answer: 1) Like a cat on a hot tin roof
**   2) Albatross around the neck**
**   3) To bell the cat**
**   4) To pay the piper.**

18) TOSS-UP. 10 points.

What pop artist said, "In the future everyone will be world-famous for fifteen minutes"?

Answer: Andy Warhol.

18) BONUS. 30 points. 10 points each.

Listen to the following lines; then identify the poet and poem and correct the historical inaccuracy in the stanza: "Then felt I like some watcher of the skies / When a new planet swims into his ken; / Or like stout Cortez when with eagle eyes / He stared at the Pacific—and all his men / Looked at each other with a wild surmise—/ Silent, upon a peak in Darien."

Answer: John Keats / "On First Looking Into Chapman's Homer" / Balboa, not Cortez, discovered the Pacific Ocean.

19) TOSS-UP. 10 points.

After being formed by the confluence of the Tigris and Euphrates rivers, into which gulf does the Shatt al-Arab River system empty?

Answer: Persian Gulf.

19) BONUS. 20 points. 10 points each.

Name the highest waterfall in the world and the country in which it is located.

Answer: Angel Falls / Venezuela.

20) TOSS-UP. 20 points after the first clue. 10 after the second.

Which word am I?
1) My name is a corruption of a Greek word meaning "unconquerable."
2) I am a mineral composed solely of carbon and I am the hardest naturally occurring substance known to man.

Answer: A diamond.

20) BONUS. 20 points. 5 points each.

In which sport is each of the following trophies awarded to the championship team?
1) Stanley Cup
2) Vince Lombardi Trophy
3) Grey Cup
4) Davis Cup

Answer: 1) Professional ice hockey (National Hockey League)
2) Professional football (National Football League)

3) **Professional football (Canadian Football League)**
4) **Tennis.**

21) TOSS-UP. 10 points.

Identify both the "tiller of the soil" who became the first person in the Bible to commit a murder and his brother, "the keeper of the sheep," whom he killed.

Answer: Cain killed his brother Abel.

21) BONUS. 20 points. 5 points each.

Identify the explorers of each of the following areas.
1) Alaska in 1741
2) New Caledonia in 1774
3) Victoria Falls in 1855
4) Quebec (City) and New France in 1608

Answer: 1) Vitus Johassen Bering (Semyon Dezhnyov did so in 1648)
2) James Cook
3) David Livingstone
4) Samuel de Champlain

22) TOSS-UP. 10 points.

Name the earliest known fully developed system of writing, actually picture symbols found on clay tablets, probably developed by Sumerians and literally defined as "wedge-shaped."

Answer: Cuneiform (cuniform).

22) BONUS. 20 points. 5 points each.

Name the Russian author of *The Three Sisters*, and then name the 3 sisters in this play.

Answer: Anton Chekhov / Olga, Masha, and Irina (Prozorov).

23) TOSS-UP. 10 points.

The pressure exerted by one millimeter of mercury is sometimes referred to as one _____, a word that comes from the name of the Italian inventor of the barometer. What is this word?

Answer: Torricelli (abbreviated torr; after Evangelista Torricelli).

23) BONUS. 20 points. 10 points each.

What 2 boxers were involved in the famous "long count" in their fight on September 22, 1927, in which the winner was given about 14 seconds to rise from a knockdown when the loser failed to go to a neutral corner?

Answer: Jack Dempsey and Gene Tunney (Dempsey lost).

24) TOSS-UP. 10 points.

Identify the U.S. President who said, "Given a chance to go forward with the policies of the last eight years, we shall soon, with the help of God, be in sight of the day when poverty will be banished from this nation." He said this in 1928.

Answer: Herbert Hoover.

24) BONUS. 25 points. 5 points each.

Which amendments are known by the following nicknames?
1) Susan B. Anthony Amendment
2) Doctrine of Residual Powers or Reserved Powers
3) Lame Duck Amendment
4) Prohibition Amendment
5) Due Process Amendment

Answer: 1) 19th Amendment
2) 10th Amendment
3) 20th Amendment
4) 18th Amendment
5) 5th Amendment.

25) TOSS-UP. 10 points.

Name the most populous city in the largest U.S. state.

Answer: Anchorage, Alaska.

25) BONUS. 20 points. 5 points each.

Identify each of the following, all of which include the word "lone."
1) Tonto's *Kemo Sabe*
2) Charles Lindbergh's nickname

3) A nickname for Texas

4) A two-word phrase for a person who prefers to live and work independently of others

Answer: 1) The Lone Ranger
2) The Lone Eagle
3) The Lone Star State
4) Lone wolf.

CATEGORY TOSS-UP. 100 points. 10 points each. 10 points deducted for an incorrect answer.

Give the name of the U.S. state that has been omitted in the title of each of the following songs.

1) "On, _____!"
2) "My Old _____ Home"
3) "_____ on My Mind"
4) "I Love _____"
5) "I Love You, _____"
6) "Carry Me Back to Old _____"
7) "The _____ Waltz"
8) "Home Means _____"
9) "When It's Iris Time in _____"
10) "_____, My Home Sweet Home"

Answer: 1) Wisconsin
2) Kentucky
3) Georgia
4) New York
5) California
6) Virginia (Virginny)
7) Tennessee ("Missouri Waltz" is not acceptable)
8) Nevada
9) Tennessee
10) West Virginia.

ROUND FOUR

1) TOSS-UP. 10 points.

What European leader is credited with first saying, *"Du sublime au ridicule il n'y a qu'un pas"* ("From the sublime to the ridiculous is but a step")?

Answer: Napoleon.

1) BONUS. 20 points. 5 points each.

Name the 3 Confederates immortalized on Georgia's Stone Mountain, and name either the sculptor who in 1923 started carving the figures or the sculptor who in 1968 completed the project.

Answer: Jefferson Davis, General Robert E. Lee, and General Thomas J. "Stonewall" Jackson / Gutzon Borglum (Augustus Lukeman worked on the project from 1925 to 1928) or Walter Kirtland Hancock.

2) TOSS-UP. 10 points.

Identify the mammal called the "spiny anteater" that is one of 2 mammals that lay and incubate eggs. The other mammal is the duckbill platypus.

Answer: Echidna.

2) BONUS. 20 points. 10 points each.

Answer each of the following.
1) In which ocean is zero degrees longitude, zero degrees latitude found?
2) Near which continent is this point located?

**Answer: 1) Atlantic Ocean
2) Africa (near São Tomé, south of Ghana and west of Gabon).**

3) TOSS-UP. 10 points.

This college in Provo, Utah, whose students are known as "Cougars," is controlled by the Church of Jesus Christ of Latter-day Saints and is the largest Mormon operated university school. Name it.

Answer: Brigham Young University.

3) BONUS. 20 points. 10 points each.

Answer each of the following.
1) What award is given for a record that sells a half million copies?
2) What award is given for a record that sells a million copies?

Answer: 1) Platinum Record
2) Gold Record.

4) TOSS-UP. 10 points.

Where is the Mohorovicic discontinuity or Moho located?

Answer: At the bottom of the earth's crust, or on the boundary between the earth's crust and its mantle.

4) BONUS. 30 points. 10 points each.

The capital of Sudan is located at the confluence of 2 rivers. Name this city and the 2 rivers.

Answer: Khartoum / Blue Nile and White Nile.

5) TOSS-UP. 10 points.

What is the name of Prospero's grotesque slave in Shakespeare's *The Tempest*?

Answer: Caliban.

5) BONUS. 30 points. 10 points each.

Identify each of the following Biblical personages or groups.
1) The name of the high priest of the Jews who presided at the ecclesiastical hearing that condemned Jesus to death
2) The name of the high court and chief legislative council of the ancient Jewish nation, which tried Jesus and possibly at least ratified His death sentence
3) The Roman procurator of Judea who tried and condemned Jesus to death

Answer: 1) (Joseph) Caiaphas
2) Sanhedrin
3) Pontius Pilate.

6) TOSS-UP. 30 points after the first clue. 20 after the second. 10 after the third.

Identify the artist who painted all of the following.
1) *Portrait of Madame Récamier* (1799) and *The Oath of the Horatii* (1785)
2) *The Death of Socrates* (1787) and *The Return of Brutus* (1789)
3) *The Tennis Court Oath* (1790) and *The Death of Marat* 1793)

Answer: Jacques Louis David.

6) BONUS. 25 points. 5 points each. Point total stops at the first mistake.

Name the 5 oceans of the world in the order of their size from the largest to the smallest.

Answer: Pacific, Atlantic, Indian, Arctic, and Antarctic (some oceanographers believe that there are just 3 oceans—the Pacific, the Atlantic, and the Indian—and that all other bodies of water belong to these 3; others consider there to be 4 oceans, omitting the Antarctic as a separate body.)

7) TOSS-UP. 10 points.

Edwin P. Hoyt's biography *The Improper Bostonian* is about a famous physician, scientist, philosopher, poet, novelist, and *bon vivant* who was the father of a Supreme Court Justice. Name this versatile man who as a poet wrote "The Chambered Nautilus" (1858) and "Old Ironsides" (1830).

Answer: Dr. Oliver Wendell Holmes.

7) BONUS. 20 points. 10 points each.

Name the abode of the blessed after death in Greek mythology and the great hall of immortality where Odin received and feasted the souls of warriors slain heroically in battle in Norse mythology.

Answer: Elysium (or Elysian Fields or Isles of the Blessed) and Valhalla.

8) TOSS-UP. 10 points.

According to a story by Aulus Gellius, which Roman slave escaped certain death when thrown into the arena with a lion because the

lion recognized him as the person who had extracted a thorn from its
foot and refused to harm him?

Answer: Androcles (or Androclus).

8) BONUS. 30 points. 10 points each.

According to several sources, which 3 Knights of the Round Table
found the Holy Grail?

**Answer: Bors (Sir Bors de Ganis), Galahad, and Perceval
(Percival or Parsifal).**

9) TOSS-UP. 30 points after the first clue. 20 after the second. 10 after the third.

What's my name?
1) I was born Elizabeth Ann Bayley in New York City in 1774. In
   1808, I established the Paca Street School in Baltimore, one of the
   first Catholic elementary schools in the U.S.
2) I was known as the "Mother of the Parochial School System in the
   U.S." In 1814, I established the first Orphan Asylum of Philadelphia, the nation's first Catholic child-care institution.
3) In 1809, I founded the Sisters of Charity of Saint Joseph in
   Emmitsburg, Maryland.

Answer: Saint Elizabeth Ann (Mother) Seton.

9) BONUS. 30 points. 10 points each.

Identify each of the following architectural terms from the definition.
1) The front of a building
2) Any horizontal band decorated with sculpture on the outside wall
   between the architrave and the cornice
3) The main area within a church extending from the main entrance
   to the transept

Answer: 1) Façade
2) Frieze
3) Nave.

10) TOSS-UP. 10 points.

To which U.S. Cabinet Secretary does the Bureau of the Census
report?

Answer: Secretary of Commerce.

10) BONUS. 20 points. 10 points each.

Name the 2 newspapers that first published the Pentagon Papers.

Answer: *New York Times* **and** *Washington Post*.

11) TOSS-UP. 10 points.

What kind of a "snowman" is a *Yeti*?

Answer: Abominable (Snowman).

11) BONUS. 20 points. 5 points each.

Identify each of the following concerning Roy Rogers.
1) The name of his second wife (since 1947)
2) The name of his horse, sometimes called "the smartest horse in the movies"
3) The name of his dog, a German shepherd
4) The name of his wife's horse

Answer: 1) Dale Evans (his first wife, Arlene Rogers, died from childbirth complications in 1946)
2) Trigger (formerly known as Golden Cloud)
3) Bullet
4) Buttermilk.

12) TOSS-UP. 10 points.

What name is associated with both the opera *Hansel and Gretel* (1893) and Arnold Dorsey?

Answer: Engelbert Humperdinck (the author of the opera and the pseudonym of Arnold Dorsey).

12) BONUS. 20 points. 5 points each.

Identify the dog that belongs to each of the following.
1) Dennis the Menace
2) Hi and Lois
3) Charlie Brown
4) Little Orphan Annie

Answer: 1) Ruff
2) Dawg
3) Snoopy
4) Sandy.

13) TOSS-UP. 10 points.

Identify the Venetian born in 1775 whose 12 volumes of *Memoirs* tell of his romantic exploits. This name today designates "a promiscuous man; a libertine; a rake."

Answer: (Giovanni) Casanova.

13) BONUS. 20 points. 10 points each.

Name the 2 writers of the 1848 *Communist Manifesto*.

Answer: Karl Marx and Friedrich Engels.

14) TOSS-UP. 10 points.

Of George Eliot, George Orwell, and George Sand, which one is a man?

Answer: George Orwell.

14) BONUS. 20 points. 5 points each.

Name the 4 symphonic movements set as a classical standard by Joseph Haydn.

Answer: *Allegro, andante, scherzo,* and *finale*.

15) TOSS-UP. 30 points after the first clue. 20 after the second. 10 after the third.

Who am I?
1) I was a Spanish artist born in 1893, and my surname in Spanish means "he looked."
2) I was an abstract and surrealist painter and am known for *The Hunter* (*Catalan Landscape*, 1923-1924) and *Women and Bird in the Moonlight* (1949).
3) I am also known for *Dutch Interior* (1928) and *Personages and a Dog in Front of the Sun* (1949).

Answer: Joan Miró.

15) BONUS. 25 points. All or nothing.

Name the 5 books called the Pentateuch, which constitute the Torah of Jewish religion.

Answer: Genesis, Exodus, Leviticus, Numbers, and Deuteronomy.

16) TOSS-UP. 10 points.

Which game is played with 15 men (stones, checkers, or counters) on a board with 24 spear-shaped sections called *points*, and in which moves are determined by a throw of the dice?

Answer: Backgammon.

16) BONUS. 20 points. 5 points each.

Identify the subject of each of the following biographies.
1) *One Brief Shining Moment* by William Manchester
2) *The Last Lion* by William Manchester
3) *The Far Side of Paradise* by Arthur Mizener
4) *Willa* by Phyllis C. Robinson

Answer: 1) John F. Kennedy
2) Winston Spencer Churchill
3) F. Scott Fitzgerald
4) Willa Cather.

17) TOSS-UP. 30 points after the first clue. 20 after the second. 10 after the third.

I am a city in the U.S. What's my name?
1) I am named after the youngest signer of the U.S. Constitution, who helped found the city.
2) I am located at the confluence of the Mad, the Great Miami, and the Stillwater rivers (and Wolf Creek).
3) I am called the "Birthplace of Aviation" because Orville and Wilbur Wright's experiments here in their bicycle shop led to the first successful flight of a heavier-than-air plane at Kitty Hawk, North Carolina.

Answer: Dayton (Ohio; after Jonathan Dayton).

17) BONUS. 30 points. 10 points each.

Name the 3 North Carolina capes which jut into the Atlantic Ocean from the Outer Banks.

Answer: Cape Hatteras, Cape Lookout, and Cape Fear.

18) TOSS-UP. 10 points.

After Alexander the Great died in 323 B.C., Aristotle, fearing an anti-Macedonian reaction in Athens, decided to retire to Chalcis, for he did not want Athens to "sin twice against philosophy." According to Aristotle, which "first sin against philosophy" occurred in 399 B.C.?

Answer: The death of Socrates by requiring him to drink hemlock.

18) **BONUS. 20 points. 5 points each.**

Name the only 4 U.S. States which border on Mexico.

Answer: California, Arizona, New Mexico, and Texas (from west to east).

19) **TOSS-UP. 10 points.**

In which Ohio city is President William McKinley buried, a city in which the National Professional Football Hall of Fame is located?

Answer: Canton.

19) **BONUS. 30 points. 10 points each.**

Fill in the missing word in each of the following statements by Theodore Roosevelt.
1) "I wish to preach, not the doctrine of ignoble ease, but the doctrine of the _____ life." (April 10, 1899)
2) "I am as strong as a _____ moose and you can use me to the limit." (June 27, 1900)
3) "There is a homely adage which runs, 'Speak softly and carry a big _____; you will go far.'" (September 2, 1901)

Answer: 1) "strenuous"
           2) "bull"
           3) "stick."

20) **TOSS-UP. 30 points after the first clue. 20 after the second. 10 after the third.**

What is my name?
1) My pseudonym means "Eve of the Dawn," and my code number is H21.
2) I was born in 1876 in The Netherlands and became a dancer. My name at birth was Margaretha Geertruida Zelle.
3) I pretended to be a Javanese temple dancer and was executed as a German spy by a French firing squad on October 15, 1917.

Answer: Mata Hari.

20) **BONUS.** 20 points. 5 points each.

Identify the following concerning WWII propaganda broadcasting.
1) The nickname for the American, Mildred Elizabeth Gillars, who broadcast for the Nazis
2) The pseudonym for the American, Iva Ikuko Toguri d'Aguino, who broadcast for the Japanese (pardoned by President Gerald Ford on his last day in office in 1977)
3) The nickname for the Briton, William Joyce, who broadcast for the Germans
4) The name of the song that Swedish-born singer, Lala Anderson, sang as the theme song for the German Army radio station

Answer: 1) **Axis Sally**
2) **Tokyo Rose**
3) **Lord Haw Haw**
4) **"Lili Marlene."**

21) **TOSS-UP.** 30 points after the first clue. 20 after the second. 10 after the third.

What is my name?
1) My real name was Charles Louis de Secondat.
2) I wrote the *Lettres persanes* (*Persian Letters*; 1721).
3) I wrote *De l'esprit des lois* (*The Spirit of the Laws*; 1748).

Answer: (Baron de la Brède et de) Montesquieu.

21) **BONUS.** 20 points. 10 points each.

Name the author and the title of the religious allegory that includes the following line: "They went then till they came to the Delectable Mountains, which mountains belong to the Lord of that hill of which we have spoken before."

Answer: *The Pilgrim's Progress* by **John Bunyan.**

22) **TOSS-UP.** 10 points.

Which branch of physics is concerned with the nature and properties of light and vision?

Answer: Optics.

22) **BONUS.** 20 points. 10 points each.

Answer each of the following concerning the Moon.
1) What is the color of its sky at all times?

2) Compared with the Earth, why has the Moon changed so little over a billion years?

Answer: 1) Black
2) Because there is no weather (for there are nei-
ther clouds, nor air, nor water).

23) TOSS-UP. 10 points.

In the Mother Goose nursery rhyme, what did Simple Simon, on his way to the fair, say first of all to the pieman?

Answer: "Let me taste your ware."

23) BONUS. 20 points. 5 points each.

With which university is each of the following school songs associated?
1) "Far Above Cayuga's Waters"
2) "On the Banks of Old Raritan"
3) "Roar, Lion, Roar"
4) "The Stein Song"

Answer: 1) Cornell University
2) Rutgers University
3) Columbia University
4) University of Maine.

24) TOSS-UP. 10 points.

Although it was not a time of complete intellectual stagnation and cultural decline, what name is given to "the period from the end of classical civilization to the revival of learning in the West" that lasted from about 476 to about 1500?

Answer: Dark Ages or Middle Ages (Dark Ages is more
properly the period from about 476 to 1000 when
there was a general lapse in intellectual activity).

24) BONUS. 20 points. 10 points each.

Name the 2 leaders of the 1848 Women's Rights Convention at Seneca Falls, New York.

Answer: Elizabeth Cady Stanton and Lucretia Mott.

25) TOSS-UP. 10 points.

If you had a one land in your garden, an entomologist would call it a *lepidopteran,* but what would you call it?

Answer: Butterfly or moth (or any insect having 4 wings with small scales).

25) **BONUS.** 30 points. 10 points each.

Identify each of the following chemical elements from its Latin name and then give its chemical symbol. All or nothing on each one.
1) *Argentum*
2) *Stannum*
3) *Ferrum*

Answer: 1) **Silver / Ag**
           2) **Tin / Sn**
           3) **Iron / Fe.**

CATEGORY TOSS-UP. 100 points. 10 points each. 10 points deducted for an incorrect answer.

Identify each of the following concerning Superman, the "Man of Steel" created by Jerry Siegel and Joe Shuster.
1) The name he was given at birth
2) The planet on which he was born
3) The town in the U.S. in which he grew up
4) The identity he assumed from his adopted parents
5) The name of the newspaper for which he works as a "mild-mannered" reporter
6) The city in which the newspaper is located
7) The editor for whom he works or the office boy with whom he is friends
8) The woman he cares about at the newspaper
9) The name of his archenemy, who resents Superman because of an accident caused by Superboy
10) The words that complete the litany "Faster than a speeding _____, more powerful than a _____, able to leap _____ at a single bound . . . . It's Superman!"

Answer: 1) **Kal-El (son of Jor-El and his wife Lara living in the city of Kandor, who died when the planet on which they lived was destroyed by an atomic fire)**
           2) **Krypton (radioactive green remnants of his planet, called kryptonite, were capable of weakening and possibly killing him; Superboy's "dog of steel" was called Krypto)**

3) Smallville, Illinois
4) Clark Kent (from John or Jonathan and Martha, or Mary, Kent on April 10, 1926)
5) *Daily Planet*
6) Metropolis (he attended Metropolis University before becoming a reporter)
7) Perry White or Jimmy Olsen
8) Lois Lane (he dated Lana Lang as Superboy and he dated the mermaid Lori)
9) Lex Luthor
10) Bullet / locomotive / tall buildings.

ROUND FIVE

1) TOSS-UP. 10 points.

Which branch of the Federal Government was established by the Connecticut, or "Great," Compromise?

Answer: Congress (or the legislative branch).

1) BONUS. 20 points. 10 points each.

The Soviet Union established diplomatic relations with several European governments prior to 1934 when it became a member of the League of Nations. In which year under which President did the U.S. accord the Soviet Union diplomatic recognition?

Answer: 1933 / Franklin Roosevelt.

2) TOSS-UP. 30 points after the first clue. 20 after the second. 10 after the third.

Identify the well-known American artist from the following paintings.
1) *Mr. and Mrs. Thomas Mifflin* (1773) and *The Siege of Gibraltar* (1791)
2) *Boy with a Squirrel* (1765) and *The Death of Major Pierson* (1791)
3) *Watson and the Shark* (1778) and *The Death of the Earl of Chatham* (1781)

Answer: John Singleton Copley.

2) BONUS. 20 points. 5 points each.

Identify the assassin or would-be assassin of each of the following.
1) Lee Harvey Oswald
2) George Wallace
3) Dr. Martin Luther King, Jr.
4) George Moscone and Harvey Milk

Answer: 1) **Jack Ruby (Jacob Rubenstein)**
2) **Arthur Herman Bremer**
3) **James Earl Ray**
4) **Dan White.**

3) TOSS-UP. 10 points.

In which country did U.S. forces finally capture Emilio Aguinaldo in March, 1901, and defeat his army soon thereafter? This leader who had once helped U.S. forces defeat the Spanish felt betrayed when the U.S. broke its promise to make his country independent.

Answer: Philippines (called the Philippine Insurrection or the Philippine-American War).

3) BONUS. 20 points. 10 points each.

Name not only the city from which she came but also the person who, according to the Bible, was changed into a pillar of NaCl as punishment for her curiosity and disobedience (Genesis 19:26).

Answer: Sodom / Lot's wife.

4) TOSS-UP. 10 points.

In which city are Tiananmen (T'ien An Men) Square, the Great Hall of the People, the Forbidden City, and the Gate of Heavenly Peace?

Answer: Peking (or Beijing, China).

4) BONUS. 20 points. 10 points each.

Give both the French and English names of the 2 "banks" separated by the Seine River, one of which is the center of student life and an academic center, the other a merchant and artisan center.

Answer: Rive Gauche and Rive Droite / Left Bank and Right Bank.

5) TOSS-UP. 10 points.

Name the state in southeastern Mexico on the Bay of Campeche (on the Gulf of Mexico) from which a trademark for a very pungent condiment sauce made of red peppers takes its name.

Answer: Tabasco.

5) BONUS. 20 points. 5 points each.

Identify the sports teams associated with each of the following nicknames.
1) "The Purple People Eaters" (1970's)
2) "The Gashouse Gang" (1930's)

3) "Murderer's Row" (1927)
4) "The Hogs" (1980's)

Answer: 1) Minnesota Vikings (Professional Football)
**   2) St. Louis Cardinals (Professional Baseball)**
**   3) New York Yankees (Professional Baseball)**
**   4) Washington Redskins (Professional Football).**

6) TOSS-UP. 10 points.

Identify the paratrooper's battle cry derived from the name of an Apache Indian chief. It is the Spanish equivalent of Jerome.

Answer: Geronimo.

6) BONUS. 20 points. 5 points each.

Identify the following concerning Thomas Buchanan Read's poem about a Civil War battle.
1) The Union general whose ride is celebrated in the poem
2) The town in Virginia from which this general supposedly rode to the battle site
3) The number of miles this general supposedly rode to rally his troops
4) The name of the Civil War general's horse which covered the distance "mostly on the gallop"

Answer: 1) "Sheridan's Ride" (1864)
**   2) Winchester (at the Battle of Cedar Creek October 19, 1864)**
**   3) 20 ("and Sheridan twenty miles away")**
**   4) Rienzi.**

7) TOSS-UP. 10 points.

Which football coach said, "Winning is not the most important thing about football—it's the only thing"? (He also said, "Winning isn't everything, but wanting to win is.")

Answer: Vince Lombardi (at least attributed to him).

7) BONUS. 20 points. 5 points each.

Identify the following.
1) The queen of England (1516-1558) who said, "When I am dead and opened, you shall find 'Calais' lying in my heart."

2) The queen of France (1755-1793) who said, *"Qu'ils mangent de la brioche!"*
3) The queen of England (1533-1603) who said, "I know I have the body of a weak and feeble woman, but I have the heart and stomach of a king, and of a king of England too."
4) The queen of Egypt (c. 1495-1475 B.C.) who said, "So as regards these two great obelisks, / Wrought with electrum by my majesty for my father Amun, / They are each of one block of hard granite / Without seam, without joining together!"

Answer: 1) Mary I (Tudor)
2) Marie Antoinette
3) Elizabeth I
4) Hatshepsut.

8) TOSS-UP. 10 points.

Name the American author whose Brook Farm experience was recalled in a fictional account entitled *The Blithedale Romance* (1852).

Answer: Nathaniel Hawthorne.

8) BONUS. 20 points. 5 points each.

Identify each of the following concerning a knight of the Round Table.
1) The knight who was successful in his quest of the Holy Grail because of his purity and nobility of spirit and whose name means today "any man regarded as very pure and noble"
2) The name of his father or mother
3) The name of his seat at the Round Table, especially reserved for the purest knight
4) The name of his forefather, who supposedly carried the Holy Grail from Palestine to Great Britain

Answer: 1) Sir Galahad
2) Sir Lancelot (du Lac) or Princess Elaine (the Fair of Astolat)
3) *Siege Perilous*
4) Joseph of Arimathea.

9) TOSS-UP. 10 points.

She was linked with the assassination plot to kill President Abraham Lincoln, and she became the first woman in U.S. history to be hanged. Name this boarding house owner who conspired with John Wilkes Booth.

Answer: Mary Surratt.

9) BONUS. 20 points. 10 points each.

Give the meaning of the word *Galápagos* and tell which country owns these islands.

Answer: Turtles (Tortoises) / Ecuador.

10) TOSS-UP. 30 points after the first clue. 20 after the second. 10 after the third.

What's my name?
1) I fought in the first Arab-Israeli war of 1948 and served as the Israeli minister of agriculture from 1959 to 1964 and as chief of staff from 1953 to 1958.
2) I was the supreme commander of the Israeli forces in the Arab-Israeli (Sinai-Suez) war of 1956, and I was the Israeli foreign minister from 1977 to 1979.
3) I lost an eye during a battle in Lebanon during WWII.

Answer: Moshe Dayan.

10) BONUS. 20 points. 10 points each.

Name the first person to appear on the cover of *Time* magazine, on March 3, 1923, and the person to appear on the cover in 1928 as the first "Man of the Year." The first served in the U.S. House of Representatives for 46 years and was known as "Uncle Joe"; the second was the first person to make a solo nonstop flight across the Atlantic Ocean (May 20-21, 1927).

Answer: Joseph Gurney Cannon and Charles Augustus Lindbergh.

11) TOSS-UP. 10 points.

In the philosophy of which German philosopher and mathematician is each person and thing a *monad*, an ultimate unit of being?

Answer: Gottfried Wilhelm von Leibni(t)z (known as monadism, monadology, or leibnizism).

11) BONUS. 30 points. 10 points each.

Translate the following 2 phrases and tell with which fighter these phrases are associated: *No más* and *manos de piedras.*

Answer: "No more" / "hands of stone" / Roberto Duran.

12) TOSS-UP. 10 points.

According to the Romans, what year was "the last year of confusion," for it was the year Julius Caesar set at 445 days in order to realign the calendar with the seasons?

Answer: 46 B.C.

12) BONUS. 30 points. 10 points each.

Identify the country or area designated by the Roman name.
1) Gaul
2) Hibernia
3) Hispania

Answer: 1) France (Belgium, northern Italy, and southern Netherlands were part of this area in ancient times)
2) Ireland
3) Spain and the Iberian Peninsula (but also the poetic name for Spain).

13) TOSS-UP. 10 points.

Identify the presidential candidate who said, "These unhappy times call for the building of ... plans ... that build from the bottom up and not from the top down, that put their faith once more in the forgotten man at the bottom of the economic pyramid."

Answer: Franklin D. Roosevelt (1932).

13) BONUS. 20 points. All or nothing.

Name the 3 South American countries crossed by the equator.

Answer: Brazil, Colombia, and Ecuador.

14) TOSS-UP. 10 points.

Which singer from which group said in 1966, "We're more popular than Jesus Christ now"?

Answer: John Lennon of the Beatles.

14) BONUS. 20 points. 10 points each.

Name the 2 in Greek mythology who were imprisoned in the palace of King Minos at Cnossus. One of them following his escape lived peacefully in Sicily after his pursuer, King Minos, was either killed by scalding water or suffocated in a bath. The other, this person's son, fell into the sea and drowned when he flew too close to the sun, and melted his wings made of feathers set in beeswax.

Answer: Daedalus and Icarus.

15) TOSS-UP. 10 points.

Name the only U.S. state capital with a 3-word name.

Answer: Salt Lake City (Utah).

15) BONUS. 30 points. 10 points each.

Identify the German classical composer of each group of works.
1) *Brandenburg Concertos*, *French Suites*, and *Well-Tempered Clavier*
2) *Fidelio, Eroica*, and *Missa Solemnis*
3) *Julius Caesar, Water Music*, and *Messiah*

Answer: 1) Johann Sebastian Bach
2) Ludwig van Beethoven
3) George Frideric Handel.

16) TOSS-UP. 10 points.

What is the full name of the NASDAQ system?

Answer: National Association of Securities Dealers' Automated Quotations system.

16) BONUS. 20 points. 10 points each.

Name the location in Georgia that served as the southern White House for Franklin D. Roosevelt, and name his summer home located in New Brunswick, Canada, at the entrance to Passamaquoddy Bay.

Answer: Warm Springs / Campobello Island.

17) TOSS-UP. 10 points.

Which fictional character is addressed by 3 witches as a thane of Glamis, a thane of Cawdor, and finally as the King of Scotland? This character appears in a play by Shakespeare.

Answer: Macbeth.

17) BONUS. 30 points. 10 points each.

Identify each of the following Jacksons.
1) I was the author of the statement, "Nobody can save us but us," and the leader of Operation PUSH (People United to Save Humanity) and project EXCEL, or Push for Excellence.
2) I played in the film *The Wiz*, and along with my brothers made such songs as "The Love You Save" and "Never Can Say Goodbye" famous.
3) I became a U.S. senator from the state of Washington in 1953 and was known as "Scoop."

Answer: 1) Jesse
2) Michael
3) Henry (Martin).

18) TOSS-UP. 10 points.

Give the year of the presidential election in which the G.O.P. was divided by a Bull Moose to equal a Democratic victory.

Answer: 1912.

18) BONUS. 20 points. 5 points each.

Identify the state in which each of the following ski resorts is located.
1) Crested Butte
2) Jackson Hole
3) Sun Valley
4) Squaw Valley

Answer: 1) Colorado (Crested Butte)
2) Wyoming (Jackson)
3) Idaho (Ketchum)
4) California (Squaw Valley).

19) TOSS-UP. 30 points after the first clue. 20 after the second. 10 after the third.

Identify the following Italian-American religious person.
1) I established the Missionary Sisters of the Sacred Heart (M.S.C.) in 1880, originally for the instruction of poor children.
2) I founded Columbus Hospital in New York City and Columbus Hospital in Chicago in 1905.
3) I was born in Lombardy, Italy, in 1850, and in 1950, Pope Pius XII named me the patron saint of immigrants.

Answer: Saint Francis Xavier (Mother) Cabrini.

19) **BONUS.** 30 points. 10 points each.

Fill in the missing word in each of the following statements by Theodore Roosevelt.
1) A man who is good enough to shed his blood for his country is good enough to be given a _____ deal afterwards. More than that no man is entitled to, and less than that no man shall have." (July 4, 1903)
2) Men with the _____ are often indispensable to the well-being of society, but only if they know when to stop raking the muck." (April 14, 1906)
3) "We stand at _____ and we battle for the Lord." (June 17, 1912)

Answer: 1) "square"
2) "muckrake"
3) "Armageddon."

20) **TOSS-UP.** 10 points.

He lived in England during the time of the Great Fire of London, helped develop the British navy, and wrote a diary which covered the period from 1660 to 1669. Name this English writer whose diary is the most famous in the English language.

Answer: Samuel Pepys.

20) **BONUS.** 20 points. 10 points each.

Identify the poet of the following lines and the animal referred to twice in the first line: "_____! _____ ! burning bright / In the forests of the night, / What immortal hand or eye, / Could frame thy fearful symmetry?"

Answer: William Blake / Tiger ("Tiger! Tiger!" in *Songs of Experience*).

21) **TOSS-UP.** 30 points after the first clue. 20 after the second. 10 after the third.

What noun am I?
1) I am derived from a Latin word meaning "a deviation."
2) In astronomy, I mean "a small apparent displacement of a heavenly body, caused by the motion of the earth in its orbit."

3) In optics, I mean "a blurring or distortion in an image."

Answer: Aberration.

21) BONUS. 20 points. 10 points each.

When this U.S. astronaut accomplished a space "first," he said, "That may have been one small step for Neil, but it's a heck of a big leap for me." Who was he and what did he accomplish?

Answer: Bruce McCandless / He took the first untethered "walk" in space (in a Manned Maneuvering Unit).

22) TOSS-UP. 10 points.

Name either person who in 1966 in Oakland, California, founded the militant organization called the Black Panthers.

Answer: Huey P. Newton or Bobby G. Seale.

22) BONUS. 20 points. 10 points each.

Name the only 2 Confederate state capitals not captured by Union forces during the Civil War. One was east of the Mississippi and the other was west of the river.

Answer: Tallahassee (Florida) and Austin (Texas).

23) TOSS-UP. 10 points.

The French phrase *venez m'aider* is the probable origin of what word that is the international radio-telephone signal word for help used by aircraft and ships in distress?

Answer: Mayday (pseudo French *m'aider* for help me).

23) BONUS. 30 points. 10 points each.

Of which ship in which work is each of the following "Captain"?
1) Captain Smollet in a work by Robert Louis Stevenson
2) Captain Hook in a work by James B. Barrie
3) Captain Nemo in a work by Jules Verne

Answer: 1) *Hispaniola* in *Treasure Island*
2) *Jolly Roger* in *Peter Pan*
3) *Nautilus* in *20,000 Leagues Under the Sea*.

24) TOSS-UP. 10 points.

Complete the following palindrome: "Able was I ere I saw _____."

Answer: Elba.

24) BONUS. 20 points. 5 points each.

Name the Republicans Franklin D. Roosevelt defeated in the 1932, 1936, 1940, and 1944 presidential elections.

Answer: Herbert Hoover (1932); Alfred M. Landon (1936); Wendell L. Willkie (1940); and Thomas E. Dewey (1944).

25) TOSS-UP. 10 points.

What name is given to the group of nuclear-powered submarines, including the *Ohio*, that constitute the most powerful weapon of the U.S. nuclear force? The name comes from that of Neptune's three-pronged instrument.

Answer: Trident.

25) BONUS. 30 points. 10 points each.

Identify each of the following chemical elements from its Latin name, and then give its chemical symbol. All or nothing on each one.
1) *Hydrargyrum*
2) *Aurum*
3) *Plumbum*

Answer: 1) Mercury / Hg
2) Gold / Au
3) Lead / Pb.

CATEGORY TOSS-UP. 100 points. 10 points each. 10 points deducted for an incorrect answer.

Identify each of the following related to the 1960's.
1) The actress who used the nonsense word *super-califragilisticexpialidocious* and the film in which she used it
2) The 2 teams that played in the first football Super Bowl in 1967
3) Elvis Presley's wife whose name is French for "beautiful place"
4) The name of the political leader who said to the Press after losing the California's governor's race, "You won't have me to kick around anymore"
5) The name of the person who coined the phrase "black power"
6) The cellist who performed solo at the Kennedy White House
7) The name of the political leader who married Happy Murphy
8) The name given to "the humorous theorem that each person in a

hierarchy will be promoted to his level of incompetence"
9) The European political leader who proclaimed "*Vive le Québec libre!*"
10) The name of the prison camp where TV's "Hogan's Heroes" were housed

Answer: 1) Julie Andrews in *Mary Poppins*
2) Green Bay Packers defeated the Kansas City Chiefs (by a 35-10 score)
3) Priscilla Ann Beaulieu—*Beau* (beautiful) and *lieu* (place)
4) Richard Nixon
5) Stokely Carmichael
6) Pablo Casals
7) Nelson Rockefeller
8) Peter Principle
9) Charles De Gaulle
10) Stalag 13.

ROUND SIX

**980 points**

1) TOSS-UP. 10 points.

How many pecks are "a bushel and a peck"?

Answer: 5.

1) BONUS. 20 points. 5 points each.

In which book by which author does which character say to which character, "You see it's like a portmanteau word . . . there are two meanings packed up in one word"?

Answer: In *Through the Looking-Glass* by Lewis Carroll (Charles Lutwidge Dodgson), Humpty Dumpty says the line to Alice.

2) TOSS-UP. 10 points.

In which Spanish city is the Alhambra Palace located?

Answer: Granada.

2) BONUS. 20 points. 5 points each.

Identify each of the following.
1) The lake named after the founder of the city of Quebec
2) The 2 U.S. states between which it is located
3) The Canadian province in which this lake is partly located

Answer: 1) Lake Champlain (after Samuel de Champlain)
2) New York and Vermont
3) Quebec.

3) TOSS-UP. 10 points.

What is the phrase from Matthew 20:1-16 which means "at the last possible moment," referring to the "last hour of the day" when the generous owner of the vineyard hired men and paid them the same wage for a day's work as he paid those he had hired earlier in the day?

Answer: At the eleventh hour.

3) BONUS. 20 points. 5 points each.

Spell the Spanish for each of the 4 seasons of the year: spring, summer, fall, and winter.

Answer: *P-r-i-m-a-v-e-r-a, v-e-r-a-n-o, o-t-o-n-o,* and *i-n-v-i-e-r-n-o.*

4) TOSS-UP. 10 points.

Translate *"Gallia est omnis divisa in partes tres,"* the opening words of Caesar's *Gallic Wars.*

Answer: "All Gaul is divided into three parts."

4) BONUS. 30 points. 10 points each.

Answer the following concerning the Second Triumvirate legally established in 43 B.C. and renewed in 37 B.C.
1) What dominant leader in Rome formed this alliance?
2) With what 2 men did he form this alliance?
3) In the ensuing rivalry that developed in the alliance, what member allied himself with what "Queen of Kings" before they were defeated at the Battle of Actium in 31 B.C.?

Answer: 1) **Octavian (Gaius Julius Caesar Octavianus; born Gaius Octavius; called Augustus, a title of honor bestowed by the senate in 27 B.C.)**
2) **Mark Antony (Marcus Antonius) and (Marcus Aemilius) Lepidus**
3) **Antony allied himself with Cleopatra (Octavian defeated them).**

5) TOSS-UP. 10 points.

Name the U.S. President, a graduate of Williams College in Williamstown, Massachusetts, who was headed there for a reunion but never arrived because he was shot at the Baltimore and Potomac Railway Depot in Washington, D.C., on July 2, 1881.

Answer: James A. Garfield.

5) BONUS. 20 points. 10 points each.

Give the 2 French phrases for types of epilepsy, one characterized by short periods of unconsciousness but no convulsions, and the other by convulsions and loss of consciousness.

Answer: *Petit mal* (small illness) and *grand mal* (great ailment).

6) TOSS-UP. 10 points.

What is the name of George M. Cohan's World War I song with the lyrics, "Send the word, send the word _____,/That the Yanks are coming, the Yanks are coming, / The drums rum-tumming ev'rywhere"?

Answer: "Over There."

6) BONUS. 20 points. 5 points each.

Identify each of the following words for *novel*.
1) The French word for "a novel"
2) The French phrase for "a novel or romance in which actual historical characters are introduced under fictitious names" (literally, "a novel with a key")
3) The French phrase for "a long novel," usually in several volumes, which deals with many generations of a family or social group (literally "a river novel")
4) The French phrase for "a serialized story in a newspaper" (literally, "a serial story")

Answer: 1) *roman*
         2) *roman à clef*
         3) *roman-fleuve*
         4) *roman-feuilleton.*

7) TOSS-UP. 10 points.

Which English nurse earned the nicknamed of "The Lady With the Lamp"?

Answer: Florence Nightingale.

7) BONUS. 20 points. 5 points each.

Listen to the lines from the following poem and then give the following information: "Lo! in that house of misery / A lady with a lamp I see / Pass through the glimmering gloom, / And flit from room to room."
1) The name of the poem

2) The author of the poem
3) The war in 1854 in which the lady in the poem played a major role
4) The city in which she was born

Answer: 1) "Santa Filomena" (which means "Saint Night-ingale")
2) Henry Wadsworth Longfellow
3) The Crimean War (between Great Britain and France against Russia)
4) Florence, Italy (she was born there on May 12, 1820, and named for the city).

8) TOSS-UP. 10 points.

What is the term used to designate the property of matter to remain at rest or to maintain its state of motion without change unless acted upon by some external force?

Answer: Inertia.

8) BONUS. 20 points. 5 points each.

Identify the location of each of the following medical facilities.
1) Mayo Clinic
2) Menninger Psychiatric Clinic
3) Hughston Orthopaedic Clinic and Hughston Sports Medicine Hospital
4) Johns Hopkins Hospital and Medical School

Answer: 1) Rochester, Minnesota
2) Topeka, Kansas
3) Columbus, Georgia
4) Baltimore, Maryland.

9) TOSS-UP. 10 points.

Which dog breed is a Dandie Dinmont, one derived from Sir Walter Scott's novel *Guy Mannering*? Farmer Dandie Dinmont raises 2 of these dogs, whose name literally means "earth dog." They have drooping ears, a shaggy grayish or brownish coat and short legs.

Answer: (Dandie Dinmont) Terrier.

9) BONUS. 20 points. 5 points each.

Identify the name by which the inhabitants of the following cities or countries are known.

1) Liverpool
2) Moscow
3) Naples
4) Cyprus

Answer: 1) **Liverpudlians**
           2) **Muscovites (Moscovites)**
           3) **Neapolitans**
           4) **Cypriots (Cypriotes, or Cyprians).**

10) TOSS-UP. 10 points.

What "golden" bird is sometimes called the "King of the Birds" because it seems to symbolize both freedom and power?

Answer: Golden eagle.

10) BONUS. 30 points. 10 points each.

Identify each of the following terms used in ballet.
1) A practice wooden bar on a ballet studio wall
2) A jump from one foot to the other as one foot is "thrown" for power
3) A dance for two persons; a duet

Answer: 1) Barre
           2) Jeté
           3) Pas de deux.

11) TOSS-UP. 10 points.

Name the clear thick fluid resembling the white of an egg that is located between the adjacent bones of a movable joint.

Answer: Synovial fluid (or synovia).

11) BONUS. 20 points. 10 points each.

What are the 2 Latin phrases used to describe a government existing by fact, and not by choice or right and a government recognized as right and lawful?

Answer: *De facto* and *de jure*.

12) TOSS-UP. 10 points.

Which court case involving a white engineer denied admission to the University of California Medical School at Davis concluded with a ruling prohibiting the use of quotas in admission decisions but supporting their use as a factor for consideration?

Answer: Bakke Case (*Regents of the University of California v. Allan Bakke.*)

12) BONUS. 30 points. 10 points each.

Identify the country or area designated by the Roman name.
1) Hesperia
2) Helvetia
3) Caledonia

Answer: 1) Spain (the Western Land: the ancient Greek name for Italy and the Roman writers' name for Spain and sometimes for Italy)
2) Switzerland
3) Scotland.

13) TOSS-UP. 10 points.

What grammatical error is made in the sentence "I ain't got no money"?

Answer: Double negative.

13) BONUS. 20 points. 5 points each.

Name the country involved in a 1915 dispute with the U.S., and name the ABC powers who unsuccessfully attempted mediation at a meeting in Niagara Falls, Canada.

Answer: Mexico (engaged in the dispute when the U.S. intervened in Mexican affairs by landing troops in Veracruz on April 25, 1915) and Argentina, Brazil, and Chile (the ABC powers).

14) TOSS-UP. 10 points.

Name the Supreme Court case of 1819 in which the court ruled that a charter is a contract which the Constitution protects from state legislative interference. This case involved a college granted a charter as a private school and the state of New Hampshire's efforts to revoke the charter and make it a state university.

Answer: *Dartmouth College v. Woodward.*

14) BONUS. 30 points. 10 points each.

Identify the German classical composer of each group of the following works.

1) *Hungarian Dances, A German Requiem,* and *Alto Rhapsody*
2) *Parsifal, The Flying Dutchman,* and *A Faust Overture*
3) *Thus Spake Zarathustra, Don Quixote,* and *Metamorphoses*

Answer: 1) **Johannes Brahms**
2) **Richard Wagner**
3) **Richard Strauss.**

15) TOSS-UP. 10 points.

In which Tennessee city was the Sunsphere the focal point of the 1982 World's Fair and "Energy Turns the World" its theme?

Answer: Knoxville.

15) BONUS. 20 points. 5 points each.

Name the U.S. city associated with each World's Fair center of attraction and theme.

1) Trylon and Perisphere / "Building the World of Tomorrow"
2) The Space Needle / "Man in the Space Age"
3) Wonderwall / "The World of Rivers—Fresh Water as a Source of Life"
4) Unisphere / "Peace Through Understanding"

Answer: 1) **New York (1939-1940)**
2) **Seattle (1962)**
3) **New Orleans (1984)**
4) **New York (1964-1965).**

16) TOSS-UP. 10 points.

Which fictional character did C.S. Forester feature in *Beat to Quarters, Flying Colours,* and *A Ship of the Line*?

Answer: Captain Horatio Hornblower.

16) BONUS. 20 points. 10 points each.

Name the "Brown Bomber" and his 1946 opponent, the "Pittsburgh Kid," about whom he said, "He can run but he can't hide." The "Brown Bomber" won in the 8th round.

Answer: Joe Louis / Billy Conn.

17) TOSS-UP. 10 points.

Name the first American satellite in space (January 31, 1958).

Answer: *Explorer I.*

17) BONUS. 30 points. 10 points each.

Identify each of the following Jacksons.
1) I became a well-known gospel singer called the "Queen of Gospel Song."
2) I became known as "Mr. October" in baseball, and I had a candy bar named after me.
3) I wrote the short story "The Lottery" (1948), a classic American story.

Answer: 1) **Mahalia**
         2) **Reggie**
         3) **Shirley.**

18) TOSS-UP. 10 points.

In which month and year was Archduke Francis Ferdinand, the heir to the thrones of Austria-Hungary (Hapsburg thrones), assassinated by a Serbian nationalist, an event which led to the outbreak of WWI?

Answer: June (28), 1914.

18) BONUS. 20 points. 5 points each.

Identify each of the following concerning World War I.
1) The name of the Bosnian Serb assassin
2) The name of the town in which the assassination occurred
3) The ruler of Austria-Hungary who declared war on Serbia after his heir and nephew had been assassinated
4) The name of the country which was known as the Kingdom of Serbs, Croats, and Slovenes, and given its present name in 1929

Answer: 1) **Gavrilo Princip**
         2) **Sarajevo, Bosnia (at the Princip Bridge over the Miljacka River where the assassination took place stand two footprints—Princip's footprints—embedded in the concrete sidewalk; now Sarajevo, Yugoslavia)**
         3) **Francis Joseph (Franz Josef I)**
         4) **Yugoslavia.**

19) TOSS-UP. 10 points.

What is the only even prime number?

Answer: 2.

19) **BONUS. 30 points. 5 points each. Point total stops at the first mistake.**

Name the 6 planets closest to the sun starting with the closest.

Answer: Mercury, Venus, Earth, Mars, Jupiter, and Saturn.

20) **TOSS-UP. 10 points.**

After having witnessed brutality to horses in Russia, Henry Bergh, a New York philanthropist, founded the ASPCA in 1866. What is the full name of this society?

Answer: American Society for the Prevention of Cruelty to Animals.

20) **BONUS. 25 points. 5 points each.**

Identify the last name of each of the following sets of American brothers associated with the "Wild West."
1) Morgan, James, Virgil, and Wyatt
2) Frank and Jesse
3) Ike, Phineas (Finn), and Billy
4) Cole, Jim, John, and Bob
5) Emmett, Robert (Rob), Frank, William, and Gratton (Grat)

Answer: 1) Earp
       2) James
       3) Clanton
       4) Younger
       5) Dalton.

21) **TOSS-UP. 10 points.**

Identify the map projection named after West German historian Arno _____. His map projection is unlike Mercator's, for Africa (not Europe) dominates the center and the equator passes through the middle (not the bottom third).

Answer: Peters Projection.

21) **BONUS. 30 points. 15 points each.**

Two phrases from John Donne's *Devotions upon Emergent Occasions* have been used as movie titles, one of which is also the title of an Ernest Hemingway novel. Give the 2 phrases by completing the blanks in the following excerpts from Meditation XVII: "_____, entire of itself; every man is a piece of the continent, . . . I am involved in mankind; and therefore never send to know _____; it tolls for thee."

Answer: "No man is an island" / "for whom the bell tolls."

22) TOSS-UP. 10 points.

In which town in Virginia was the "Battle of the Crater" fought on July 30, 1864?

Answer: Petersburg.

22) BONUS. 20 points. 10 points each.

In which mountains in which state did Washington Irving's Rip Van Winkle live?

Answer: Catskills in New York.

23) TOSS-UP. 10 points.

What name did the French poet Tristan Tzara give to the art movement in painting, sculpture, and literature that defied convention and stressed absurdity. The name literally means "hobby-horse" in French.

Answer: Dada (dadaism).

23) BONUS. 30 points. 10 points each.

Of which ship in which work is each of the following "Captain"?
1) Captain Wolf Larsen in a work by Jack London
2) Captain Ahab in a work by Herman Melville
3) Captain William Bligh in a work by Charles Nordhoff and James Norman Hall

Answer: 1) *Ghost* in *The Sea Wolf*
2) *Pequod* in *Moby Dick*
3) H.M.S. *Bounty* in *Mutiny on the Bounty*.

24) TOSS-UP. 30 points after the first clue. 20 after the second. 10 after the third.

Who am I?
1) I wrote the book *One World* in 1943 outlining my ideas on

international cooperation.

2) I was known as the "Barefoot Boy from Wall Street."

3) I was the Republican candidate for President of the U.S. in 1940.

Answer: Wendell Lewis Willkie.

24) BONUS. 20 points. 5 points each.

Each of the following works is the only *chef d'oeuvre* of its author. Identify the writer of each.

1) *To Kill a Mockingbird*
2) *Gone With the Wind*
3) *A Confederacy of Dunces*
4) *The Rubáiyát*

Answer: 1) **Harper Lee**
2) **Margaret Mitchell**
3) **John Kennedy Toole**
4) **Omar Khayyám (translated by Edward FitzGerald).**

25) TOSS-UP. 10 points.

Identify the Washington, D.C., school, that is the world's only liberal arts college for the deaf. Its students are nicknamed the "Bisons."

Answer: Gallaudet College.

25) BONUS. 20 points. 10 points each.

Identify the play by William Shakespeare in which the following lines appear, and identify the character whose name is missing in the lines: "Let me have men about me that are fat; / Sleek-headed men, and such as sleep o'nights; / Yond' _____ has a lean and hungry look; / He thinks too much: such men are dangerous."

Answer: *Julius Caesar*/Cassius (The lines were said by Caesar).

CATEGORY TOSS-UP. 100 points. 10 points each. 10 points deducted for an incorrect answer.

Complete each of the following nursery rhymes.

1) "Jack Sprat could eat no fat, / His wife could eat no lean; / And so betwixt (between) them both (you see), / They _____!"
2) "Wee Willie Winkie runs through the town, / Upstairs and downstairs in his nightgown, / Rapping at the window, crying

through the lock, / Are the children in their beds, for now it's
_____?

3) "Little Miss Muffet/ Sat on a tuffet, / Eating her (some) curds and
   whey; / There (Along) came a spider, / Who sat down beside her
   / And _____."

4) "There was an old woman who lived in a shoe, / She had so many
   children she didn't know what to do; / She gave them some broth
   without any bread; / She whipped them all soundly and
   _____."

5) "High diddle diddle/ The cat and the fiddle, / The cow jumped over
   the moon; / The little dog laughed / To see such craft (sport) / And
   the _____."

6) "Jack and Jill went up the hill / To fetch a pail of water; / Jack fell
   down and broke his crown, / And _____."

7) "There once were two cats of Kilkenny, / Each thought there was
   one cat too many; / So they fought and they bit, / Till, excepting
   their nails / And the tip of their tails / Instead of two _____."

8) "Tom, Tom, the piper's son, / Stole a pig and away did run! / The
   pig was eat, and Tom was beat, / And Tom went _____."

9) "Pussy cat, pussy cat, where have you been? / I've been to London
   to look at the queen. / Pussy cat, pussy cat, what did you there?/
   I frightened a _____."

10) Mary had a little lamb, / Its fleece was white as snow; / And every-
    where that Mary went / The _____."

Answer: 1) **licked the plate (platter) clean**
          2) **eight o'clock (or ten o'clock)**
          3) **frightened Miss Muffet away**
          4) **put (sent) them to bed**
          5) **dish ran away with the spoon**
          6) **Jill came tumbling after**
          7) **cats, there weren't any**
          8) **howling down the street (crying down the street)**
          9) **little mouse under her chair**
          10) **lamb was sure to go.**

ROUND SEVEN

1) TOSS-UP. 10 points.

Name the river, mentioned in the Old and New Testament, in which Jesus Christ was baptized by John the Baptist (Matthew 3:13-17).

Answer: Jordan River.

1) BONUS. 30 points. 10 points each.

Identify the following efforts to stabilize the German economy following WWI.
1) The plan of April, 1924, that scheduled gradual German reparation payments to its former enemies
2) The plan of February, 1929, that revised the first plan and reduced the amount of German reparation payments
3) The conference of June, 1932, that proposed cancellation of 90% of the reparation payments demanded in the second plan

Answer: 1) Dawes Plan
2) Young Plan
3) Lausanne Conference.

2) TOSS-UP. 10 points.

About which vice presidential candidate did Mark Hanna bemoan, "There would be only one heartbeat between that wild-eyed madman—that damned cowboy—and the Presidency of the United States"?

Answer: Theodore Roosevelt.

2) BONUS. 20 points. 10 points each.

Identify each of the following.
1) The country formerly called Abyssinia
2) This country's capital

Answer: 1) Ethiopia
2) Addis Ababa.

3) TOSS-UP. 20 points after the first clue. 10 after the second.

What's my name?
1) I was thrown into jail in 1832 for 6 months for depicting King Louis Phillipe in a caricature as Gargantua gorging himself on the earnings of French workers.
2) I was a French lithographer, caricaturist, and painter—a pioneer in realism—and I am probably best known for *The Third-Class Carriage*.

Answer: Honoré Daumier.

3) BONUS. 20 points. 5 points each.

Identify the country whose flag is known as the *tricolore* (tricolor), and then, using the language spoken in the country, give the 3 colors in its flag.

Answer: France / *Bleu, blanc, et rouge.*

4) TOSS-UP. 10 points.

Which word designates the bicameral legislative body of Japan, which consists of the House of Representatives and the House of Councillors?

Answer: Diet.

4) BONUS. 20 points. 5 points each.

Identify each of the following legislative bodies.
1) The bicameral legislative body of Great Britain, which consists of the House of Commons and the House of Lords
2) The bicameral legislative body of the Soviet Union, which consists of the Council of the Union and the Council of the Nationalities
3) The unicameral legislature of Israel
4) The bicameral legislative body of Canada, which consists of the Senate and the House of Commons

Answer: 1) Parliament
2) Supreme Soviet
3) Knesset
4) Parliament.

5) TOSS-UP. 10 points.

In botany, it is a group of shrubs or herbs of the Mediterranean region which have spiny or toothed leaves with flowers ranging from white to purple; in architecture, it is the leafy decoration resembling this plant, used especially on the capitals of Corinthian columns. Name it.

Answer: Acanthus.

5) BONUS. 20 points. 10 points each.

Grover Cleveland, in referring on March 1, 1886, to the Tenure of Office Act, said, "After an existence of nearly twenty years of innocuous desuetude these laws are brought forth." Define "innocuous" and "desuetude."

Answer: Innocuous means "harmless" or "having no adverse effect," and desuetude means "lapsing into inexistence" or "state or condition of disuse."

6) TOSS-UP. 10 points.

What is the name of the figure of speech in which one thing is directly likened to another as in the phrase "a heart as big as a house"?

Answer: Simile.

6) BONUS. 20 points. 5 points each.

Identify each of the following concerning the life of a handicapped American woman.
1) The blind, deaf, and mute woman born near Tuscumbia, Alabama, in 1880, who conquered her physical handicaps caused by brain fever at 19 months
2) The woman who became the teacher of this handicapped child when she was seven years old
3) The play and movie that told the story of how this teacher used the sense of touch to help this woman
4) The school, located in Cambridge, Massachusetts, from which this handicapped woman graduated *cum laude* in 1904

Answer: 1) Helen Adams Keller
        2) Anne Sullivan (Macy; Mary Agnes "Polly" Thomson replaced her in 1936)
        3) *The Miracle Worker*
        4) Radcliffe College.

7) TOSS-UP. 10 points.

Which U.S. institution, whose students are nicknamed the "Falcons," is called the "West Point of the Air"? This Academy is located 8 miles north of Colorado Springs, Colorado.

Answer: U.S. Air Force Academy.

7) BONUS. 30 points after the first clue. 20 after the second. 10 after the third.

Who am I?
1) I was the son of Peleus and Thetis in Greek mythology.
2) I was dressed in women's clothing and sent to live with King Lycomedes on the island of Skiros (Scyros) so that I would not participate in the Trojan War.
3) My mother dipped me in the River Styx at birth to make me immortal but the water did not touch my heel, the spot where Paris' arrow struck and killed me.

Answer: Achilles.

8) TOSS-UP. 10 points.

The Alpine belt is an area where earthquakes occur. On which 2 continents is this belt located?

Answer: Europe and Asia.

8) BONUS. 20 points. 10 points each.

What is the name of the world's highest mountain that is not part of a range, and in which country is it located?

Answer: Mount Kilimanjaro (or Mount Kibo) is located in Tanzania.

9) TOSS-UP. 10 points.

Although he had not killed anyone nor held anyone for ransom, he was found guilty under California's "Little Lindbergh" law, which provided for the death penalty if "bodily harm" were used during a kidnapping. This person became a *cause célèbre* in Cell 2455 on Death Row in San Quentin. What is the name of this sex offender, known as the "Red Light Bandit," who was executed on May 2, 1960?

Answer: Caryl Chessman.

9) BONUS. 20 points. 10 points each.

Which "Boss" and which "Hall" of the 1870's and 1880's did William

O. Bartlett, editorial writer for the New York *Sun*, expose with the slogan: "No king, no clown / To rule this town!"

Answer: "Boss" Tweed and Tammany Hall.

10) TOSS-UP. 10 points.

Identify the plant, *Taraxacum officinale*, native to Eurasia, that was named from the French words meaning "the tooth of the lion."

Answer: Dandelion (*dent de lion*).

10) BONUS. 30 points. 10 points each.

Identify each of the following terms in ballet.
1) A full turn of the body while standing on one foot
2) A group of dancers that performs as an ensemble for a ballet company
3) A jump straight upward, during which the dancer repeatedly crosses his legs and sometimes beats them together

Answer: 1) Pirouette
2) Corps de ballet
3) Entrechat.

11) TOSS-UP. 10 points.

Identify the Quaker, nicknamed the "Great Humanitarian," who as head of the U.S. Food Administration directed efforts in Europe following WWI and eventually became President.

Answer: Herbert Clark Hoover.

11) BONUS. 30 points. 10 points each.

Who shot and killed which person on July 11, 1804, in Weehawken, and in which state did this famous incident occur?

Answer: Aaron Burr shot and killed Alexander Hamilton in a duel (Hamilton died on July 12) in New Jersey.

12) TOSS-UP. 10 points.

Name the sea god of Greek mythology from whom the word meaning "a person who readily changes his appearance, character, or principles" is derived.

Answer: Proteus (protean in the adjective form).

12) BONUS. 20 points. 5 points each.

Identify the following words that have come from literary characters with similar traits.
1) The word that means "vain, empty, noisy boasting or bragging; arrogant pretention" and is derived from a character in Edmund Spenser's *The Faerie Queen*
2) The word that means "a boastful, swashbuckling soldier" and is derived from the title character in a play by Plautus
3) The adjective that means "boastful, witty and brazen" and is derived from a character in Shakespeare's *Henry IV* (Parts I and II) and *The Merry Wives of Windsor*
4) The word that means "arrogant boasting, or pretentious, blustering talk" and is derived from a character in Boiardo's *Orlando Innamorato* (1487) and Ariosto's sequel *Orlando Furioso* (1532)

Answer: 1) Braggadocio (after Braggadochio)
2) Miles gloriosus
3) Falstaffian (from Falstaff)
4) Rodomontade (rodomontado, rhodomontade; from Rodomont).

13) TOSS-UP. 10 points.

What is the official motto of the United States, adopted on July 30, 1956?

Answer: In God We Trust.

13) BONUS. 20 points. 5 points each.

Name 4 of the first 8 commissioners in the history of professional baseball.

Answer: Judge Kenesaw Mountain Landis (1921-1944); Albert B. "Happy" Chandler (1945-1951); Ford C. Frick (1951-1965); William D. Eckert (1965-1969); Bowie K. Kuhn (1969-1984); Peter V. Ueberroth (1984-1989); A. Bartlett Giamatti (1989); and Francis "Fay" Vincent (1989-).

14) TOSS-UP. 10 points.

Identify the leader of 450 Confederate guerrilla raiders who, on August 21, 1863, shot every man and boy in sight and burned the town of Lawrence, Kansas, killing about 150.

Answer: William Clarke Quantrill (leader of Quantrill's Raiders).

14) BONUS. 30 points. 10 points each.

Name his work, the location in which it is set, and the author who won the 1928 Pulitzer Prize in literature, an award given for the first time for a work set outside the United States.

Answer: *The Bridge of San Luis Rey* / Lima, Peru / Thornton Niven Wilder.

15) TOSS-UP. 10 points.

What is the 2-word term for "a method of finding the position of an aircraft or ship without astronomical observations, as by using compass readings and other previously recorded data"?

Answer: Dead reckoning.

15) BONUS. 20 points. 5 points each.

In which U.S. state is each of the following cities located?
1) East Chicago
2) East Cleveland
3) East Moline
4) East Saint Louis

Answer: 1) Indiana
2) Ohio
3) Illinois
4) Illinois.

16) TOSS-UP. 10 points.

Identify the South American country whose name means "equator."

Answer: Ecuador.

16) BONUS. 20 points. 5 points each.

Identify each of the following South American countries.
1) The country whose name comes from the Latin word for "silver"
2) The country formerly called *Alto Perú*, Upper Peru, by the Spaniards
3) The country whose name means "Little Venice" in Spanish
4) The country whose name is derived from an Indian word that means "place where the land ends" or "deepest part of the earth"

Answer: 1) Argentina
2) Bolivia
3) Venezuela
4) Chile.

17) TOSS-UP. 10 points.

He wrote, "I have entered on an enterprise which is without precedent, and will have no imitator. I propose to show my fellows a man as nature made him, and this man shall be myself." Who is this French author, sometimes called the "Father of European Romanticism," who wrote the above in his *Les Confessions* (1781-1788)?

Answer: Jean Jacques Rousseau.

17) BONUS. 30 points. 10 points each.

Identify each of the following art movements from the description.
1) A western European artistic and literary movement of the early 20th century, characterized by the rejection of traditional conventions, by nihilistic satire, and by the intention to shock through irrationality and fantastic or abstract creations
2) An early 20th century movement in painting marked by the use of bold, often distorted forms and vivid colors, from the French for "wild beast"
3) A style of painting and sculpture developed in Paris in the early 20th century and characterized by the reduction and separation of subjects into abstract and geometric structures

Answer: 1) Dadaism (dada, or Dada; from the French for "hobbyhorse")
2) Fauvism (Les Fauves)
3) Cubism.

18) TOSS-UP. 10 points.

Identify not only the author of *Keeping Faith* but also the author of *First Lady From Plains*. He served as U.S. President and she was the First Lady.

Answer: Jimmy Carter and Rosalynn Carter.

18) BONUS. 20 points. 10 points each.

Identify the 2 poets from the given stanzas.

1) From "A Valediction Forbidding Mourning": "If they be two, they are two so / As stiff twin compasses are two; / Thy soul, the fixt foot, makes no show / To move, but doth if the other do."

2) From "A Red, Red Rose": "O, my Luve is like a red, red rose, / That's newly sprung in June. / O, my Luve is like the melodie, / That's sweetly played in tune."

Answer: 1) John Donne
       2) Robert Burns.

19) TOSS-UP. 10 points.

Name a temple of Sumerian origin in the form of a pyramidal tower with each story smaller than the one below it.

Answer: Ziggurat (also zikkurat or zikurat).

19) BONUS. 20 points. 10 points each.

Name the tree in the Garden of Eden bearing the forbidden fruit which was tasted by Adam and Eve (Genesis 2:17; 3:6-24) and the tree in the Garden of Eden bearing fruit, which if eaten, gave everlasting life (Genesis 2:9; 3:22).

Answer: Tree of knowledge of good and evil (or tree of knowledge) and the tree of life.

20) TOSS-UP. 10 points.

Which Russian composed *The Firebird* in 1910?

Answer: Igor Stravinsky.

20) BONUS. 20 points. 5 points each.

Identify the composer of each of the following works.
1) *The Nutcracker* (1892)
2) *Prelude to the Afternoon of a Faun* (1892-1894)
3) *From the New World* (1893)
4) *Shéhérazade* (1888)

Answer: 1) Peter Ilich Tchaikovsky
       2) Achille-Claude Debussy
       3) Antonín Dvorák
       4) Nikolai Rimsky-Korsakov.

21) TOSS-UP. 10 points.

What is the mathematical name for a straight line that connects 2 nonadjacent vertices of a polygon?

Answer: Diagonal.

21) **BONUS. 30 points. 5 points each.**

Answer each of the following.
1) From 1302 until the 1789 Revolution in France, which groups were represented in the "Three Estates" of the States-General?
2) Which group did Edmund Burke call the "Fourth Estate," while speaking in Parliament when he said, "And there sits the Fourth Estate, more important than them all"?
3) Which group is today identified as the "Fifth Estate"?

Answer: 1) Clergy, nobility, and the commoners
2) Journalism, or the press
3) Scientists, or the Mafia, or the Underworld.

22) **TOSS-UP. 20 points after the first clue. 10 after the second.**

Which word am I?
1) I am a sculpture, often a profiled head, carved in relief on a background of another color on a gem or shell.
2) I mean a "small theatrical role or brief appearance by a prominent actor or actress often limited to a single scene on a TV show or in a motion picture."

Answer: Cameo (Cameo role or cameo bit).

22) **BONUS. 20 points. 5 points each.**

Identify each of the following.
1) The 2 South American countries which do not border on Brazil
2) The 2 landlocked South American countries

Answer: 1) Chile and Ecuador
2) Bolivia and Paraguay.

23) **TOSS-UP. 10 points.**

Give the month, day, and year of the death of Julius Caesar.

Answer: March 15, 44 B.C.

23) **BONUS. 30 points. 10 points each.**

Give the city and state of the 3 existing U.S. mints.

Answer: Philadelphia, Pennsylvania (since 1792); Denver, Colorado (since 1906); and San Francisco, California (1854-1955 and since 1965).

24) TOSS-UP. 10 points.

Which title was first used by the counts of Viennois and Auvergne, whose coat of arms bearing three dolphins was later adopted by the French crown princes? This title was then used from 1349 to 1830 as the official title of the eldest son of the King of France, the heir apparent to the French throne.

Answer: Dauphin.

24) BONUS. 30 points. 10 points each.

Each of the following works is the *chef d'oeuvre* of its author. Identify the writer of each.
1) *Call It Sleep*
2) *The Invisible Man*
3) *The Bell Jar*

Answer: 1) Henry Roth
2) Ralph Ellison
3) Sylvia Plath.

25) TOSS-UP. 10 points.

Identify the Central American country whose name is derived from that of a Roman Catholic feast meaning "Holy Saviour of the World."

Answer: El Salvador (from the feast of *San Salvador del Mundo*).

25) BONUS. 30 points. 10 points each.

Identify each of the following concerning the vice presidency of the U.S.
1) The first Vice President to resign, who did so in 1832 for political reasons, and the President he was serving
2) The second Vice President to resign, who did so in 1973 after being charged with accepting bribes while serving as a Baltimore County Executive and as governor of Maryland, and the President he was serving
3) The man who replaced him as Vice President in 1973, and the number of the amendment that allows a President to fill a vacancy in the office of Vice President

Answer: 1) John C. Calhoun and Andrew Jackson
2) Spiro Agnew and Richard Nixon
3) Gerald Ford and 25th Amendment.

CATEGORY TOSS-UP. 100 points. 10 points each. 10 points deducted for an incorrect answer.

Identify each of the following individuals associated with the French Revolution.
1) The French king who was guillotined in 1793
2) The French queen who was guillotined in 1793
3) The revolutionary leader who said, *"Il nous faut de l'audace, encore de l'audace, toujours de l'audace"* ("Audacity, audacity, always audacity") and was guillotined in 1794
4) The "Father of Modern Chemistry," who was guillotined in 1794
5) The provincial girl, a Girondist supporter, who stabbed to death a revolutionary leader in his bathtub and was guillotined in 1793
6) The notorious revolutionary leader who was stabbed to death in 1793 in his bathtub by a young woman from the provinces
7) The Jacobin leader, known as the "Incorruptible," who was elected to the 12-man Committee of Public Safety in 1793, but against whom his fellow Jacobins conspired, and who was guillotined in 1794
8) The revolutionary leader known as the "Tribune of the People" and the "French Demosthenes"
9) The moderate leader who was elected president of the National Assembly in 1790, was excommunicated by the Pope, and fled to America in 1794
10) The commander in chief of the armed forces who helped end the Reign of Terror, or his assistant whose artillery cleared the streets of Paris "with a whiff of grapeshot" on October 5, 1795, establishing the Directory

Answer: 1) Louis XVI
2) Marie Antoinette
3) George Jacques Danton
4) Antoine Lavoisier
5) Charlotte Corday
6) Jean Paul Marat
7) Maximilien Robespierre
8) Comte de Mirabeau (Honoré Gabriel Victor Riguetti)
9) Talleyrand (Charles Maurice de Talleyrand-

Périgord, Prince de Bénévent)
10) Vicomte de Barras (Paul François Jean Nicolas
Barras) or Napoléon.

ROUND EIGHT

1) TOSS-UP. 10 points.

In what environment did *fluvial* civilizations develop?

Answer: Along the banks of a river.

1) BONUS. 20 points. 5 points each.

Give the Japanese words that carry the following literal meanings.
1) "Divine wind" or "God wind"
2) "belly cutting"
3) "a man power carriage"
4) "exalted gate" or "honorable door" (i.e., of the Imperial Palace)

Answer: 1) Kamikaze
2) Hara-kiri (hari-kari)
3) Jinrikisha (jinriksha, jinricksha, or jinrickshaw)
4) Mikado (Mikado).

2) TOSS-UP. 10 points.

Name one of the 2 ships, an Italian and a Swedish liner, that collided on July 25, 1956, off Nantucket Island, Massachusetts, with over 50 lives lost. One of the ships has the same name as the capital of Sweden.

Answer: *Andrea Doria* and the *Stockholm*.

2) BONUS. 20 points. 5 points each.

Identify the ships described in each of the following.
1) The U.S. battleship that exploded on February 15, 1898, in the Havana Harbor, Cuba, with over 260 lives lost
2) The ship that struck an iceberg and sank on April 15, 1912, in the North Atlantic with more than 1,490 lives lost
3) The ship that was sunk by a German submarine on May 7, 1915, off the coast of Ireland with over 1,195 lives lost
4) The U.S. nuclear submarine that sank on April 10, 1963, in the North Atlantic with 129 dead

Answer: 1) *Maine*
2) *Titanic*
3) *Lusitania*
4) U.S.S. *Thresher.*

3) TOSS-UP. 10 points.

In which country did Faisal rule as the first king (1921-1933) after the British took his country from the Ottoman Empire?

Answer: Iraq.

3) BONUS. 20 points. 10 points each.

Identify each of the following.
1) The American sometimes called the "Father of the Hydrogen Bomb"
2) The Soviet "Father of the Hydrogen Bomb"

Answer: 1) Edward Teller
2) Andrei Dmitriyevich Sakharov.

4) TOSS-UP. 10 points.

Give the names of the father and mother of a foal.

Answer: Sire and dam.

4) BONUS. 20 points. 5 points each.

What is the national anthem of each of the following countries?
1) United States
2) Great Britain
3) France
4) Canada

Answer: 1) "The Star-Spangled Banner"
2) "God Save the Queen" (or "King")
3) "La Marseillaise"
4) "O Canada."

5) TOSS-UP. 10 points.

Name the national hero known as the "Apostle of Agrarian Reform" and the "Attila of the South" who occupied Mexico City with Pancho Villa in 1914 and was murdered by Colonel Jésus Guajardo in 1919.

Answer: Emiliano Zapata [His motto was "Land, Liberty,

and Death to the *hacendados*" (landowners)].

5) BONUS. 30 points. 10 points each.

Name the 3 ballets Russian-American composer Igor Fyodorovich Stravinsky produced in Paris in collaboration with Sergei Diaghilev in 1910, 1911, and 1913.

Answer: *The Firebird* **(1910),** *Petrouchka* **(1911), and** *The Rite of Spring* **(1913).**

6) TOSS-UP. 10 points.

The Latin word *videlicet* is abbreviated *viz.* What is the meaning of this word?

Answer: Namely (that is to say).

6) BONUS. 20 points. 10 points each.

Identify each of the following.
1) The U.S. judge who presided over the Watergate affair
2) The judge who presided over the largest corporate divestiture in history—the split of American Telephone and Telegraph into 8 smaller divisions

Answer: 1) Judge John Sirica
2) Judge Harold Greene (born Heinz Grünhaus).

7) TOSS-UP. 10 points.

Who is famous for saying "*Cogito, ergo sum*" ("I think, therefore I am")?

Answer: René Descartes (Who first said "*Cogito, ergo sum, cogito*" is not known).

7) BONUS. 20 points. 5 points each.

Identify each of the following.
1) The family whose baby was kidnapped and then murdered in the 1930's
2) The state in which the kidnapping occurred in Hopewell
3) The year it occurred in March
4) The person who committed the crime

Answer: 1) (Charles) Lindbergh, Jr., family
2) New Jersey

3) 1932
4) **Richard Bruno Hauptmann.**

8) TOSS-UP. 10 points.

Who was the first presidential nominee of the Republican Party? His name completes the 1856 slogan, "Free Soil, Free Men, Free Speech, _____."

Answer: (John C.) Frémont.

8) BONUS. 20 points. 5 points each.

Identify the state in which each of the following golf courses is located.
1) Augusta National Golf Club
2) Pinehurst Country Club
3) Pebble Beach Golf Links
4) Merion Golf Course

Answer: 1) Georgia (Augusta)
2) North Carolina (Pinehurst)
3) California (Pebble Beach)
4) Pennsylvania (Ardmore).

9) TOSS-UP. 30 points after the first clue. 20 after the second. 10 after the third.

What is my name?
1) I was a mountain nymph, the daughter of the river-god Peneus (Peneius) in Greek mythology.
2) Thanks to a lead-tipped arrow shot by Eros (Cupid), I could love neither god nor mortal. Apollo, however, called after me, "I am the lord of Delphi, and I love you," but I cherished my freedom and did not want to be married.
3) After I screamed for my father to help me, Apollo changed me into a laurel tree, which he promised would remain eternally green and which he adopted as his symbol.

Answer: Daphne.

9) BONUS. 20 points. 10 points each.

Name the barber of Seville and the woman with whom Count Almaviva is madly in love in either Pierre Augustin Caron de Beaumarchais' play *The Barber of Seville* or Gioacchino Rossini's *opera buffa* (comic opera) of the same name.

Answer: Figaro and Rosine (or Rosina).

10) TOSS-UP. 10 points.

Which medal is given as the highest honor by the American Chemical Society? This medal is named after an English clergyman and chemist who, along with Carl Wilhelm Scheele, first discovered a gas he called "dephlogisticated air," later renamed oxygen by Antoine Lavoisier?

Answer: Priestley Medal (after Joseph Priestley).

10) BONUS. 30 points. 10 points each.

Who, during the Civil War, made each of the following statements?
1) "I can't spare this man—he fights."
2) "He has lost his left arm, but I have lost my right arm."
3) "No terms except an unconditional and immediate surrender can be accepted. I propose to move immediately upon your works."

Answer: 1) President Abraham Lincoln (about General Ulysses S. Grant)
2) General Robert E. Lee (about General Thomas J. "Stonewall" Jackson)
3) General Ulysses S. Grant (to General Simon Bolivar Buckner at Fort Donelson).

11) TOSS-UP. 10 points.

When James Butler "Wild Bill" Hickok was shot and killed by Jack McCall in Deadwood, Dakota Territory, on August 2, 1876, he was holding a hand of cards that has become known as the "Dead Man's Hand." Of which 2 ranks of cards did he have pairs?

Answer: Aces and eights (Ace of diamonds and ace of clubs, eight of spades and eight of clubs. The other card was the queen of hearts).

11) BONUS. 20 points. 10 points each.

Answer each of the following.
1) Which country was formerly called Mesopotamia?
2) What is this country's capital?

Answer: 1) Iraq
2) Baghdad.

12) TOSS-UP. 10 points.

Name the summer educational program of public lectures, concerts, and dramatic performances that originated in 1814 at a New York lake and later lent its name to such activities in other locations.

Answer: Chautauqua.

12) BONUS. 20 points. 5 points each.

What 4 words appeared on the wall during the feast of Belshazzar of Babylon and were interpreted by Daniel (Daniel 5) to mean that the kingdom of Belshazzar was to be divided and given to the Medes and Persians?

Answer: *Mene, Mene, Tekel, Upharsin* **(or** *Parsin***); meaning, "numbered, numbered, weighed, (and) divided").**

13) TOSS-UP. 10 points.

What word am I? I am the sea nymph in Homer's *Odyssey* who kept Odysseus on my island of Ogygia for seven years on his way home from Troy. I am an orchid of the North Temperate Zone. I am a type of music, usually satirical ballads, sung by the natives of Trinidad. And I am Jacques Cousteau's oceanographic ship.

Answer: Calypso.

13) BONUS. 20 points. 5 points each.

Identify each of the following professional athletes from the nickname.
1) The basketball player known as the "Big O"
2) The baseball player known as "The Splendid Splinter"
3) The tennis player known as "The Iceman"
4) The race car driver known as the "Stock Car Racing King"

Answer: 1) Oscar Robertson
            2) Ted Williams
            3) Bjorn Borg
            4) Richard Petty.

14) TOSS-UP. 20 points after the first clue. 10 after the second.

Which word or name am I?
1) I am an archaic word for "a meadow," or I am a word for "an alcoholic liquor made of fermented honey and water."

2) I am the last name of an American psychological anthropologist, and the name for a lake in northwest Arizona and southeast Nevada.

Answer: Mead.

14) BONUS. 20 points. 5 points each.

Identify the Broadway play based on each of the following works.
1) *I Am a Camera* and stories by Christopher Isherwood
2) *Liliom*
3) *The Apartment*
4) *Les Romantiques*

Answer: 1) *Cabaret*
**   2) *Carousel***
**   3) *Promises, Promises***
**   4) *The Fantasticks.***

15) TOSS-UP. 10 points.

What is the word for "a social visit, or meeting, as between vessels at sea," "a herd or school of whales," or "a woman's shapely leg"?

Answer: Gam.

15) BONUS. 20 points. 5 points each.

In which country did each of the following rulers abdicate?
1) Diocletian in 305
2) Charles IV in 1808
3) Nicholas II in 1917
4) Carol II in 1940

Answer: 1) Rome (Roman Empire)
**   2) Spain**
**   3) Russia**
**   4) Rumania.**

16) TOSS-UP. 10 points.

How much would a person who weighs 100 pounds on Earth weigh on Mercury—about 17, 37, 57, or 77 pounds?

Answer: 37.

16) BONUS. 20 points. 10 points each.

Identify each of the following.
1) The world's highest capital of an independent country
2) The country in which it is located

Answer: 1) La Paz
       2) Bolivia.

17) TOSS-UP. 20 points after the first clue. 10 after the second.

What's my name?
1) I frequently have 13 columns of beads strung on parallel wires in a rectangular frame for use in mathematical calculations.
2) I am the oldest known mechanical computing aid, having been used in China and other Asian countries as early as the 6th century B.C.

Answer: Abacus (called *suan pan* or *soo poin* in Chinese).

17) BONUS. 30 points. 10 points each.

Identify each of the following art movements from the description.
1) A style of painting developed in France in the 1870's, characterized chiefly by short brush strokes of bright colors to represent the effect of light on objects
2) A 20th century literary and artistic movement that stresses the significance of the unconscious and juxtaposes seemingly unrelated objects
3) A style of decoration and architecture of the late 19th and early 20th centuries, characterized by the use of flowing, sinuous lines

Answer: 1) Impressionism
       2) Surrealism (from the French for "beyond realism")
       3) Art nouveau (from the French for "new art").

18) TOSS-UP. 10 points.

Name the law or principle of Dutch-born mathematician that explains the lift of an airplane wing, the curve of a baseball, and why a ping pong ball cannot be blown out of a funnel.

Answer: Bernoulli's law or principle.

18) BONUS. 20 points. 10 points each.

Identify each of the following concerning the ancient Roman calendar.

1) The term for the 15th day of March, May, July, and October and the 13th day of the other months
2) The term for the 7th day of March, May, July, and October, and the 5th day of the other months

Answer: 1) Ides
      2) Nones.

19) TOSS-UP. 10 points.

What field or discipline has sometimes been called the "Mother of the Arts"?

Answer: Architecture.

19) BONUS. 20 points. 5 points each.

Give the complete name for the following NCAA colleges or universities from their abbreviations.
1) UNLV
2) UTEP
3) CCNY
4) UNCC

Answer: 1) University of Nevada at Las Vegas
      2) University of Texas at El Paso
      3) City College of New York
      4) University of North Carolina at Charlotte.

20) TOSS-UP. 10 points.

Who said, "We shall go on to the end. . . . We shall defend our Island, whatever the cost may be. . . . We shall never surrender" in a speech to the House of Commons on June 4, 1940.

Answer: Winston Churchill.

20) BONUS. 20 points. 10 points each.

Identify each of the following.
1) The word for "the branch of agriculture dealing with the science and economics of field crop production, and soil management"
2) The word for "the art or science of growing flowers, fruits, vegetables, and shrubs"

Answer: 1) Agronomy
      2) Horticulture.

21) TOSS-UP. 10 points.

Name the only U.S. Vice President buried in Washington, D.C., who is also the only Vice President whose surname has become part of the English language, in a word which means "to divide a voting area (state, county, or city) into election districts so as to give one political party an electoral majority in as large a number of districts as possible."

Answer: Elbridge Gerry (*gerrymander* is the word).

21) BONUS. 20 points. 5 points each.

Give the translation of each of the following Latin phrases.
1) *Requiescat in pace*
2) *Dominus vobiscum*
3) *Gloria in Excelsis Deo*
4) *Pater Noster*

Answer: 1) **May he (or she) rest in peace**
2) **The Lord be with you**
3) **Glory in the highest to God (Glory be to God on high)**
4) **Our Father (the Lord's Prayer).**

22) TOSS-UP. 10 points.

Name that temperature of a gas above which it cannot be liquefied by pressure alone, regardless of the amount applied.

Answer: Critical temperature.

22) BONUS. 30 points. 10 points each.

Identify each of the following.
1) The highest point on the earth's surface
2) The lowest spot on the earth's surface
3) The deepest part of any of the Earth's oceans

Answer: 1) **Mt. Everest (Asia)**
2) **Shore of the Dead Sea (SW Asia)**
3) **Mariana Trench (accept the Mindanao Trench).**

23) TOSS-UP. 30 points after the first clue. 20 after the second. 10 after the third.

Which French author of novels, plays, and essays am I?

1) I wrote *Exile and the Kingdom* and *The Fall*.
2) I wrote *The Myth of Sisyphus* and *The Plague*.
3) I wrote *The Stranger* and *Caligula*.

Answer: Albert Camus.

23) **BONUS. 20 points. 10 points each.**

Identify each of the following.
1) The name for the type of painting or sculpture which portrays the Virgin Mary mourning over the dead body of Christ
2) The name of the Italian artist whose work of this genre was exhibited at the New York World's Fair in 1964-1965

**Answer: 1) *Pietà*
2) Michelangelo.**

24) **TOSS-UP. 10 points.**

What is measured at 32 feet per second per second?

Answer: A falling body, or a body's acceleration (the acceleration of a falling body due to the earth's gravitational attraction, near the surface of the earth).

24) **BONUS. 30 points. 5 points each.**

Fill in the blanks of at least 6 of the following 8 to complete the Camp Fire Law: "Worship _____. Seek _____. Give _____. Pursue _____. Be _____. Hold on to _____. Glorify _____. Be _____."

Answer: God / Beauty / Service / Knowledge / Trustworthy / Health / Work / Happy.

25) **TOSS-UP. 10 points.**

Which of the words in parentheses in the following sentence is correct? "It is I who (is, am, are) going with the group."

Answer: Am.

25) **BONUS. 20 points. 5 points each.**

Which word qualifies each of the following days of the week in the observation of Lent?
1) _____ Tuesday, *Mardi gras*, or the last day before Lent
2) _____ Wednesday, or the first day of Lent

3) _____ Sunday, or the Sunday of Holy Week
4) _____ Friday, or the day of Christ's crucifixion

Answer: 1) Shrove
       2) Ash
       3) Palm or Passion
       4) Good.

CATEGORY TOSS-UP. 100 points. 10 points each. 10 points deducted for an incorrect answer.

Identify the U.S. President in office during each of the following events.
1) U.S. acquisition of Hawaii, Guam, Puerto Rico, and the Philippines
2) Commodore Perry's departure for Japan to open that country to world trade
3) Ending of the Korean War
4) The Cherokee Indians' forced march to Oklahoma on the "Trail of Tears"
5) Congressional approval of the Missouri Compromise
6) Completion of the Brooklyn Bridge
7) Teapot Dome scandal
8) Failure of the Bay of Pigs invasion
9) Freeing of 52 U.S. hostages held by Iran for 444 days
10) Battle of the Little Big Horn

Answer: 1) William McKinley (1898)
       2) Millard Fillmore (1852)
       3) Dwight Eisenhower (1953)
       4) Martin Van Buren (1838-1839; accept Andrew Jackson, although the "Trail of Tears" more specifically refers to the forced removal of the Cherokee Indians from their homeland in the East to Oklahoma)
       5) James Monroe (1820)
       6) Chester Arthur (1883)
       7) Warren Harding (1923)
       8) John Kennedy (1961)
       9) Ronald Reagan (1981)
      10) Ulysses Grant (1876).

ROUND NINE

1) TOSS-UP. 10 points.

What Biblical name for the resin that comes from an evergreen tree is used today to mean "something comforting, soothing, or healing"?

Answer: Balm of Gilead (also called Mecca balsam; Jeremiah 8:22; Ezekiel 27:17).

1) BONUS. 20 points. 5 points each.

Lake Michigan is the largest body of fresh water solely in the U.S. and the only Great Lake that is wholly in the U.S. It is surrounded by 4 states. Name these states.

Answer: Michigan, Wisconsin, Illinois, and Indiana.

2) TOSS-UP. 10 points.

Name the South African surgeon who performed the first successful human heart transplant on December 3, 1967.

Answer: Dr. Christiaan Barnard.

2) BONUS. 20 points. 5 points each.

Give the Celsius equivalent for each of the following Fahrenheit temperatures.
1) 0 degrees for the freezing point of an ice, salt, and water mixture
2) 32 degrees for the freezing point of pure water
3) 98.6 degrees for the normal temperature of the human body
4) 212 degrees for the boiling point of water

Answer: 1) –18 degrees (–17.8 to 1 decimal point)
2) 0 degrees
3) 37 degrees
4) 100 degrees.

3) TOSS-UP. 10 points.

Which mythological figure brought Aphrodite a beauty potion from

Hades, opened the jar, was overcome by the vapors, and was revived by Eros, whom she later married? She became immortal.

Answer: Psyche.

3) BONUS. 20 points. 5 points each.

Identify the U.S. President who was embarrassed by each of the following who was involved in or accused of some type of "impropriety."
1) Albert Bacon Fall
2) Bert Lance
3) Richard Allen
4) Billie Sol Estes

**Answer: 1) Warren Harding
2) Jimmy Carter
3) Ronald Reagan
4) Lyndon Johnson.**

4) TOSS-UP. 10 points.

Because of their use of motifs such as garbage cans and other images of everyday American life, what other name is given to the group of 8 American painters called "The Eight"?

Answer: The Ashcan School (also known as the Revolutionary Black Gang and the Apostles of Ugliness).

4) BONUS. 20 points. 5 points each.

Who wrote each of the following classics?
1) *Iliad*
2) *Odyssey*
3) *Georgics*
4) *Decameron*

**Answer: 1) Homer
2) Homer
3) Vergil (Virgil)
4) Boccaccio.**

5) TOSS-UP. 30 points after the first clue. 20 after the second. 10 after the third.

Which country am I?
1) I am "like a teardrop from the chin of India" (others consider me

to be shaped like a pearl, a pear, or a mango).

2) I am an island nation in the Indian Ocean whose name in Sinhalese means "the resplendent land."

3) I was known as Serendip and Taprobane to ancient navigators and later was named Ceylon.

Answer: Sri Lanka.

5) BONUS. 30 points. 10 points each.

Identify each of the following concerning the novel *The Scarlet Letter*.

1) The author

2) The city in which the novel is set

3) The woman who bears a child out of wedlock and thereafter is punished by being made to stand for three hours before the pillory and to wear the scarlet letter "A" on her breast for adultery

Answer: 1) Nathaniel Hawthorne
2) Boston (in the 17th century; 1640's)
3) Hester Prynne.

6) TOSS-UP. 10 points.

He changed Lady Macbeth's cry in Shakespeare's *Macbeth* from "Out, damn'd spot!" to "Out, crimson spot!" in his *Family Shakespeare* (1807). Name this English editor and physician whose name today means "to expurgate; to remove passages considered offensive, as from a book."

Answer: Thomas Bowdler (bowdlerize).

6) BONUS. 20 points. 5 points each.

Identify the Russian leader who said each of the following.

1) "If you don't like us, don't accept our invitations, and don't invite us to come and see you. Whether you like it or not, history is on our side. We will bury you." (1956)

2) "A single death is a tragedy, a million deaths is a statistic."

3) "The dictatorship of the Communist Party is maintained by recourse to every form of violence." (1924)

4) "The policy of peaceful coexistence, as regards its social content, is a form of intense economic, political, and ideological struggle of the proletariat against the aggressive forces of imperialism in the international arena." (1961)

Answer: 1) Nikita Khrushchev
2) Joseph Stalin (at least attributed to him)
3) Leon Trotsky
4) Nikita Khrushchev.

7) TOSS-UP. 10 points.

Identify the speaker who said, ". . . a little cocker spaniel dog in a crate that [was] sent all the way from Texas. Black and white spotted. And our little girl—Trisha, the six-year-old—named it Checkers. And you know, the kids love the dog, and I just want to say this right now, that regardless of what they say about it, we're gonna [sic] keep it!"

Answer: Richard Nixon (1952).

7) BONUS. 20 points. 10 points each.

Answer each of the following.
1) What is the translation of *la salle des miroirs*?
2) In which European palace is this room located, a site which was used for the signing of the peace treaty on June 28, 1919, that ended World War I?

Answer: 1) The Hall of Mirrors
2) In the Palace of Versailles (France).

8) TOSS-UP. 30 points after the first clue. 20 after the second. 10 after the third.

What word am I?
1) I am "a chest for holding ammunition."
2) I am "a two-wheeled ammunition wagon."
3) I am "a water tight structure inside which construction work under water is carried on."

Answer: Caisson.

8) BONUS. 20 points. 10 points each.

Identify each of the following.
1) The first black American singer to perform at the Met
2) The woman who resigned from the Daughters of the American Revolution and helped to sponsor a concert at the Lincoln Memorial after the D.A.R. allegedly refused to permit this singer to perform in Constitution Hall in Washington, D.C., in 1939 because of her race

Answer: 1) Marian Anderson
2) Eleanor Roosevelt.

9) TOSS-UP. 10 points.

It has been said that the greatest thinker of ancient times tutored the greatest soldier of ancient times. Name both this teacher who lived in Athens and this Macedonian leader.

Answer: Aristotle and Alexander the Great.

9) BONUS. 30 points. 10 points each.

Which word for an animal is derived from each of the following?
1) From the Greek for "terrible (frightful) lizard"
2) From the Greek for "river horse"
3) From the Greek / New Latin for "flat-footed"

Answer: 1) Dinosaur
2) Hippopotamus
3) Platypus.

10) TOSS-UP. 10 points.

Which amendment states that "no person shall be elected to the office of the President more than twice"?

Answer: Amendment 22.

10) BONUS. 30 points. 10 points each.

Who, during the Civil War, made each of the following statements?
1) "The Father of Waters goes unvexed to the sea."
2) "It is well that war is so terrible, or we would grow too fond of it."
3) "Hold the fort! I am coming!"

Answer: 1) President Abraham Lincoln (about the Mississippi)
2) General Robert E. Lee (on seeing a Federal charge repulsed at Fredericksburg)
3) General William Tecumseh Sherman (from Kennesaw Mountain to General John Murray Corse at Alatoona Pass).

11) TOSS-UP. 10 points.

What is the word from the Spanish which applies to "a type of

Spanish fiction in which the rogue-hero and his adventures are depicted with broad realism and humor (or satire)"? *Gil Blas* and *Moll Flanders* are examples of this genre of fiction.

Answer: Picaresque.

11) BONUS. 30 points. 10 points each.

Name either the present or former capital of each of the following countries.
1) Brazil
2) Ivory Coast
3) Pakistan

Answer: 1) Brasília or Rio De Janeiro
**   2) Yamoussoukro (not recognized by the U.S.) or Abidjan**
**   3) Islamabad or Karachi.**

12) TOSS-UP. 20 points after the first clue. 10 after the second.

What am I?
1) I am a Schwarzchild Singularity Class 1.
2) I am a hypothetical celestial body, supposedly an invisible star so condensed that neither light nor matter can escape from my intense gravitational field.

Answer: Black Hole.

12) BONUS. 20 points. 10 points each.

Identify each of the following.
1) The former mayor of Chicago who served from 1955 until 1976
2) The county in which he was head of the Democratic organization

Answer: 1) Richard Joseph Daley
**   2) Cook County.**

13) TOSS-UP. 10 points.

What's the weather like if *il fait du vent*?

Answer: It's windy.

13) BONUS. 30 points. 10 points each.

In the field of mathematics or measurement, with what is each of the following numbers identified?

1) The approximation 1.732
2) 3, 4, 5
3) 1,760

Answer: 1) The square root of three
2) The Pythagorean triple
3) The number of yards in one mile.

14) TOSS-UP. 10 points.

Name the New Jersey university, whose students are nicknamed the "Tigers," of which Woodrow Wilson was once the president.

Answer: Princeton.

14) BONUS. 30 points. 10 points each.

Identify each of the following and the state in which each is located.
1) The name of the lowest point in the United States
2) The name of the highest point in the United States
3) The name of the highest point in the contiguous United States

Answer: 1) Death Valley, California
2) Mount McKinley, Alaska
3) Mount Whitney, California.

15) TOSS-UP. 10 points.

Identify the following by naming the text or the author: "I swear by Apollo the Physician, by Asclepius, by Health, by Panacea, and by all the gods and goddesses, making them my witnesses, that I will carry out, according to my ability and judgment, this oath and this indenture."

Answer: *The Physician's Oath (The Hippocratic Oath)*, or Hippocrates.

15) BONUS. 20 points. 5 points each.

In which country did each of the following rulers abdicate?
1) Leopold III in 1951
2) Faruk I in 1952
3) King Michael in 1947
4) Todor Zhivkov in 1989

Answer: 1) Belgium
2) Egypt

    3) **Rumania**
    4) **Bulgaria.**

16) TOSS-UP. 10 points.

Identify the state whose only Revolutionary War battle took place at Coochs Bridge (September 3, 1777). After the battle of Brandywine in Pennsylvania, the British did seize Wilmington, and the state's capital was then moved from New Castle to Dover.

Answer: Delaware.

16) BONUS. 20 points after the first clue. 10 after the second.

What is my name?
1) My observations of political life led me to say, "Power is the ultimate aphrodisiac."
2) I became the first Jewish Secretary of State, received the Nobel Peace Prize in 1973, and have been called the "Modern-day Metternich."

Answer: Henry Alfred (Heinz Alfred) Kissinger.

17) TOSS-UP. 10 points.

In mathematics, what irrational number is used as the base for natural logarithms?

Answer: *e*.

17) BONUS. 20 points. 10 points each.

Name his country of origin and the author of *Cry, the Beloved Country*.

Answer: South Africa / Alan Stewart Paton.

18) TOSS-UP. 10 points.

Who said, "For everything you have missed you have gained something else; and for everything you gain, you lose something," a statement made in his 1841 essay "Compensation"?

Answer: Ralph Waldo Emerson.

18) BONUS. 20 points. 10 points each.

Name the 2 famous bare-knuckled pugilists, one nicknamed "Gentleman Jim" and the "Dancing Master" and the other the

"Boston Strong Boy." These 2 heavyweights fought on September 7, 1892, in the first title bout in which padded gloves were used, with "Gentleman Jim" winning by a knockout in the 21st round.

Answer: Jim Corbett and John L. Sullivan.

19) TOSS-UP. 10 points.

In which field would one find the names of Marie Taglioni, Fanny Elssler, Melissa Hayden, Anna Pavlova, and Dame Margot Fonteyn?

Answer: Ballet (dance).

19) BONUS. 20 points. 5 points each.

According to Empedocles, the Greek doctor, poet, and philosopher, what were the 4 basic elements of matter?

Answer: Earth, air, fire, and water.

20) TOSS-UP. 30 points after the first clue. 20 after the second. 10 after the third.

Who am I?
1) I was married secretly to Missouri Senator Thomas Hart Benton's daughter Jessie in 1841.
2) I was the first presidential nominee of the Republican Party in 1856 and lost to James Buchanan in the election.
3) I was renowned for my explorations in the West and was known as the "Pathfinder."

Answer: John Charles Frémont.

20) BONUS. 30 points. 10 points each.

Identify each of the following U.S. WWII military leaders from the following nicknames.
1) "Old Blood and Guts"
2) "Beau Brummel of the Army," "Buck Private's Gary Cooper," or "The Napoleon of Luzon"
3) "Bull"

Answer: 1) George S. Patton
2) Douglas MacArthur
3) William F. Halsey.

21) TOSS-UP. 10 points.

How many times is the capacity of a pipe increased if the diameter is doubled?

Answer: 4.

21) BONUS. 30 points. 10 points each.

Identify the playwright and his nationality for each of the following plays.
1) *A Doll's House* (1879)
2) *The Threepenny Opera* (1928)
3) *La Machine Infernale* (*The Infernal Machine*; 1936)

Answer: 1) Henrik Ibsen—Norwegian
2) Bertolt (Bertold) Brecht—German
3) Jean Cocteau—French.

22) TOSS-UP. 10 points.

Name the painting stolen from the Louvre in August, 1911, which was found under Vicenzo Peruggia's hotel room bed in December, 1913. This painting by Leonardo da Vinci was finished in 1506 and bought by François I, king of France.

Answer: The *Mona Lisa* (or *La Joconde* or *La Gioconda*).

22) BONUS. 20 points. 10 points each.

Who initiated on March 12, 1933, a series of radio talks beginning with "My friends . . .," and what were these talks called?

Answer: Franklin D. Roosevelt / Fireside Chats.

23) TOSS-UP. 30 points after the first clue. 20 after the second. 10 after the third.

With which historical novel am I associated?
1) I was born Charles de Baatz in Gascony, France, served magnificently in the army during the reign of Louis XIII and Louis XIV, and was killed during a siege at Maastricht in the Netherlands.
2) I was also known as Seigneur d'Artagnan.
3) My life furnished the material and the inspiration for a historical novel by Alexandre Dumas, père.

Answer: *Les Trois Mousquetaires* (*The Three Musketeers*).

23) BONUS. 30 points. 10 points each.

Give the surname for each of the following George Washingtons.
1) The American civil engineer and West Point officer who directed the completion of the Panama Canal
2) The American botanist, chemurgist, and educator who was known as the "Father of Chemurgy" and "the Plant Doctor"
3) The American designer of a popular carnival ride that was the hit of the Chicago exposition in 1893

Answer: 1) George Washington Goethals
           2) George Washington Carver
           3) George Washington Gale Ferris.

24) TOSS-UP. 10 points.

Only one of the mythological Gorgons was mortal. Name her.

Answer: Medusa.

24) BONUS. 20 points. 10 points each.

Give the French and English names for either of the following: 1. "A gambling card game in which the betting is on two groups of cards played on a table marked with two diamond-shaped spots on which the bets are placed." 2. "A novel by Stendhal (Henri Marie Beyle) in which Julien Sorel, the young hero, is executed for attempted murder."

Answer: Rouge et noir and red and black or *Le Rouge et le Noir*, and *The Red and the Black*—the book and the game bear the same name.

25) TOSS-UP. 10 points.

Who is the founder of the Holy Spirit Association for the Unification of World Christianity, or the Unification Church?

Answer: The Reverend Sun Myung Moon.

25) BONUS. 20 points. 5 points each.

For which artist was each of the following a model?
1) Yvette Guilbert
2) Françoise Gilot
3) Duchess of Alba
4) Lisa del Gioconda or Lisa Gherardini

Answer: 1) Henri de Toulouse-Lautrec
2) Pablo Picasso
3) Francisco de Goya
4) Leonardo da Vinci.

CATEGORY TOSS-UP. 100 points. 10 points each. 10 points deducted for an incorrect answer.

Identify the country in which each of the following notable fossils was first discovered. Then identify the last item.
1) Java Man
2) Heidelberg Man
3) Peking Man
4) Swanscombe Man
5) Steinheim Man
6) Neanderthal Man
7) Solo Man
8) Broken Hill Man (formerly called Rhodesian Man)
9) Cro-Magnon Man
10) The name for the earliest humanlike creature, a term which means "southern ape."

Answer: 1) Indonesia (accept Java)
2) Germany
3) China
4) England
5) Germany (West Germany)
6) Germany (Neander Valley, near Düsseldorf, West Germany)
7) Indonesia (near Surakarta)
8) Zambia (formerly Northern Rhodesia; near Lusaka)
9) France (near Brive)
10) Australopithecus.

ROUND TEN

1) TOSS-UP. 10 points.

What Asian leader was known as the "Romantic Revolutionary," the "Great Helmsman," and the "Founder of Communist China"?

Answer: Mao Tse-tung (or Mao Zedong).

1) BONUS. 20 points. 5 points each.

Give the name of the fictional bird, its generic type, the voice of the bird, and the name of the cat created by Bob Clampett. This fictional bird is famous for the line, "I tawt I taw a puddy tat."

Answer: Tweety Pie / (Yellow) canary / Mel Blanc / Sylvester the Cat (Sylvester P. Pussycat).

2) TOSS-UP. 10 points.

What is the name of the battle in Gordon W. Prange's work *Miracle at _____*, a battle fought on June 4, 1942, that was the turning point of the war in the Pacific and one of America's great victories?

Answer: Midway.

2) BONUS. 20 points. 5 points each.

Identify the subject of each of the following Pulitzer Prize biographies.
1) *Crusader in Crinoline* by Forrest Wilson—1942
2) *Admiral of the Ocean Sea* by Samuel Eliot Morison—1943
3) *The American Leonardo* by Carleton Mabee—1944
4) *Son of the Wilderness* by Linnie Marsh Wolfe—1946

**Answer: 1) Harriet Beecher Stowe
2) Christopher Columbus
3) Samuel F. B. Morse
4) John Muir.**

3) TOSS-UP. 10 points.

What name is given to the use of language in "A Man, a Plan, a Canal, Panama"?

Answer: Palindrome (spelled the same backwards and forwards).

3) BONUS. 20 points. 5 points each.

Answer each of the following concerning a pre-WWII agreement.
1) What is the name of the pact or agreement which has come to mean "the epitome of a humiliating, dishonorable act of appeasement or surrender"?
2) In which year was this pact signed?
3) The area of which country was ceded to which country according to the pact in order to ensure "peace in our time"?

Answer: 1) Munich Pact or Munich Agreement
2) 1938 (September 30)
3) The Sudetenland of Czechoslovakia / ceded to Germany.

4) TOSS-UP. 10 points.

Identify the U.S. city once featured in the jingle: "Mary had a little lamb,/And when she saw it sicken,/She shipped it off to Packingtown, / And now it's labeled chicken." This city is the same one described in Upton Sinclair's *The Jungle* (1906).

Answer: Chicago.

4) BONUS. 20 points. 10 points each.

Which Canadian capital city founded in 1882, was first named Pile of Bones and renamed in honor of Queen Victoria of England from the Latin word for "Queen," and of which province is this the capital?

Answer: Regina / Saskatchewan.

5) TOSS-UP. 10 points.

Name the 1801 automatic pattern loom that was capable of weaving cloth with intricate patterns? This machine used punched cards to produce a pattern and was a forerunner of the computer.

Answer: Jacquard loom (after Joseph Marie Jacquard).

5) BONUS. 25 points. 5 points each.

Identify the following Greeks who became known as "Fathers."
1) Father of Greek Tragedy
2) Father of History, Father of Greek Prose, Father of Lies
3) Father of Medicine
4) Father of Comedy
5) Father of Epic Poetry, Father of Poetry, Father of Song

Answer: 1) Aeschylus (or Thespis)
**   2) Herodotus**
**   3) Hippocrates**
**   4) Aristophanes**
**   5) Homer (Orpheus is sometimes called the Father**
**   of Poetry).**

6) TOSS-UP. 10 points.

Name the Spanish-born artist who is noted for his paintings *The Sacrament of the Last Supper* (1956) and *The Temptation of Saint Anthony*, and for his two famous surrealist motion pictures *The Golden Age* (*L'Age d'or*, 1931) and *An Andalusian Dog* (*Un Chien andalou*, 1918), which he made in collaboration with Luis Buñuel?

Answer: Salvador Dali.

6) BONUS. 20 points. 10 points each.

The Olympic symbol consists of 5 interlocking rings or circles that represent the sporting friendship of all peoples.
1) What are the names of the 5 continents that the rings symbolize?
2) What are the colors of the 5 rings?

Answer: 1) Africa, Asia, Australia, Europe, and (North and
**   South) America**
**   2) Black, blue, green, red, and yellow.**

7) TOSS-UP. 10 points.

The cedar of which Middle Eastern country provided the material that Solomon used in building his temple (II Chronicles 2:8, or I Kings 5:6)?

Answer: Lebanon.

7) BONUS. 20 points. 10 points each.

By what names are the male dancer and the principal or leading female dancer in ballet known?

Answer: Danseur and (prima) ballerina (danseuse is a female ballet dancer and is not a correct answer).

8) TOSS-UP. 30 points after the first clue. 20 after the second. 10 after the third.

What's my name?
1) The daughter of an Albanian grocer, I was born Agnes Gonxha Bojaxhiu in 1910 in what is now Skopje, Yugoslavia.
2) I am known as the "Saint of the Gutters."
3) I founded the Order of the Missionaries of Charity in Calcutta, India, in 1948, and in 1979 I won the Nobel Prize for peace for helping the poor.

Answer: Mother Teresa.

8) BONUS. 30 points. 10 points each.

Name the 3 terrifying sisters of Greek mythology, whose hair was enmeshed with serpents, whose hands were of brass, and whose bodies were covered with scales. They were so ugly that the sight of them turned the beholder to stone.

Answer: Stheno (Sthenno), Euryale, and Medusa (they are the Gorgons).

9) TOSS-UP. 10 points.

Which phrase from Matthew 5:13 designates "any person or persons regarded as representative of the finest or noblest elements of society"? Christ, in the Sermon on the Mount, used the phrase in reference to His disciples.

Answer: Salt of the earth (salt having been used in religious ceremonies as a symbol of goodness and incorruptibility).

9) BONUS. 20 points. 10 points each.

Name the first black coach to win an NCAA Division I national championship in basketball and the school at which he coached.

Answer: John Thompson / Georgetown University.

10) TOSS-UP. 30 points after the first clue. 20 after the second. 10 after the third.

Who am I?
1) I said, "Hear me my warriors; my heart is sick and sad. Our chiefs are killed, the old men are all dead. It is cold, and we have no blankets; the little children are freezing to death. Hear me my warriors; my heart is sick and sad. From where the sun now stands I will fight no more forever."
2) I was known as the "Indian Napoleon."
3) I was a Nez Percé Indian who became famous for a military retreat of my people through Idaho and Montana in an attempt to reach Canada. I surrendered at the battle of Bear Paw Mountains, Montana, on October 5, 1877.

Answer: Chief Joseph (Hinmaton-Yalaktit, "Thunder Rolling in the Heights").

10) BONUS. 30 points. 10 points each.

Identify the U.S. President who was embarrassed by each of the following who was involved in or accused of some type of "impropriety."
1) Sherman Adams
2) William Worth Belknap
3) Edwin Meese

Answer: 1) Dwight Eisenhower
        2) Ulysses Grant
        3) Ronald Reagan.

11) TOSS-UP. 10 points.

Name the Jewish historian and author of *The Antiquities of the Jews* (completed A.D. 93), a 20-volume history of the Jews from their beginnings to the close of the reign of Nero.

Answer: Flavius Josephus (born Joseph ben Matthias).

11) BONUS. 30 points. 10 points each.

Who wrote each of the following classics?
1) *Works and Days*
2) *Odes* and *Epodes* and *Satires*
3) *Bucolics*

Answer: 1) Hesiod

2) Horace
3) Vergil (Virgil).

12) TOSS-UP. 20 points after the first clue. 10 after the second.

What is my name?
1) According to the Bible, I was the son of Nun and originally named Osgea (Hoshea). I was renamed, and my new name meant "God saves" or "Yahweh is deliverance."
2) I led the Israelites across the Jordan and conquered Palestine after the death of Moses.

Answer: Joshua.

12) BONUS. 30 points. 10 points each.

Identify each of the following concerning the novel *The Scarlet Letter*.
1) The elderly physician to whom the adulteress had been married and who returns to seek out the adulterer
2) The daughter who was born out of wedlock
3) The clergyman with whom she committed adultery and who, after seven years of silence, confesses his guilt on the scaffold and dies in her arms

Answer: 1) Roger Chillingworth (the Scholar Prynne)
2) Pearl
3) Arthur Dimmesdale.

13) TOSS-UP. 10 points.

Name the Roman Emperor who in 313 granted Christians freedom to practice their religion and who in 325 called the First Nicene Council.

Answer: Constantine the Great.

13) BONUS. 30 points. 10 points each.

In the field of mathematics or measurement, with what is each of the following numbers identified?
1) 62 $\frac{1}{2}$
2) The approximation .3010
3) 1,728

Answer: 1) The number of pounds for one cubic foot of water

2) The logarithm of two to the base ten
3) The number of cubic inches in one cubic foot.

14) TOSS-UP. 10 points.

How many degrees Fahrenheit is a temperature of 20 degrees Celsius?

Answer: 68 degrees Fahrenheit.

14) BONUS. 20 points. 5 points each.

Name 4 of the 6 Triple Crown winners in horseracing since 1940.

Answer: Whirlaway (with Eddie Arcaro; 1941); Count Fleet (with Johnnie Longden; 1943); Assault (with Willie Mehrtens; 1946); Citation (with Eddie Arcaro; 1948); Secretariat (with Ron Turcotte; 1973); Seattle Slew (with Jean Cruquet; 1977); and Affirmed (with Steve Cauthen, 1978).

15) TOSS-UP. 10 points.

What president of Columbia University wrote *Crusade in Europe*?

Answer: Dwight Eisenhower.

15) BONUS. 30 points. 5 points each.

Name the 6 U.S. capitals which end in the letter *a* or in the letters *ia* and give their states.

Answer: Atlanta, Georgia; Topeka, Kansas; Augusta, Maine; Helena, Montana; Columbia, South Carolina; and Olympia, Washington.

16) TOSS-UP. 10 points.

Between which 2 states is the Chesapeake Bay located?

Answer: Maryland and Virginia.

16) BONUS. 20 points. 10 points each.

You may be "between a rock and hard place" if you can't identify each of the following. This allusion refers to a strait through which Homer's Odysseus had to sail.
1) The name and description of the peril located on the Italian side of the Strait of Messina

2) The name and description of the peril located on the Sicilian side of the Strait of Messina

Answer: 1) Scylla was a rock personified as a ravenous sea monster (which barked like a dog and terrified sailors with its 12 feet and 6 heads, each with 3 rows of teeth)
      2) Charybdis was a whirlpool (which swallowed the waters of the sea three times a day and threw them up again).

17) TOSS-UP. 10 points.

What is the name of the particular temperature and pressure in which all 3 states of matter—solid, liquid, and gas—exist in contact and in equilibrium with one another?

Answer: Triple point.

17) BONUS. 30 points. 10 points each.

Name either the present capital or the former name of the present capital of each of the following countries.
1) Gambia
2) Mozambique
3) Burma

Answer: 1) Banjul or Bathurst (former name)
      2) Maputo or Lourenço Marques (former name)
      3) Yangon or Rangoon (former name).

18) TOSS-UP. 10 points.

He was the first and only person to have received 2 Nobel Prizes by himself, one in chemistry and one in peace. He is called the "High Priest of Vitamin C" for his work using high doses of this vitamin to fight a variety of diseases from cancer to the common cold. Name him.

Answer: Linus Pauling.

18) BONUS. 30 points. 10 points each.

Identify the 3 great 17th century French playwrights during France's "Golden Age of Literature"—France's Classical Age. They are the authors of *Le Cid*, *Phèdre*, and *Le Misanthrope*.

Answer: (Pierre) Corneille, (Jean) Racine, and Molière (Jean Baptiste Poquelin).

19) TOSS-UP. 10 points.

Name the Oscar Wilde character whose countenance remains fair and innocent despite his villainy and who wanted his picture to grow old while he remained forever young. This Faustian young man's cold and cruel remark to Sibyl Vane prompted this actress to kill herself.

Answer: Dorian Gray (in *The Picture of Dorian Gray*).

19) BONUS. 30 points. 10 points each.

Which word for an animal is derived from each of the following?
1) From the Mayan word for "man of the forest"
2) From the New Latin for "breast-tooth"
3) From the Greek for "nose horn"

Answer: 1) Orangutan
2) Mastodon
3) Rhinoceros.

20) TOSS-UP. 10 points.

What is the number representing the ratio of the speed of a body to the speed of sound in the surrounding medium, such as air, through which the body is moving?

Answer: Mach number (after Ernst Mach).

20) BONUS. 30 points. 10 points each.

Identify each of the following U.S. WWII military leaders from the following nicknames.
1) "Hap" and "Father of the U.S. Air Force"
2) "The Flying Tiger" and "Old Leather Face"
3) "Doughboy's General" and "G.I.'s General"

Answer: 1) Henry H. Arnold
2) Claire Lee Chennault
3) Omar Nelson Bradley.

21) TOSS-UP. 10 points.

To which American artist working for the New York *Journal* on assignment in Cuba during the Spanish-American War did William Randolph Hearst supposedly say, "You furnish the pictures and I'll furnish the war"? This artist became famous for his paintings and sculptures of cowboys and Indians of the Old West.

Answer: Frederic Sackrider Remington.

21) **BONUS. 30 points. 10 points each.**

Identify the playwright and his nationality for each of the following plays.
1) *The Skin of Our Teeth* (1942)
2) *Waiting for Godot* (1948)
3) *Saint Joan* (1923)

Answer: 1) Thornton Niven Wilder—American
2) Samuel Beckett—Irish
3) George Bernard Shaw—English (born in Ireland).

22) **TOSS-UP. 10 points.**

What part of speech is the word *than* in the following sentence? "He is somewhat more intelligent than a gorilla."

Answer: Conjunction.

22) **BONUS. 20 points. 10 points each.**

Which 2 elements make up more than 74% of the rocks in the earth's crust?

Answer: Oxygen (46.6%) and silicon (27.7%).

23) **TOSS-UP. 10 points.**

Name the South Carolina University in Greenville denied its tax exempt status because of its policy of racial segregation by a Supreme Court ruling of 1983.

Answer: Bob Jones University (*Bob Jones v. the United States*).

23) **BONUS. 20 points. 5 points each.**

Give the names of the 4 representatives who signed the Munich Pact or Munich Agreement on September 30, 1938, which approved of the ceding of the Sudetenland of Czechoslovakia to Germany.

Answer: Adolf Hitler (Germany), Benito Mussolini (Italy), Neville Chamberlain (Great Britain), and Édouard Daladier (France).

24) TOSS-UP. 10 points.

Name the vocal and instrumental duo who grew up together in Forest Hills, New York, and who are noted for their albums *Sounds of Silence* and *Bridge Over Troubled Water*, and for the song "Mrs. Robinson" in the film *The Graduate*.

Answer: (Paul) Simon and (Art) Garfunkel.

24) BONUS. 30 points. 10 points each.

Identify each of the following artists from their given real names.
1) Tiziano Vecellio
2) Domenikos Theotokopoulos
3) _____ de Buonarroti Simoni

Answer: 1) Titian
        2) El Greco
        3) Michelangelo.

25) TOSS-UP. 10 points.

He is known as the "Father of the Green Revolution." Name this American plant breeder and pathologist who won the 1970 Nobel Prize for peace for developing high-yield miracle wheat grains that greatly increased grain yields in India and Mexico.

Answer: Norman Ernest Borlaug.

25) BONUS. 30 points. 10 points each.

According to French philosopher Montesquieu in his major work *De l'Esprit des lois* (*The Spirit of the Laws*; 1748), what are the 3 basic types of government?

Answer: Monarchy (led by a king or queen; based on honor), republic (an aristocracy or a democracy; based on virtue), and despotism (controlled by a tyrant; based on fear).

CATEGORY TOSS-UP. 100 points. 10 points each. 10 points deducted for an incorrect answer.

Identify the animal described in each of the following.
1) The world's largest animal ever
2) The world's smallest dog
3) The world's heaviest domestic dog

4) The world's slowest moving land mammal
5) The world's fastest animal at a distance of less than 1,000 yards
6) The world's fastest animal at a distance of more than 1,000 yards
7) The world's smallest bird
8) The world's largest living bird
9) The world's longest living vertebrate animal
10) The world's fastest flying small bird (appropriately named)

Answer: 1) **Blue whale**
        2) **Chihuahua**
        3) **St. Bernard (accept Mastiff)**
        4) **Sloth**
        5) **Cheetah**
        6) **Antelope (Gazelle)**
        7) **Hummingbird**
        8) **Ostrich**
        9) **Tortoise (Turtle)**
      10) **Swift.**

ROUND ELEVEN

1) TOSS-UP. 10 points.

Which Biblical figure is sometimes portrayed in Mexican piñatas? At noon on the day before Easter children beat, hang, and burn these images of this figure.

Answer: Judas Iscariot.

1) BONUS. 20 points. 10 points each.

Identify the 2 food items named after the famous Australian soprano Dame Nellie Melba (Helen Porter Mitchell Armstrong).

Answer: Peach melba (created for her by Auguste Escoffier, the French chef) and melba toast.

2) TOSS-UP. 10 points.

What U.S. establishment was created by Congress on August 10, 1846, and named after British scientist James _____, who left a fortune for the establishment of a place for the "increase and diffusion of knowledge among men"? This institution is sometimes called "America's Attic."

Answer: Smithsonian Institution.

2) BONUS. 25 points. 5 points each.

Identify each of the following U.S. cities with the nickname "Big." Each city is either a capital city or one of the 3 largest in its state.
1) The Big Apple
2) The Big A
3) The Big Heart of Texas
4) The Big D
5) The Big Orange

Answer: 1) New York
2) Atlanta
3) Austin
4) Dallas
5) Los Angeles.

3) TOSS-UP. 10 points.

Name the "King of the Elephants" in Jean and Laurent de Brunhoff's series of stories introduced in 1931 and based on a tale created by Parisian pianist Cecile Sabouraud.

Answer: Babar.

3) BONUS. 20 points. 10 points each.

Name the largest natural satellite in our solar system and the planet this satellite orbits.

Answer: Ganymede orbits Jupiter.

4) TOSS-UP. 10 points.

Which word from Roman history designates "a surgical operation to remove a fetus from the uterus by cutting through the mother's abdominal wall and uterine walls"? This word is derived from a similar operation that supposedly brought a Roman leader into the world, about 100 B.C.

Answer: Caesarean or Caesarean section (after Julius Caesar).

4) BONUS. 20 points. 5 points each.

Identify each of the following words from Roman history from the given definition or description.
1) "lavish; rich; sumptuous, especially pertaining to food" (from a Roman general and consul, c. 117-56 B.C., noted for his elegant and luxurious living)
2) "a guide who shows and explains the history and curiosities of a place to sightseers" (so derived from the traditional talkativeness of most guides and formed from the name of Rome's greatest orator, 106-43 B.C.)
3) "classical; correct; brilliant; elegant; pertaining to the highest point in the literature of a country" (from the first emperor, 27 B.C.-A.D. 14, of Rome whose reign was called the golden age of Latin literature)
4) "a wealthy, generous patron, especially of the arts" (from a Roman, actually an Etruscan statesman, c. 70-8 B.C., who was a generous patron of Virgil and Horace)

Answer: 1) Lucullan (after Lucius Licinius Lucullus)

2) cicerone (after Marcus Tullius Cicero)
3) Augustan (after Augustus Caesar)
4) Maecenas (after Gaius Cilnius Maecenas).

5) TOSS-UP. 10 points.

"The Game" was played between these 2 teams on December 28, 1958. The score was 23-17, and it was Alan Ameche who scored the winning touchdown on a 1-yard plunge in the first "sudden death game" for the National Football League title. Identify the 2 teams, nicknamed the "Colts" and the "Giants," who played in this game.

Answer: Baltimore (Colts) and the New York (Giants).

5) BONUS. 20 points. 10 points each.

Identify the animal, *Corvus corax*, who was a visitor from "the Night's Plutonian shore" and the single word, containing a long o and the consonant r, that was this visitor's repetitive message in a poem by Edgar Allan Poe.

Answer: The raven / "Nevermore."

6) TOSS-UP. 20 points after the first clue. 10 after the second.

Who am I?
1) I was a Louisiana Frenchman, born near New Orleans in 1818. I served as superintendent of the U.S. Military Academy for five days, but was removed after declaring my loyalty to the South if Louisiana seceded from the Union.
2) I directed the opening bombardment of the Civil War and was nicknamed the "Hero of Fort Sumter," and after helping win the first Battle of Bull Run, I was nicknamed the "Hero of Manassas."

Answer: P(ierre) G(ustave) T(outant) Beauregard.

6) BONUS. 20 points. 5 points each.

Identify each of the following concerning William Jennings Bryan.
1) The nickname beginning with "Great" by which this political and religious leader was known
2) The name given to his famous speech, the one presented in 1896 at the Chicago Democratic National Convention in which he argued for free silver by saying, "You shall not press down upon the brow of labor this crown of thorns, you shall not crucify mankind upon a cross of gold."

3) The President he served and the Cabinet position he held, a position from which he resigned in fear that U.S. policies would lead to war with Germany (specifically he thought that the second *Lusitania* note was too provocative)

4) The weekly newspaper he edited and published from 1901 to 1913

Answer: 1) **"Great Commoner"**
2) **"Cross of Gold" Speech**
3) **Woodrow Wilson and Secretary of State**
4) *The Commoner.*

7) TOSS-UP. 10 points.

Which British word for a *peddler* is the same as the surname of an English poet and translator of Homer, of an American ornithologist and author, and of an American pioneer nicknamed "Johnny Appleseed"?

Answer: Chapman (George Chapman, Frank Michler Chapman, and John Chapman).

7) BONUS. 20 points. 10 points each.

Name the 2 books of the Bible dedicated to an unknown *Theophilus*, whose name means "friend of God."

Answer: The Gospel of Luke or the Acts of the Apostles.

8) TOSS-UP. 10 points.

What word means "an abnormal stone, or deposit formed in the body, as in the gall bladder, kidney, or urinary bladder," or designates a method of calculation in mathematics? This word comes from the Latin and etymologically means "pebble" or "small stone."

Answer: Calculus.

8) BONUS. 30 points. 5 points each.

Identify each of the following concerning Sir Arthur Conan Doyle's Sherlock Holmes.
1) The address of Sherlock Holmes in London, England
2) The assistant with whom Holmes lives
3) The U.S. Supreme Court Justice for whom Holmes was named
4) The type of cap, cape, or pipe used by Holmes
5) The "Napoleon of Crime," the arch enemy of Holmes
6) The movie actor who played Holmes in 14 movies between 1939

and 1946 with Nigel Bruce as Holmes' assistant

Answer: 1) 221B Baker Street
   2)   Dr. John Watson
   3)   Oliver Wendell Holmes, Jr. (the name of Sherlock was from the name of a popular English cricket player)
   4)   Deer-stalker cap, Inverness cape, or calabash pipe
   5)   Professor (James) Moriarty
   6)   Basil Rathbone.

9) TOSS-UP. 30 points after the first clue. 20 after the second. 15 after the third. 10 after the fourth.

What word am I?
1) In architecture, I am the top projection of a cornice or the circular chandelier hanging from the ceiling of a church.
2) In electricity, I am a faint glow near the surface of an electrical conductor at high voltage, indicating an electrical breakdown in the surrounding gas.
3) In astronomy, I am a faintly white or colored luminous ring of light seen around a celestial body, especially the outermost portion of the sun's atmosphere.
4) In botany, I am the crownlike part of a flower.

Answer: Corona.

9) BONUS. 20 points. 10 points each.

Identify each of the following.
1) The first animal in space, a dog aboard *Sputnik II* on November 2, 1957
2) The 2 chimpanzees that were sent into space by the U.S. from Cape Canaveral on May 28, 1959, and became the first primates to return to earth

Answer: 1) Laika
   2)   Abel and Baker.

10) TOSS-UP. 20 points after the first clue. 10 after the second.

What is my name?
1) I am a code carved on a stone column and discovered in Susa, Iran, in 1901.

2) I was one of the first law codes in history and was developed by a king who ruled Babylon for 43 years from about 1792 to 1750 B.C.

Answer: Code of Hammurabi.

10) **BONUS. 20 points. 10 points each.**

Give the author and the title of the symbolical moral fable in which a group of British schoolboys, shipwrecked on a tropical Pacific island, shake off their civilized behavior and revert to a state of savagery and cruelty.

Answer: William Arthur Golding's *The Lord of the Flies.*

11) **TOSS-UP. 10 points.**

He had only 3 months of formal schooling; was considered "addled" by his teachers because he asked so many questions; challenged a chemistry book of the time; printed a small local newspaper, the *Weekly Herald*, in the baggage car of a train; set fire to the baggage car by a chemical experiment; and invented an electric vote-recording machine. Name this American who became known as the "Wizard of Menlo Park."

Answer: Thomas Alva Edison.

11) **BONUS. 20 points. 5 points each.**

Identify the person responsible for the formula $E=MC^2$. Then identify each part of the formula.

Answer: Albert Einstein / E stands for energy / M stands for mass / C^2 stands for speed of light squared.

12) **TOSS-UP. 10 points.**

Name the future President of the U.S. who as a vice-presidential nominee was defeated along with Ohio Governor James M. Cox by Warren Harding and Calvin Coolidge in the 1920 presidential election.

Answer: Franklin Roosevelt.

12) **BONUS. 20 points. 10 points each.**

Name the highest mountain chain in the world, and then name the longest mountain chain on a continent.

Answer: Himalayas / Andes (longest mountain chain in the world is the Mid-Atlantic Ridge, located mostly underwater).

13) TOSS-UP. 10 points.

In which U. S. city is the "Magnificent Mile" located, an area that stretches from Michigan Avenue to Oak Street?

Answer: Chicago.

13) BONUS. 20 points. 10 points each.

Identify each of the following.
1) The "prehistoric man," called *Eoanthropus dawson*, or Dawn Man, pieces of which were discovered between 1908 and 1912
2) The country in which this "find of the missing link" took place, a discovery proved to be a hoax by tests conducted from 1949-1959

Answer: 1) Piltdown Man (near Sussex)
2) England.

14) TOSS-UP. 10 points.

Name the only 2 eagles that breed in the United States and Canada.

Answer: Golden eagle and bald eagle.

14) BONUS. 25 points. 5 points each.

Answer each of the following war-related items.
1) What is the translation of the French rallying cry *Ils ne passeront pas*, which was issued as an Order of the Day?
2) What leader issued this order?
3) With which battle is this cry associated?
4) With which war is this cry associated?
5) What is the Spanish equivalent that was used as the Republican motto during the Spanish Civil War?

Answer: 1) "They shall not pass"
2) Marshal Henri Philippe Pétain
3) Verdun
4) World War I
5) *No pasarán!*

15) TOSS-UP. 10 points.

Name the mythological Titan who stole fire from Olympus and gave it to man.

Answer: Prometheus.

15) BONUS. 25 points. 5 points each.

Identify each of the following from Greek mythology concerning Prometheus, who brought fire to humans.
1) The deity who, according to Aeschylus, punished him for doing so
2) The personal punishment the deity inflicted upon him
3) The animal that came each day for 30 years to eat part of the Titan's body
4) The part of the body that was eaten by the animal each day and renewed by the deity each night
5) The person who in some legends released the Titan from his imprisonment

Answer: 1) Zeus
      2) chained him to a rock on Mount Caucasus
      3) eagle or vulture
      4) liver
      5) Hercules (or Heracles).

16) TOSS-UP. 10 points.

Which private, coeducational university located in Waltham, Massachusetts, was named for a former U.S. Supreme Court Justice, and was established as the first nonsectarian institution of higher education sponsored by the American Jewish community? Its students are nicknamed the "Judges."

Answer: Brandeis University (after Louis Dembitz Brandeis).

16) BONUS. 20 points. 10 points each.

Give the *nom de plume* under which financial journalist George J.W. Goodman writes and complete the name of his book *The Money _____*, a 1968 analysis of the stock market.

Answer: Adam Smith / *The Money Game*.

17) TOSS-UP. 20 points after the first clue. 10 after the second.

Who am I?
1) I was allegedly the first person who suggested that it was possible to circumnavigate the world, and Columbus possibly quoted me later in a letter to the King and Queen of Spain.

2) I was born in England about 1214 and my most important work was *Opus Majus* (*Longer Work*).

Answer: Roger Bacon.

17) BONUS. 30 points. 10 points each.

Name the highest and lowest points in South America and the country in which both are located. The highest point in South America is also the highest mountain in the western hemisphere.

Answer: Mount Aconcagua / Península Valdés / Argentina.

18) TOSS-UP. 10 points.

I was born in Italy in 1452, but I died and was buried in a small chapel at Amboise in France in 1519. King François I wanted to surround himself with famous representatives of Renaissance culture, and I, a well-known Italian artist, spent my last two years in his presence. What's my name?

Answer: Leonardo da Vinci.

18) BONUS. 20 points. 10 points each.

Identify each of the following.
1) The person known as the "George Washington of South America" and the "Liberator (*El Libertador*) of South America"
2) The country in which he was born, the first South American country he liberated, in 1813

**Answer: 1) Simón Bolívar
2) Venezuela.**

19) TOSS-UP. 10 points.

Name the British general and governor of Massachusetts whose orders resulted in the first battle of the American Revolutionary War. His soldiers, having been ordered to seize colonial arms, suffered heavy losses at Lexington and Concord, and after more losses at Bunker Hill, he was recalled to England.

Answer: Thomas Gage.

19) BONUS. 20 points. 10 points each.

Name the English author of the novel *Lost Horizon* and the Himalayan mountain valley kingdom in the novel.

Answer: James Hilton / Shangri-La.

20) TOSS-UP. 10 points.

Complete the following line from Shakespeare's *A Midsummer Night's Dream*: "Shall we their fond pageant see? / Lord, what fools these _____!"

Answer: "mortals be!"

20) BONUS. 20 points. 5 points each.

Identify each of the following concerning the Lone Ranger. John Reid was his real name, and Clayton Moore played the role the most often.
1) The Indian who helped the Lone Ranger survive the ambush, or the actor who played the role on TV
2) The name of the Lone Ranger's horse and the name of the Indian's horse
3) The Gioacchino Antonio Rossini piece used as the theme song of the Lone Ranger
4) The Indian name meaning "trusty scout" or "faithful friend" given to the Lone Ranger by his Indian sidekick

Answer: 1) Tonto, or Jay Silverheels
2) Silver and Scout (earlier it was White Feller, or Paint)
3) *The William Tell Overture*
4) Kemo Sabe.

21) TOSS-UP. 30 points after the first clue. 20 after the second. 10 after the third.

Which island am I?
1) My main city is actually a small village named Hanga Roa.
2) I am located in the South Pacific about 2,300 miles (3,700 kilometers) west of Chile.
3) I am the site of over 600 large stone statues carved out of the hard volcanic rock by an unknown sculptor.

Answer: Easter Island.

21) BONUS. 30 points. 5 points each.

Identify each of the following concerning the Nixon administration and the "Saturday Night Massacre."

1) The Chief of Staff of President Nixon's administration
2) The Special Prosecutor who wanted the subpoenaed White House tapes
3) The Attorney General who was ordered by the chief of staff to dismiss the Special Prosecutor but who resigned instead
4) The Deputy Attorney General who also resigned because he would not dismiss the Special Prosecutor
5) The Solicitor General who did fire the Special Prosecutor
6) The month and year of the Saturday Night Massacre

Answer: 1) **Alexander Haig**
2) **Archibald Cox**
3) **Elliot Richardson**
4) **William Ruckelshaus**
5) **Robert Bork**
6) **October (20) 1973.**

22) TOSS-UP. 10 points.

Some say *Omnia vincit amor,* or "Love conquers all," but which U.S. state has the motto *Labor Omnia Vincit,* or "Work Conquers All"? This state is known as the "Sooner State."

Answer: Oklahoma.

22) BONUS. 20 points. 5 points each.

Name the song, other than "The Star Spangled Banner," played before each of the following events. Each song is associated with a state or country.
1) Kentucky Derby
2) Preakness
3) Belmont Stakes
4) Any Expos baseball game

Answer: 1) **"My Old Kentucky Home"**
2) **"Maryland, My Maryland"**
3) **"Sidewalks of New York"**
4) **"O Canada."**

23) TOSS-UP. 10 points.

Name the pact, also known as the Pact of Paris, signed on August 27, 1928, that renounced war "as an instrument of national policy" and was eventually signed by 62 nations. The American originator of the pact won the Nobel Peace Prize in 1929. This pact is named for Calvin Coolidge's Secretary of State and France's Foreign Minister.

Answer: Kellogg-Briand Pact (Treaty).

23) **BONUS.** 25 points. 5 points each.

Identify each of the following concerning William Jennings Bryan.
1) The 3 years he ran for the presidency
2) The 2 candidates who defeated him

Answer: 1) 1896 and 1900 (by William McKinley) and 1908 (by William H. Taft)
2) William McKinley and William H. Taft.

24) **TOSS-UP.** 10 points.

What phrase from the field of zoology means "a social hierarchy in which each person's status is determined by one's aggressiveness, wealth, or power as compared to others"? This phrase alludes to the status created when more aggressive birds peck dominated birds without fear of retaliation.

Answer: Pecking order or peck order.

24) **BONUS.** 30 points. 10 points each.

Identify each of the following artists from their given real names.
1) Donato Di Niccolo di Betto Bardi
2) Rafaello Santi (or Sanzio)
3) Jacopo Robusti

Answer: 1) Donatello
2) Raphael
3) Tintoretto.

25) **TOSS-UP.** 10 points.

Which country borders the Red Sea, and is surrounded by Egypt, Libya, Chad, Central African Republic, The Congo, Uganda, Kenya, and Ethiopia?

Answer: Sudan.

25) **BONUS.** 20 points. 5 points each.

Identify each of the following.
1) The animals that symbolize the Democratic and Republican

Parties
2) The animal that symbolized New York's Tammany Society
3) The name of the cartoonist of *Harper's Weekly* who created and popularized these symbols

Answer: 1) **Donkey and Elephant**
        2) **Tiger**
        3) **Thomas Nast.**

CATEGORY TOSS-UP. 100 points. 10 points each. 10 points deducted for an incorrect answer.

Identify each of the following concerning William Shakespeare's *Hamlet*.
1) The country in which the play is set
2) The castle in which most of the play takes place
3) The name of Prince Hamlet's uncle, who, for having killed Hamlet's father, is later killed by Hamlet
4) The mother of Hamlet, who marries the uncle after her husband's death and who dies from a poisonous drink
5) The woman who is wooed by Hamlet and later goes mad and drowns
6) The two friends of Hamlet who accompany him to England with a warrant for his death but who are killed instead
7) The man who is hiding behind the tapestry (arras) and whom Hamlet accidentally kills
8) The son whose father is killed accidentally by Hamlet
9) The king of Norway who comes to claim the crown of the country in which the play is set
10) The actual cause of Hamlet's death

Answer: 1) **Denmark**
        2) **Elsinore**
        3) **Claudius**
        4) **Queen Gertrude**
        5) **Ophelia**
        6) **Rosencrantz and Guildenstern**
        7) **Polonius**
        8) **Laertes**
        9) **Fortinbras**
       10) **Poison on the rapier of Laertes.**

ROUND TWELVE

1) TOSS-UP. 10 points.

Which Japanese word means "(may you live for) 10,000 years," and is a patriotic salute to the Japanese emperor? This word is also used as a battle cry or a cry of enthusiasm.

Answer: Banzai.

1) BONUS. 20 points. 10 points each.

Franklin D. Roosevelt was governor of New York before he became President of the United States. Name the first 2 Presidents following Franklin Roosevelt who were former governors and name their states.

Answer: Jimmy Carter of Georgia, and Ronald Reagan of California.

2) TOSS-UP. 10 points.

In literature, who "shall never vanquish'd be until / Great Birnam Wood to high Dunsinane Hill / Shall come against him"?

Answer: Macbeth.

2) BONUS. 30 points. 10 points each.

Identify the author of the following lines, the title of the poem in which they appear, and the meaning of the title: "So live, that when thy summons comes to join/The innumerable caravan, which moves/ To that mysterious realm, where each shall take/His chamber in the silent halls of death, / Thou go not, like the quarry-slave at night, / Scourged to his dungeon, but, sustained and soothed / By an unfaltering trust, approach thy grave, / Like one who wraps the drapery of his couch / About him, and lies down to pleasant dreams."

Answer: William Cullen Bryant / "Thanatopsis" (1821)/ "A view of death."

3) TOSS-UP. 10 points.

Which planet is the 4th planet from the sun, is known as "The Red Planet," and is named after the Roman god of war?

Answer: Mars.

3) BONUS. 30 points. 10 points each.

Identify each of the following roads.
1) The road built in 1937-1939 from Lashio, Burma, to Kunming, China, and used to supply China in its war against Japan
2) The road the Allied forces completed in 1945 from Myitkyina, Burma, to Ledo, India
3) The road renamed by Chiang Kai-shek in honor of General Joseph W. _____, commander of U.S. forces in the China-Burma-India theatre during WWII

Answer: 1) Burma Road
       2) Ledo Road
       3) Stilwell Road (formerly the Ledo Road).

4) TOSS-UP. 10 points.

What is the name of the annual award established in 1945 and given by the Mystery Writers of America to the year's best mystery? This award is named for the American author of "The Gold Bug" (1843).

Answer: The Edgar (or the Edgar Allan Poe Award; Poe is considered to be the "Father of the Modern Detective Story," and his "The Murders in the Rue Morgue" is sometimes considered to be the first detective story).

4) BONUS. 20 points. 10 points each.

Name the principal food source of the panda and the principal food source of the koala bear.

Answer: Bamboo / eucalyptus.

5) TOSS-UP. 10 points.

What mathematical word did John Napier coin from 2 Greek words, *logos*, meaning "ratio," and *arithmos*, meaning "number"?

Answer: Logarithms.

5) BONUS. 30 points. 10 points each.

Answer each of the following questions concerning Julius Caesar.
1) What phrase is used to imply that "the conduct of important persons must be free of even the suspicion of wrongdoing"?
2) Which wife of the person mentioned in the phrase was accused of wrongdoing?
3) What action did she commit that occasioned this accusation?

Answer: 1) **Caesar's wife must be above suspicion**
           2) **Pompeia**
           3) **Pompeia was in charge of sacred services for Bona Dea ("the good goddess") and possibly allowed a man Publius Clodius into the all-women affair; (Publius Clodius was also on trial for having had an affair with Pompeia; he was acquitted, but Caesar divorced her).**

6) TOSS-UP. 10 points.

Name the mountain known as the "Tiger of the Alps," which was successfully climbed by Englishman Edward Whymper and party on July 14, 1865. It is located on the Swiss-Italian border near Zermatt, Switzerland.

Answer: The Matterhorn (Mont Cervin in French and Monte Cervino in Italian).

6) BONUS. 20 points. 10 points each.

Name the only 2 English monarchs since William I who were not crowned in Westminster Abbey. They were never coronated at all.

Answer: Edward V and Edward VIII.

7) TOSS-UP. 30 points after the first clue. 20 after the second. 10 after the third.

What famous pair are we?
1) We were legendary Greek lovers written about by Lord Byron and Christopher Marlowe.
2) I was a young man of Abydos and my beloved was a priestess of Aphrodite in Sestos, on the other side of the Hellespont Strait.
3) We met secretly at night. My beloved guided me in my swim across the Hellespont by a lamp lit in her tower until one night the wind extinguished it. I drowned, and she threw herself to her

death in the sea.

Answer: Hero and Leander.

7) BONUS. 20 points. 10 points each.

Which 2 phrases from Greek mythology designate in psychology "a daughter's abnormal fondness for her father" and "a son's abnormal fondness for his mother"? The first is named for the daughter of Agamemnon and Clytemnestra, and the latter for the son of King Laius and Jocasta.

Answer: Electra Complex and Oedipus Complex.

8) TOSS-UP. 10 points.

Name the Israelite who was the first king of Israel (c. 1020-1000 B.C.).

Answer: Saul.

8) BONUS. 20 points. 5 points each.

Identify each of the following countries on the South American continent.
1) The northernmost country
2) The southernmost country
3) The easternmost country
4) The westernmost country

Answer: 1) Colombia
        2) Chile
        3) Brazil
        4) Peru.

9) TOSS-UP. 10 points.

Name the last monarch of the line founded by Ptolemy in the 4th century B.C. in Egypt.

Answer: Queen Cleopatra (Cleopatra VII Philopator, 69-30 B.C.).

9) BONUS. 20 points. 10 points each.

Name the author of the *Aeneid*, and give the number of books it contains.

Answer: Vergil (Virgil) / 12.

10) TOSS-UP. 10 points.

What is the name for a number representing the relative position of an element in the periodic table, a chart in which the elements are arranged in the order of their nuclear charges?

Answer: Atomic number.

10) BONUS. 20 points. 10 points each.

Between which countries were the First and Second Opium Wars fought? The First War (1839-1842) ended with the treaties of Nanking (1842) and the Bogue (1843), while the Second War (1856-1860) ended with the signing of the Peking Convention (1860) in which the Chinese agreed to observe the Treaties of Tientsin (1858).

Answer: First Opium War was between China and Great Britain (the victor) / the Second Opium War was between China and Great Britain-France (the victors).

11) TOSS-UP. 10 points.

Which U.S. state, whose name is derived from two Choctaw words, is known as the "Land of the Red People (Men)"?

Answer: Oklahoma.

11) BONUS. 20 points. 10 points each.

Translate the Latin phrase *In hoc signo vinces*, and identify the Roman leader who used these words on his standards after seeing them on a flaming cross in the heavens on the eve of his battle near Rome in A.D. 312.

Answer: In (Under) this sign (standard) shalt thou conquer / Constantine I, the Great.

12) TOSS-UP. 10 points.

From which Shakespearean play are the following lines taken: "How sharper than a serpent's tooth it is / To have a thankless child. Away, away!" The character who made this statement had three daughters.

Answer: *King Lear*.

12) BONUS. 20 points. 10 points each.

What are the Latin phrases for "an acceptable person" and "an unacceptable person" used especially for ambassadors or other representatives who are either acceptable or not to the government to which they are sent?

Answer: *Persona grata* and *persona non grata.*

13) TOSS-UP. 10 points.

In light, any color may theoretically be produced with a mixture of no more than 3 colors, known as the additive colors. What are they?

Answer: Red, blue, and green.

13) BONUS. 25 points. 5 points each.

Identify each of the following actors or actresses from the given nickname and description.
1) The American actor known as "The Man of a Thousand Faces"
2) The American actor known as "The Great Profile"
3) The French actress knows as "The Sex Kitten"
4) The French actress known as "The Divine Sarah"
5) The English actress, born on the Isle of Jersey and known as "The Jersey Lily"

Answer: 1) Lon Chaney
           2) John Barrymore
           3) Brigitte Bardot
           4) Sarah Bernhardt
           5) Lillie Langtry.

14) TOSS-UP. 10 points.

Which Canadian province is named after Princess Louise Caroline _____, the 4th daughter of Queen Victoria and the wife of the Canadian governor general, Marquis of Lorne? This is the most western of the Canadian Prairie Provinces.

Answer: Alberta.

14) BONUS. 20 points. 10 points each.

Identify the "Army" defeated in the "Battle of Anacostia Flats" by the troops under the command of General Douglas MacArthur, Chief of Staff, and his aide, Major Dwight Eisenhower, and the city in which this victory was won with bayonets and tear gas on July 28-29, 1932.

Answer: "Bonus Army" or "Bonus Expeditionary Forces"
(indigent veterans who were demanding that Congress immediately pay their entire federal war bonuses) / Washington, D.C.

15) TOSS-UP. 10 points.

Name the animal capable of killing mice, rats, and snakes, including cobras and other venomous varieties. In Kipling's *The Jungle Book*, Teddy had one named Rikki-Tikki-Tavi.

Answer: Mongoose.

15) BONUS. 25 points. 5 points each.

Identify the location of each of the following camps.
1) Camp Pendleton
2) Camp Lejeune
3) Camp David
4) Camp Hill (a city; home of the BOMC)
5) The comic strip in which Camp Swampy is featured

Answer: 1) California
2) North Carolina
3) Maryland
4) Pennsylvania
5) *Beetle Bailey*.

16) TOSS-UP. 10 points.

Which American songwriter is famous for his "Begin the Beguine" and musicals such as *Fifty Million Frenchmen* (1929), *Can-Can* (1953), and *Silk Stockings* (1955)?

Answer: Cole Porter.

16) BONUS. 20 points. 5 points each.

Identify the person for each of the following achievements in space.
1) First man in space (April, 1961)
2) First woman in space (June, 1963)
3) First American in space (May, 1961)
4) First American in orbit (February, 1962)

Answer: 1) Yuri Gagarin
2) Valentina V. Tereshkova

3) Alan Shepard
4) John H. Glenn.

17) TOSS-UP. 10 points.

Which 2 groups fought the battle of Marathon, in which the victor defeated a force more than twice its size?

Answer: Athenians (with their Allies, the Plataeans) and the Persians.

17) BONUS. 25 points. 5 points each.

Identify each of the following concerning the battle of Marathon.
1) The king whose superior forces under Datis and Artaphernes were defeated
2) The actual leader of the victorious forces
3) The date of the battle within 10 years
4) The swift runner who was sent from Marathon to Sparta (150 miles) to bring help, who returned to Marathon, and who then was sent from Marathon to Athens to announce the victory
5) The number of miles or kilometers he ran from Marathon to Athens

Answer: 1) **King Darius I of Persia**
2) **Miltiades (Callimachus was nominally in charge)**
3) **490 B.C. (accept 480 - 500 B.C.)**
4) **Pheidippides**
5) **About 25 miles or 40 kilometers (a marathon today is 26 miles 385 yards, or 42.2 kilometers).**

18) TOSS-UP. 10 points.

It was drafted in 1776, adopted by Congress in 1777, and ratified in 1781. Name this first constitution of the United States.

Answer: Articles of Confederation.

18) BONUS. 20 points. 5 points each.

Identify each of the following concerning "The Great Locomotive Chase" of the Civil War.
1) The Confederate locomotive belonging to Georgia's Western and Atlantic Railroad that was hijacked by 22 Union soldiers during the Civil War in April, 1862, for the purpose of breaking the vital rail link between Marietta, Georgia, and Chattanooga, Tennessee

2) The leader of the Union raiding party
3) The name of the Confederate locomotive that chased the stolen locomotive and caught it
4) The leader of the Confederate pursuers

Answer: 1) *The General*
2) **James J. Andrews**
3) *The Texas*
4) **William A. Fuller.**

19) TOSS-UP. 10 points.

Choose the correct verb from the choices in the parentheses: The announcer said, "He should have (going, went, gone) to the bullpen earlier."

Answer: Gone.

19) BONUS. 20 points. 5 points each.

Identify each of the following from Matthew 26:36 and Mark 14:32.
1) The garden or orchard site of the betrayal and arrest of Jesus
2) The hill on whose side the garden is located
3) The 3 apostles who went with Jesus into the garden when He prayed
4) The person who in the garden betrayed Jesus with a kiss

Answer: 1) **Garden of Gethsemane (whose name means "oil press or vat")**
2) **Mount of Olives (or Mount Olivet)**
3) **Peter and the 2 sons of Zebedee, James and John**
4) **Judas Iscariot.**

20) TOSS-UP. 10 points.

This college named after a general working for the Freedmen's Bureau is a predominately black institution located in Nashville, Tennessee. Name this school from which historian W.E.B. DuBois graduated. Its students are nicknamed the "Bulldogs."

Answer: Fisk University.

20) BONUS. 20 points. 10 points each.

What is the absolute temperature scale based on the Celsius degree, and what is the absolute temperature scale based on the Fahrenheit degree?

Answer: Kelvin scale / Rankine scale.

21) TOSS-UP. 10 points.

Which 2 colors are used on the sign for a Fallout Shelter?

Answer: Black and yellow.

21) BONUS. 20 points. 5 points each.

Identify the winner of the World Cup in soccer in each of the following years.
1) 1962
2) 1966
3) 1970
4) 1974

Answer: 1) Brazil
2) England
3) Brazil
4) West Germany.

22) TOSS-UP. 10 points.

What cotton fabric is named from the French phrase translated as "cord of the king," although the fabric itself was developed in England?

Answer: Corduroy (*cord du roi*).

22) BONUS. 20 points. 5 points each.

Identify the U.S. Presidents elected in each of the following years, each of whom died in office.
1) 1840
2) 1860
3) 1880
4) 1900

Answer: 1) William Henry Harrison
2) Abraham Lincoln
3) James A. Garfield
4) William McKinley.

23) TOSS-UP. 10 points.

Who was the founder and first president of the Southern Christian Leadership Conference (SCLC)?

Answer: Martin Luther King, Jr.

23) BONUS. 25 points. 5 points each.

Identify each of the following leaders.
1) The second president of the SCLC (1968 to 1977)
2) The founder and national director of the Congress of Racial Equality (CORE) from 1942 until 1966
3) The executive secretary of the National Urban League from 1961 to 1971
4) The executive secretary of the National Association for the Advancement of Colored People (NAACP) from 1955 to 1977, known as "Mr. Civil Rights"
5) The first woman president of the NAACP, who took office in 1984

Answer: 1) Rev. Ralph David Abernathy
2) James Leonard Farmer
3) Whitney M. Young, Jr.
4) Roy Wilkins
5) Enolia P. McMillan.

24) TOSS-UP. 10 points.

What is the name of General Winfield Scott's plan used by the North during the Civil War for strangling the Confederacy by a coastal blockade and winning control of the Mississippi River? The name is the same as that of a large tropical South American snake.

Answer: "Anaconda policy" or "plan."

24) BONUS. 25 points. 5 points each.

Identify each of the following measures.
1) The number of feet in one statute mile
2) The number of feet in one yard
3) The number of feet in one fathom
4) The number of square feet in one square yard
5) The number of feet in one furlong

Answer: 1) 5,280
2) 3

3) 6
4) 9
5) 660.

25) TOSS-UP. 30 points after the first clue. 20 after the second. 10 after the third.

Who am I?
1) I was born Isadore Baline in Russia in 1888.
2) I first achieved success with the lyrics for *Marie from Sunny Italy* (1907).
3) I received the U.S. government medal for Merit in 1945 for the Broadway musical *This is the Army* (1942), and I wrote a big theatrical success called *Annie Get Your Gun* (1946).

Answer: Irving Berlin.

25) BONUS. 20 points. 10 points each.

Which New York City mayor served from 1926 to 1932 and was forced to resign after a discussion with which New York governor because of widespread corruption in his administration? This mayor, who performed the marriage ceremony for comedienne Fanny Brice and showman Billy Rose, symbolized the *Roaring and Fabulous Twenties*, while this governor later became President of the U.S.

Answer: (James John) Jimmy Walker/Franklin D. Roosevelt.

CATEGORY TOSS-UP. 100 points. 10 points each. 10 points deducted for an incorrect answer.

The abacus, a device invented in China as early as the 6th century B.C., is the oldest known mechanical computing aid. Identify the computing devices invented since then or the inventors who created them.
1) A Scottish mathematician's 1617 non-mechanical device which only multiplied
2) The mechanical adding machine invented by Frenchman Blaise Pascal in 1642
3) The name of a German mathematician who invented a more advanced calculator in 1671
4) The mechanical calculator which was invented in 1834 by Charles Babbage and was a forerunner of the digital computer
5) The name of the system of mathematical logic which forms the basis for the functioning of a computer

6) The name of the developer of the first successful punch-card data processing system in about 1886 and the census tabulating machine in 1890

7) The name of the first large-scale automatic digital computer built by IBM in 1944 after being conceived by Howard A. Aiken in 1937

8) The name of the first large electronic digital computer, designed by John W. Mauchly and J. Presper Eckert and completed in 1946

9) The name of the first stored-program digital computer, which was completed in 1949 and used John Von Neumann's computer design of coded numbers

10) The name of the first computer to be built for commercial purposes, designed by Eckert and Mauchly in 1951

Answer: 1) **Napier's "bones" or "rods"**
2) **La Pascaline**
3) **Wilhelm von Leibniz (Leibnitz)**
4) **Babbage's analytical engine**
5) **Boolean algebra**
6) **Herman Hollerith**
7) **Mark I or Automatic Sequence Controlled Calculator**
8) **ENIAC or Electronic Numerical Integrator And Calculator (or Computer)**
9) **EDVAC or Electronic Discrete Variable Automatic Computer**
10) **UNIVAC I or UNIVersal Automatic Computer.**

ROUND THIRTEEN

1) TOSS-UP. 10 points.

What 1869 novel was originally titled *All's Well That Ends Well?* The author is Leo Tolstoy.

Answer: *War and Peace.*

1) BONUS. 20 points. 5 points each.

In which city and state is each of the following universities or colleges located?
1) Catholic University
2) Duquesne University
3) Oral Roberts University
4) Pepperdine University

Answer: 1) **Washington, D.C.**
2) **Pittsburgh, Pennsylvania**
3) **Tulsa, Oklahoma**
4) **Malibu, California.**

2) TOSS-UP. 10 points.

Scientists sometimes capture flies for experiments, but which athletes shag flies for practice?

Answer: **Baseball players (outfielders in particular).**

2) BONUS. 20 points. 10 points each.

Which 2 Latin phrases designate the basic conditions for U.S. citizenship, being born on the soil of the U.S., or having one parent who is a U.S. citizen.

Answer: *Jus soli* and *jus sanguinis.*

3) TOSS-UP. 10 points.

What is the name of a non-square equilateral quadrilateral?

Answer: **Rhombus.**

3) BONUS. 25 points. 5 points each.

Identify each of the following abbreviations for guided missiles.
1) ICBM
2) MIRV
3) SLBM
4) SAM
5) ABM

Answer: 1) **Intercontinental Ballistic Missile**
        2) **Multiple Independently Targeted Reentry Vehicle**
        3) **Submarine Launched Ballistic Missile**
        4) **Surface-To-Air Missile**
        5) **Antiballistic Missile.**

4) TOSS-UP. 10 points.

Name the post-World War II movement in American painting characterized by the use of color and the random or spontaneous application of paint and associated with such notable artists as Jackson Pollock, Willem de Kooning, and Robert Motherwell.

Answer: Abstract expressionism.

4) BONUS. 30 points. 10 points each.

Name the owners and the lioness featured in *Born Free*, and either of the other 2 books about the lioness born in captivity in 1956.

Answer: Joy and George Adamson / Elsa / *Living Free* or *Forever Free*.

5) TOSS-UP. 10 points.

Name the only place in the U.S. where another flag flies higher than the U.S. flag.

Answer: United Nations (New York City).

5) BONUS. 25 points. 5 points each.

In which foreign city is each of the following landmarks located?
1) Tivoli Gardens amusement park
2) Borghese Gallery and Gardens
3) Trafalgar Square
4) Saint Mark's Basilica
5) The CN Tower

Answer: 1) Copenhagen (Denmark)
2) Rome (Italy)
3) London (England)
4) Venice (Italy)
5) Toronto (Canada; Canadian National Tower).

6) TOSS-UP. 30 points after the first clue. 20 after the second. 10 after the third.

Who am I?
1) Alexander told me he was surnamed the Great, and I told him "I am _____, surnamed the Dog." Alexander also told me that if he were not Alexander, he would like to be me.
2) I was called the "Cynic," and I belonged to the Cynic school of philosophy.
3) Carrying a lantern, I walked barefoot through the streets of Greece looking for an honest man.

Answer: Diogenes.

6) BONUS. 20 points. 10 points each.

"The ability to get to the verge without getting into the war is the necessary art. If you cannot master it, you inevitably get into war. If you are scared to go to the brink, you are lost." What Secretary of State of the Eisenhower administration made the preceding statement, and what word meaning "the art of pursuing an extremely dangerous policy to the edge of catastrophe (to the brink of war) before stopping" was derived from it?

Answer: John Foster Dulles/Brinkmanship (Adlai Stevenson may have added -manship to the word).

7) TOSS-UP. 10 points.

Which name identifies the 2 military lines established by Germany in the 20th century. One was built by Paul von _____ and Erich Ludendorff during the winter of 1916-1917, during World War I, and the other was built by Adolf Hitler during the 1930's opposite the Maginot Line of France and stretched from Switzerland to Kleve in The Netherlands.

Answer: Both lines are called the Siegfried Line (the WWI line was also called the Hindenburg Line, and the WWII line was also called the German Westwall).

7) BONUS. 30 points. 10 points each.

Identify the isotopes of hydrogen from the following information.
1) The ordinary isotope which has one proton
2) The stable isotope which has one neutron in addition to the proton in its nucleus
3) The radioactive isotope which has two neutrons and one proton in its nucleus

Answer: 1) Protium
      2) Deuterium
      3) Tritium.

8) TOSS-UP. 10 points.

What is the name for a "contest between a great and a small man," a phrase derived from I Samuel 17:49-51 in the Bible, which records the defeat of a giant of a man who stood "6 cubits and a span" by a smaller man with a sling shot?

Answer: David and Goliath contest.

8) BONUS. 30 points. 10 points each.

Name the Empress of Russia, wife of Nicholas II, their youngest daughter and their only son, who was a hemophiliac. Some believe that the youngest daughter escaped, but most believe that the entire family was shot and killed by Bolsheviks on July 16 or 17, 1918.

Answer: Alexandra / Anastasia / Aleksei.

9) TOSS-UP. 10 points.

He was born in Russia, emigrated to Brooklyn, and wrote *The Foundation Trilogy* (1951-1953). Two volumes of his autobiography are entitled *In Memory Yet Green: 1920-1954* (1979) and *In Joy Still Felt: 1954-1978* (1980). Name this prolific author who has written more than 200 books.

Answer: Isaac Asimov.

9) BONUS. 30 points. 10 points each.

Identify each of the following American religious figures.
1) The first U.S. citizen, a native of Italy, to be canonized (declared a saint) by the Roman Catholic Church (in 1946)
2) The first person born in the U.S. to be canonized by the Roman

Catholic Church (in 1975)

3) The first male U.S. citizen, a native of Bohemia, to be canonized by the Roman Catholic Church (in 1977)

Answer: 1) **Saint Frances Xavier (Mother) Cabrini**
2) **Saint Elizabeth Ann (Mother) Seton**
3) **Saint John Nepomucene Neumann.**

10) TOSS-UP. 10 points.

What is the full title of Karel Capek's play *R.U.R.*?

Answer: *Rossum's Universal Robots.*

10) BONUS. 20 points. 5 points each.

Identify the author of each of the following works.
1) *The Greening of America*
2) *The Fate of the Earth*
3) *Hiroshima*
4) *Silent Spring*

Answer: 1) **Charles A. Reich**
2) **Jonathan Schell**
3) **John Hersey**
4) **Rachel Louise Carson.**

11) TOSS-UP. 10 points.

What are the 3 colors of television screen phosphors?

Answer: **Red, blue, and green.**

11) BONUS. 20 points. 5 points each.

The more advanced division of the 7 liberal arts during the Middle Ages was called the *quadrivium*. Name at least 3 of the 4 subjects that comprise this group.

Answer: **Arithmetic, geometry, astronomy, and music (harmonics).**

12) TOSS-UP. 10 points.

Name the only Canadian province or territory bordering the Pacific Ocean.

Answer: **British Columbia.**

12) BONUS. 20 points. 5 points each.

Answer each of the following concerning Dante's *Divine Comedy* (*la divina commedia*).
1) What are the 3 Canticas (canticles), or major divisions, of the *Divine Comedy*? (5 points each)
2) Each of the Canticas is divided into *cantos*. How many *cantos* are there? The number of *cantos* is symbolic of true perfection.

Answer: 1) Hell (*Inferno*), Purgatory (*Purgatorio*), and Paradise (*Paradiso*)
2) 100 (each canticle is made up of 33 *cantos*, the first *canto* of the *Inferno* serving as prologue to the whole).

13) TOSS-UP. 30 points after the first clue. 20 after the second. 10 after the third.

What word am I?
1) I am a liquid-propelled intercontinental ballistic missile of the U.S. Air Force, and a crater on the face of the moon.
2) I am the topmost cervical vertebra of the neck and support the head.
3) I am a person who carries a great burden. I am also a collection of maps or a bound volume of tables, charts, or illustrations.

Answer: Atlas (atlas).

13) BONUS. 25 points. 5 points each.

In each of the following sports, give the number of segments of playing time, the name of these divisions, and the time set for each segment.
1) Professional football
2) College basketball
3) Olympic boxing
4) Polo
5) Professional ice hockey

Answer: 1) 4 periods (quarters) of 15 minutes each
2) 2 periods (halves) of 20 minutes each
3) 3 rounds of 3 minutes each
4) 4-8 chukkers, or periods, of 7 to 7 ½ minutes each
5) 3 periods of 20 minutes each.

14) TOSS-UP. 10 points.

According to anthropologists, which of the following remains of prehistoric man are the oldest: Swanscombe Man, Java Man, Heidelberg Man, or Peking Man?

Answer: Java Man.

14) BONUS. 20 points. 5 points each.

Identify the American author of and the novel in which each of the following first lines appears.
1) "Call me Ishmael."
2) "It was Wang Lung's marriage day."
3) "Robert Cohn was once the middleweight boxing champion of Princeton."
4) "It was love at first sight."

Answer: 1) *Moby Dick* **by Herman Melville**
2) *The Good Earth* **by Pearl Buck**
3) *The Sun Also Rises* **by Ernest Hemingway**
4) *Catch-22* **by Joseph Heller.**

15) TOSS-UP. 10 points.

By what common designation is the sinoatrial node known?

Answer: Pacemaker of the heart (or sinus node).

15) BONUS. 30 points. 10 points each.

Name the 3 largest Canadian provinces in population from the largest to the smallest.

Answer: Ontario, Quebec, and British Columbia (as of 1991).

16) TOSS-UP. 30 points after the first clue. 20 after the second. 10 after the third.

Which city am I?
1) My name means today "any city or place of excessive wealth, luxury, wickedness, and vice."
2) I was a city in ancient Mesopotamia on the lower Euphrates River famed for my luxury, culture, and vice.
3) From about 1900 to 1600 B.C., I was the capital of the vast empire built by Hammurabi; the Assyrian Empire ruled me from about 975 to 626 B.C.; and King Sennacherib destroyed me in 689 B.C.

Answer: Babylon.

16) BONUS. 30 points. 10 points each.

Identify the person for each of the following achievements in space.
1) First person to make a spacewalk (March, 1965)
2) First American to make a spacewalk (June, 1965)
3) First woman to make a spacewalk and the first woman ever to make 2 space flights (July, 1984)

Answer: 1) Alexsei A. Leonov
          2) Edward H. White
          3) Svetlana Savitskaya.

17) TOSS-UP. 10 points.

What punctuation mark is used to mark a sudden break in thought, an interruption, or an abrupt change in tone?

Answer: A dash.

17) BONUS. 20 points. 5 points each.

Identify each of the following humorous abbreviations or acronyms.
1) N.Q.O.S.
2) S.W.A.K.
3) T.T.F.W.
4) Y.A.V.I.S.

Answer: 1) Not Quite Our Sort
          2) Sealed With A Kiss
          3)   Too Tacky For Words
          4) Young, Adaptable, Verbal, Intelligent, and Successful.

18) TOSS-UP. 30 points after the first clue. 20 after the second. 10 after the third.

What's my name?
1) My name means "a person or thing whose merit or beauty is neglected or unrecognized before achieving a position of importance or wealth."
2) I am the title character of a fairy tale by Charles Perrault.
3) I escaped household drudgery thanks to the help of a Fairy Godmother, and I married a prince.

Answer: Cinderella.

18) BONUS. 20 points. 5 points each.

From the given definition, identify the "humor" the ancients thought responsible for the given behavior, and give the adjective derived from this "humor." Ancient philosophers believed that the proper balance of these 4 humors or liquids was necessary for the health of the body.
1) "cheerful, confident, and optimistic; ruddy-faced"
2) "sluggish, slow, unexcitable, and stolid; self-possessed"
3) "bad-tempered or cross; peevish; cranky" or "quick-tempered or irritable; characterized by anger"
4) "gloomy, sad, or depressed"

Answer: 1) blood / sanguine
2) phlegm / phlegmatic
3) (yellow) bile / bilious or choleric
4) black bile (black bile was really a non-existent fluid thought to come from the spleen or kidney) / melancholic.

19) TOSS-UP. 10 points.

This college was established in 1740 as a charity school, became an academy in 1749, and was rechartered in 1755 as the College and Academy of _____. In 1791, it adopted its present name and became the first school in the nation to be officially designated a university. Name this Philadelphia institution whose colors are red and blue, and whose students are nicknamed the "Quakers."

Answer: University of Pennsylvania.

19) BONUS. 25 points. 5 points each.

There are 6 European capitals of independent countries which begin with the letter *b*. Name any 5 of them and their countries.

Answer: Brussels, Belgium / Berlin, Germany / Budapest, Hungary / Bucharest, Romania / Bern, Switzerland / Belgrade, Yugoslavia.

20) TOSS-UP. 10 points.

What does the Mohs hardness scale measure?

Answer: Mineral hardness.

20) BONUS. 30 points. 10 points each.

Give the common name by which each of the following contagious diseases is known.
1) Pertussis
2) Tetanus
3) Varicella

Answer: 1) Whooping cough
      2) Lockjaw
      3) Chicken pox.

21) TOSS-UP. 10 points.

With which organization are the terms Dens, Grand Cyclops, Grand Titans, Grand Dragons, and Grand Wizard associated?

Answer: Ku Klux Klan.

21) BONUS. 20 points. 5 points each.

Identify the winner of the World Cup in soccer in each of the following years.
1) 1978
2) 1982
3) 1986
4) 1990

Answer: 1) Argentina
      2) Italy
      3) Argentina
      4) West Germany.

22) TOSS-UP. 10 points.

"We're eyeball to eyeball, and I think the other fellow just blinked." Which Secretary of State said this on October 24, 1962, during the Cuban missile crisis?

Answer: Dean Rusk.

22) BONUS. 20 points. 5 points each.

Identify the U.S. Presidents elected in each of the following years.
1) 1920
2) 1940
3) 1960
4) 1980

Answer: 1) Warren G. Harding
2) Franklin D. Roosevelt
3) John F. Kennedy
4) Ronald Reagan.

23) TOSS-UP. 10 points.

What Greek-Egyptian astronomer and geographer, who wrote the *Almagest*, believed thạt the earth was the motionless center of the universe?

Answer: (Claudius Ptolemaeus) Ptolemy.

23) BONUS. 20 points. 5 points each.

Identify each of the following concerning a Washington, D.C., memorial.
1) The memorial located in Constitution Gardens which is a symbol of the nation's recognition of the men and women of its armed forces who served in the Vietnam War
2) The Yale University student who designed this memorial
3) The number of thousands of names of those who gave their lives or remain missing—the names being inscribed on this polished black granite in chronological order of the date of death, showing the war as a series of individual human sacrifices and giving each name a special place in history
4) The names of the 2 monuments toward which the memorial's walls point, thus bringing the memorial into the historical context of our country

Answer: 1) Vietnam Veterans Memorial
2) Maya Ying Lin
3) 58,000 (58,007)
4) Washington Monument and Lincoln Memorial.

24) TOSS-UP. 10 points.

What word from Greek mythology means "pertaining to dance"? This word comes from one of the 9 Muses of the arts, the Muse of the dance and of choral song.

Answer: Terpsichorean (from Terpsichore).

24) BONUS. 20 points. 10 points each.

Give the names of the 2 Spanish-language weeklies in Boston, or translate the words "The World" and "The Week" that will give you the names.

Answer: *El Mundo* and *La Semana.*

25) TOSS-UP. 10 points.

She wrote *Science and Health, with Key to the Scriptures* (1875), founded a daily newspaper, the *Christian Science Monitor* (1908), and was the founder of the Church of Christ, Scientist. Who was this New Hampshire woman born in 1821?

Answer: Mary Baker Eddy.

25) BONUS. 25 points. 5 points each.

Name the 5 U.S. states which border on the Gulf of Mexico.

Answer: Texas, Louisiana, Mississippi, Alabama, and Florida.

CATEGORY TOSS-UP. 100 points. 10 points each. 10 points deducted for an incorrect answer.

Identify each of the following concerning the Crusades.
1) The number of "numbered" Crusades undertaken from A.D. 1095 to 1291
2) The area the Christians tried to capture from the Muslims
3) The Crusade called by Pope Urban II during which Jerusalem was captured (the commoners were led by Peter the Hermit, and the knights were led by Count Robert of Flanders, Count Raymond of Toulouse, Godfrey of Bouillon, and Bohemund from Sicily)
4) The Crusade which was called by Pope Innocent III and was more an attack by the Venetians against Constantinople's establishing a Latin Empire there than an attack against the Muslims, for the Crusaders never reached the Holy Land
5) The Crusade of young boys and girls from France and Germany which never reached the Holy Land and during which most of the children died along the way or were sold into slavery
6) The Crusade led by King Louis IX of France (or Saint Louis) during which he died, resulting in his army's return to Europe
7) The Crusade called the "Crusade of Kings" as it was led by Frederick I (called Barbarossa) of Germany (Holy Roman Empire), King Philip II (called Philip Augustus) of France, and King Richard I (the Lion-Hearted) of England. Frederick I died, Philip returned home, and Richard negotiated a 5-year truce which

allowed unarmed Christians to enter the "Holy City" of Jerusalem.

8) The Crusade which was called by St. Bernard on behalf of Pope Eugenius III and led by French King Louis VII and the Hohenstaufen Emperor Conrad III of Germany (Holy Roman Empire)

9) The Crusade led by Holy Roman Emperor Frederick II, who, without a battle, enticed the Muslims to give Jerusalem to the Christians until it was seized again in 1244 by the Muslims

10) The Crusade organized by King Louis IX (Saint Louis) during which Louis and his Crusaders were captured and released only after a ransom had been paid

Answer:
1) **8 (9 counting the Children's Crusade)**
2) **Holy Land (Jerusalem and environs)**
3) **First (1095-1099)**
4) **Fourth (1201-1204)**
5) **Children's (1212)**
6) **Eighth (1270)**
7) **Third (1189-1192)**
8) **Second (1147-1149)**
9) **Sixth (1227-1229)**
10) **Seventh (1248-1254).**

ROUND FOURTEEN

1) TOSS-UP. 10 points.

In 1951, after he was removed from his position for insubordination, who said before Congress: "... like the old soldier of that ballad, I now close my military career and just fade away, an old soldier who tried to do his duty as God gave him the light to see that duty"?

Answer: General Douglas MacArthur (President Truman removed him).

1) BONUS. 20 points. 10 points each.

Identify the word that completes the following lines, and name the author: "Shall I compare thee to a _____ day? / Thou art more lovely and more temperate."

Answer: "summer's" / William Shakespeare ("Sonnet 18").

2) TOSS-UP. 10 points.

1531, 1607, 1682, 1758, 1835, 1910, and November, 1985: these dates indicate the appearance of what celestial body approximately every 76 years?

Answer: Halley's comet.

2) BONUS. 20 points. 10 points each.

Name the author of the following lines and the person he is commemorating: "O Captain! my Captain! our fearful trip is done, / The ship has weather'd every rack, the prize we sought is won; ... / But O heart! heart! heart! / O the bleeding drops of red, / When on the deck my Captain lies / Fallen cold and dead."

Answer: Walt Whitman ("O Captain! My Captain!") / Abraham Lincoln.

3) TOSS-UP. 10 points.

Which horse race is called the "Run for the Roses"?

Answer: The Kentucky Derby.

3) BONUS. 20 points. 10 points each.

Although it is not entirely surrounded by land but is connected with both the Caribbean Sea and the Gulf of Venezuela by a short channel, which body of water is considered to be the largest lake in South America, and in which country is it located?

Answer: Lake Maracaibo / Venezuela.

4) TOSS-UP. 10 points.

If the length of the edge of a cube is tripled, by how many times will its volume be increased?

Answer: Twenty-seven times.

4) BONUS. 20 points. 10 points each.

Give not only the formula for nitrous oxide but also its more common name.

Answer: N_2O / Laughing gas.

5) TOSS-UP. 10 points.

Name the style of jazz that combines elements of ragtime and blues. This music is marked by strongly accented four-four rhythm with distinctive improvisation and is usually played by a small group of musicians.

Answer: Dixieland.

5) BONUS. 20 points. 10 points each.

Fill in the 2 phrases missing in the lines of the following stanza of the "Battle Hymn of the Republic": "Mine eyes have seen the glory of the coming of the Lord; / He is trampling out the vintage where the _____ are stored; / He hath loosed the fateful lightning of His _____; / His truth is marching on."

Answer: "grapes of wrath" / "terrible swift sword."

6) TOSS-UP. 10 points.

What U.S. President enjoyed playing croquet, was known as "His Fraudulency" because of the outcome of the 1876 election, and had a wife who earned the nickname "Lemonade Lucy" for banishing alcoholic beverages from the White House and serving fruit juices and cold water instead?

Answer: Rutherford Birchard Hayes.

6) BONUS. 20 points. 10 points each.

In which country was Benigno Aquino assassinated in 1983, and who was the President of the country at that time?

Answer: Philippines / President Ferdinand E. Marcos.

7) TOSS-UP. 10 points.

Name the Black Panther Minister of Education who ran in the 1968 U.S. presidential election as a candidate for the Peace and Freedom Party. This man lived abroad from 1968, when he jumped bail following his arrest on charges of conspiracy to bomb public buildings and to commit other acts of terrorism, until 1975 when he returned to the U.S. and converted to Christianity.

Answer: Eldridge Cleaver.

7) BONUS. 20 points. 5 points each.

Identify the American author of and the novel in which each of the following first lines appears.
1) "I went back to the Devon School not long ago, and found it looking oddly newer than when I was a student there fifteen years before."
2) "To the red country and part of the gray country of Oklahoma, the last rains came gently, and they did not cut the scarred earth."

Answer: 1) *A Separate Peace* **by John Knowles**
       2) *The Grapes of Wrath* **by John Steinbeck.**

8) TOSS-UP. 10 points.

When a beam of white light passes obliquely from air into a glass prism, which color is refracted the least?

Answer: Red.

8) BONUS. 20 points. 10 points each.

Name the novels by Jane Austen in which Elizabeth Bennet and Emma Woodhouse are heroines.

Answer: *Pride and Prejudice* **and** *Emma.*

9) TOSS-UP. 10 points.

What is the total number of lines in a sonnet and in a haiku?

Answer: 17 (14 and 3).

9) BONUS. 20 points. 10 points each.

Name this West African country and its leader. He was officially nicknamed "The Elephant" because of his strength and dignity, and he ruled in the capital of Conakry from the day of independence in 1958 until his death in 1984.

Answer: Guinea / Ahmed Sekou Touré.

10) TOSS-UP. 10 points.

Name the Greek orator and patriot, known for his *Philippics*, who developed his oratorical skill by shouting above the roar of ocean waves with his mouth full of pebbles.

Answer: Demosthenes.

10) BONUS. 20 points. 5 points each.

In which city and state is each of the following universities located?
1) Purdue University
2) Rice University
3) Ball State University
4) Baylor University

Answer: 1) West Lafayette, Indiana
2) Houston, Texas
3) Muncie, Indiana
4) Waco, Texas.

11) TOSS-UP. 10 points.

What name designates the logs that Union soldiers painted black and carved to look like guns during the Civil War and today designates "hollow threats"? These "guns" that could not be fired were named after the Society of Friends, which objected to the war.

Answer: Quaker guns.

11) BONUS. 30 points after the first clue. 20 after the second. 10 after the third.

What's my name?
1) I became the longest suspension bridge in the world when I was

finished in 1931.

2) I was built for 8 lanes of traffic, but a lower deck with an additional 6 lanes was completed in 1962, making me the first 14-lane vehicular suspension bridge.

3) I span the Hudson River connecting the states of New York (at Manhattan) and New Jersey (at Fort Lee).

Answer: George Washington Bridge.

12) TOSS-UP. 10 points.

Name Hitler's private secretary, the German Nazi party leader nicknamed "Hitler's Evil Genius," the "Man Who Manipulated Hitler," and the "Brown Eminence."

Answer: Martin Bormann.

12) BONUS. 20 points. 10 points each.

In which play by which author is Madame Ranevskaya's famous Russian estate sold to pay her debts?

Answer: *The Cherry Orchard* by Anton Chekhov.

13) TOSS-UP. 10 points.

Pontius Pilate ordered that the initials I.N.R.I., representing the Latin *Iesus Nazarenus, Rex Iudaeorum*, be placed on the Cross of Calvary on which Christ was crucified (John 19:19). What is the English translation of those initials?

Answer: Jesus of Nazareth, the King of the Jews.

13) BONUS. 30 points. 10 points each.

Give the common name for each of the following contagious diseases.
1) Parotitis (parotiditis)
2) Scarlatina
3) Rubella

Answer: 1) Mumps
2) Scarlet fever
3) German measles.

14) TOSS-UP. 10 points.

What is the name for a terrestrial worm, class *Oligochaeta*, called the "fishworm," or "night crawler," or "angleworm"?

Answer: **Earthworm.**

14) BONUS. 20 points. 10 points each.

Give the year in which John Herschel Glenn, Jr., became the first American astronaut to orbit the earth, and name the state he was elected to represent in the U.S. Senate.

Answer: **1962 / Ohio.**

15) TOSS-UP. 10 points.

Name the 4 acts passed by Congress in 1798 in response to the threat of war with France which proscribed spoken or written criticism of the government, gave the President the power to banish dangerous aliens, and required a foreigner to live in the U.S. for 14 years before becoming a citizen.

Answer: **Alien and Sedition Acts.**

15) BONUS. 20 points. 10 points each.

The assassins of which country plot to kill which French leader in Frederick Forsyth's 1971 novel *The Day of the Jackal*? The plot of this novel is based on a real-life incident.

Answer: **Algeria / Charles De Gaulle.**

16) TOSS-UP. 10 points.

What is the term for 2 or more words with the same sound and spelling but different meaning?

Answer: **Homonyms.**

16) BONUS. 20 points. 10 points each.

By what other name are the Maccabiah Games known, and in which country are they held?

Answer: **The "Jewish Olympics" / Israel.**

17) TOSS-UP. 30 points after the first clue. 20 after the second. 10 after the third.

What's my name?
1) In Greek mythology, I was considered to be the patron of craftsmen and artists.

2) I was considered to be an architect and the inventor of carpentry and useful instruments such as the awl and the axe.

3) I made a golden honeycomb for the Temple of Aphrodite, yet I slew my nephew Talos (Perdix) out of jealousy. I then fled to Crete where I designed the labyrinth for the Minotaur.

Answer: Daedalus.

17) BONUS. 30 points. 5 points each. Point total stops at the first mistake.

Name the 6 largest planets in our solar system in order of size from the largest to the smallest.

Answer: Jupiter, Saturn, Uranus, Neptune, Earth, and Venus.

18) TOSS-UP. 30 points after the first clue. 20 after the second. 10 after the third.

Which religion am I?

1) Prior to 1945, I was the state religion of the country in which I am the oldest surviving religion, and unlike some religions, I have no founder.

2) My symbol is the *torii*, which is a wooden gate.

3) My name means "the way of the gods," and I am the native religion of Japan.

Answer: Shinto.

18) BONUS. 30 points. 5 points each.

Answer each of the following questions concerning a WWI telegram.

1) What name designates the telegram sent by the German Secretary of State for Foreign Affairs offering to restore lost territories to a country if it entered into the fight against the U.S.?

2) To which country did it offer this help?

3) Which 3 U.S. states—the lost territory—did Germany offer to help reconquer if it entered the fight? (5 points each)

4) In what year was the telegram sent?

Answer: 1) Zimmermann telegram (also called the Zimmermann note)
2) Mexico
3) Arizona, New Mexico, and Texas
4) 1917 (January 19; published in the U.S. on March 1, 1917).

19) TOSS-UP. 30 points after the first clue. 20 after the second. 10 after the third.

What's my name?
1) I was founded in 1849 by Paul Julius _____, originally named Israel Beer Josaphat, as a financial service in Germany, using the telegraph and even carrier pigeons to transmit daily news of the financial market.
2) I was moved to London in 1851.
3) I am today an international news-gathering agency.

Answer: Reuters.

19) BONUS. 20 points. 10 points each.

Name the 2 countries whose coastlines border on the Bay of Biscay (also called the Gulf of Vizcaya or the Gulf of Gascony).

Answer: France and Spain.

20) TOSS-UP. 10 points.

What word means "the right held by one person to use land of another for a special purpose, as a right of passage"?

Answer: Easement.

20) BONUS. 30 points. 10 points each.

Give the real names of each of the following.
1) George Eliot
2) George Orwell
3) George Sand

Answer: 1) Mary Ann (or Marian) Evans
2) Eric Arthur Blair
3) Amandine Lucie Aurore Dupin, Baroness Dudevant (accept Dupin).

21) TOSS-UP. 10 points.

Which slang word that means "paper money," or "to steal" or "to pilfer," is also the name for a common vegetable or for "odd pieces of cloth, left over after making garments, appropriated by a tailor," the latter meaning being the source for the name of the dolls that caused a sensation in 1983?

Answer: Cabbage (as in Cabbage-patch dolls).

21) BONUS. 20 points. 5 points each.

Name the 4 major civilizations of ancient Mesopotamia. One of these civilizations is credited with the invention of the cuneiform system of writing; one achieved greatness under Ashurnasirpal II; another achieved wealth under Hammurabi; and another's city-states were united in a vast organized empire under Sargon.

Answer: Sumerian, Assyrian, Babylonian, and Akkadian.

22) TOSS-UP. 10 points.

Napoleon said, *"Du sublime au ridicule il n'y a qu'un pas"* ("From the sublime to the ridiculous is but a step"). In light of this comment, which French military leader, a national hero in WWI at the Battle of Verdun, was tried for treason and eventually died in jail at 95 for having collaborated with the Germans during WWII?

Answer: Henri Philippe Pétain.

22) BONUS. 20 points. 5 points each.

Identify each of the following in relation to counties in the U.S.
1) The state which has 254 counties (the largest number)
2) The state which has 159 counties (the second largest number)
3) The name given to counties in Louisiana
4) The name given to local government units in Alaska

Answer: 1) Texas
         2) Georgia
         3) Parishes
         4) (organized) Boroughs.

23) TOSS-UP. 10 points.

Which form of pneumonia affects the kidneys, liver, intestines, and nerves and was first recognized at a July 1976 convention of the American Legion in Philadelphia, Pennsylvania?

Answer: Legionnaire's disease.

23) BONUS. 20 points. 5 points each.

Identify each of the following.
1) The king, her father, whom Queen Elizabeth II replaced on February 6, 1952 (the coronation was held on June 2, 1953)
2) The husband she married on November 20, 1947

3) Two of her 4 children

Answer: 1) **George VI**
2) **Philip Mountbatten**
3) **Charles, Anne, Andrew, and Edward.**

24) TOSS-UP. 30 points after the first clue. 20 after the second. 10 after the third.

Which French author am I?
1) I wrote *Les Chouans (The Chouans)* and *Illusions perdues (Lost Illusions)*.
2) I wrote *Le Médecin de campagne (The Country Doctor)* and *Le Père Goriot (Father Goriot)*.
3) I wrote *Eugénie Grandet* and *La Comédie humaine (The Human Comedy)*.

Answer: Honoré de Balzac.

24) BONUS. 20 points. 10 points each.

Name the 2 largest French-speaking cities in the world.

Answer: Paris and Montreal.

25) TOSS-UP. 10 points.

Name either the banks off the coast of Newfoundland, Canada, or the bank off the coast of Cape Cod, northeast from Nantucket.

Answer: Grand Banks or Georges Bank.

25) BONUS. 20 points. 5 points each.

Name the only 4 male actors who are two-time Oscar winners for Best Actor. The films in which they won their Academy Awards follow.
1) *Dr. Jekyll and Mr. Hyde* (1931-1932) and *The Best Years of Our Lives* (1946)
2) *Captains Courageous* (1937) and *Boys' Town* (1938)
3) *Sergeant York* (1941) and *High Noon* (1952)
4) *On the Waterfront* (1954) and *The Godfather* (1972)

Answer: 1) Frederic March
          2) Spencer Tracy
          3) Gary Cooper
          4) Marlon Brando.

CATEGORY TOSS-UP. 100 points. 10 points each. 10 points deducted for an incorrect answer.

Identify each of the following concerning the TV series "Star Trek."
1) The creator of this science fiction adventure
2) The century in which this adventure is set
3) The name of the starship which is on a five-year mission
4) The group which this starship represents as it explores the universe
5) The 2 enemy alien races confronted by members of the starship
6) The commander of the starship and the name of the actor who plays this role
7) The logical-thinking, half-breed Vulcan of green complexion whose father (Sarek) was an ambassador and whose mother (Amanda) was an Earth woman, and the actor who plays this role
8) The chief medical officer nicknamed "Bones," or the actor who plays him
9) The communications officer, a Bantu woman, or the actress who plays her
10) The chief engineer of European extraction, or the actor who plays him

Answer: 1) **Gene Roddenberry**
          2) **22nd century**
          3) **U.S.S. *Enterprise* (Registry Number is NCC 1701)**
          4) **United Federation of the Planets**
          5) **Klingons and Romulans**
          6) **Captain James T. Kirk played by William Shatner**
          7) **Science Officer Mr. Spock played by Leonard Nimoy**
          8) **Dr. Leonard McCoy / DeForest Kelly**
          9) **Lieutenant Uhura / Nichelle Nichols**
        10) **Montgomery Scott ("Scotty") / James Doohan.**

ROUND FIFTEEN

1010 points

1) TOSS-UP. 10 points.

Name Robert Browning's 12-book poem based on a 17th century Italian murder case. Various characters tell the story of Guido Franceschini, who kills his wife Pompilia (Comparini) and then her parents, blaming his actions on her infidelity. Pope Innocent XII, sitting in judgment, condemns Franceschini to death.

Answer: *The Ring and the Book.*

1) BONUS. 20 points. 10 points each.

Name the first book of the Old Testament and the first book of the New Testament.

Answer: Genesis and Matthew.

2) TOSS-UP. 10 points.

Which poem by Henry Wadsworth Longfellow is subtitled *A Tale of Acadie* and is based on the 1755 deportation of the French Acadian inhabitants of a Canadian region that included what are now the provinces of Nova Scotia, New Brunswick, and Prince Edward Island?

Answer: *Evangeline.*

2) BONUS. 30 points. 5 points each.

Identify the author of the following, the sport described, and then give the 4 missing names: "Outlined against a blue-gray October sky, the Four Horsemen rode / again. In dramatic lore they were known as Famine, Pestilence, / Destruction, and Death. These are only aliases. Their real names / are _____, _____, _____, and _____."

Answer: Grantland Rice (concerning a Notre Dame victory over Army in 1924) / Football / Stuhldreher, Miller, Crowley, and Layden (order not necessary).

3) TOSS-UP. 10 points.

What integer does 64 to the two-thirds power equal?

Answer: Sixteen (16).

3) BONUS. 20 points. 5 points each.

A DH may be a designated hitter in baseball, but each of the following words beginning with a DH has nothing to do with baseball. Identify each of the following.
1) A fringed, usually rectangular, flat-weave cotton carpet made in India
2) A sailing vessel with one, two, or three masts with a lateen sail used by Arabs and others on the east African, the Arabian, and the Indian coasts
3) A loincloth worn by Hindu men in India
4) The moral and religious law of Buddhism and Hinduism

Answer: 1) Dhurrie (durrie)
 2) Dhow (dow, dau)
 3) Dhoti (dhotti, dhootie, dhuti)
 4) Dharma (dhamma).

4) TOSS-UP. 10 points.

What nickname do Malcolm X, Man o'War, and the athletic teams of Cornell University have in common?

Answer: Big Red.

4) BONUS. 20 points. 10 points each.

Which university in which state was the site of the May 4, 1970, slaying of 4 students and the wounding of 10 others by National Guardsmen during a demonstration protesting U.S. involvement in Cambodia and Vietnam?

Answer: Kent State University in Ohio.

5) TOSS-UP. 10 points.

Name the American naval officer who in the 1860's became the first vice admiral, the first rear admiral, and the first four-star admiral in the U.S. Navy. This officer led a fleet that attacked and defeated the Confederate forces at Mobile Bay on August 5, 1864.

Answer: David Glasgow Farragut.

5) BONUS. 20 points maximum. 5 points each.

Name 4 of the 5 countries through which the Danube River flows.

Answer: It passes through Germany, Austria, Hungary, Yugoslavia, and Romania (it borders on Czechoslovakia, Bulgaria, and, in its delta tract, the Soviet Union).

6) TOSS-UP. 30 points after the first clue. 20 after the second. 10 after the third.

What's my name?
1) I was born in Spartanburg, South Carolina, in 1914, and I appeared on the cover of *Time* magazine 3 times, once as the "Man of the Year" in 1966.
2) I was the subject of criticism in "The Uncounted Enemy: A Vietnam Deception," a CBS broadcast.
3) I commanded U.S. forces in the Vietnam War from 1964 to 1968, and I ran unsuccessfully for governor of South Carolina in 1974.

Answer: William Childs Westmoreland.

6) BONUS. 20 points. 10 points each.

Identify the goddess of fire on the hearths of home and state in Roman mythology and the 6 women who kept the sacred fire going in the Temple in Rome.

Answer: Vesta / Vestal Virgins or Vestals.

7) TOSS-UP. 10 points.

Name either the king of England with whose reign the names of 5 ministers—Lord Clifford, Lord Ashley, the Duke of Buckingham, the Earl of Arlington, and the Duke of Lauderdale—were connected, or the word coincidentally associated with this group which means "a small group of secret plotters or intriguers organized to overturn a government or person in authority." This king ruled from 1660 to 1685.

Answer: Charles II or Cabal (the first letter of the names of the 5 ministers spell this word).

7) BONUS. 20 points. All or nothing.

Name the 3 Italian artists considered to be the 3 "Great Masters" of the High Renaissance of the 16th century. These 3 are known respectively for the *Adoration of the Three Kings*, *The Last Judgment*, and the *School of Athens*.

Answer: Leonardo da Vinci, Michelangelo, and Raphael.

8) TOSS-UP. 10 points.

What family of elements has the least reactive stable atoms?

Answer: Noble gases or inert gases (column VIII group).

8) BONUS. 20 points. 10 points each.

Between which 2 continents is the Drake Passage located? This strait lies between Cape Horn and the South Shetland Islands.

Answer: South America and Antarctica.

9) TOSS-UP. 10 points.

Which U.S. President had a serious heart attack after playing 37 holes of golf and had an operation for ileitis (a blocked intestine) a year later? He then ran successfully for reelection, but suffered a mild stroke the following year.

Answer: Dwight Eisenhower (1955, 1956, and 1957).

9) BONUS. 20 points. 10 points each.

Who invented the *Kodak* camera, and in which New York city did he establish his factory in 1880?

Answer: George Eastman in Rochester.

10) TOSS-UP. 10 points.

Give the name shared by the narrator in Herman Melville's *Moby Dick* and the son of Abraham by Hagar, the Egyptian slave of his wife Sarah (Genesis 17:18-27; 21:8-21).

Answer: Ishmael.

10) BONUS. 20 points. 5 points each.

Identify the address of each of the following residences.
1) The White House, home of the President of the United States
2) Home of the Prime Minister of England
3) Home of the Chancellor of the Exchequer of England
4) Residence of the Prime Minister of Canada

Answer: 1) 1600 Pennsylvania Avenue
2) 10 Downing Street
3) 11 Downing Street
4) 24 Sussex Drive.

11) TOSS-UP. 30 points after the first clue. 20 after the second. 10 after the third.

Who am I?
1) I fought at Chippewa and Lundy's Lane in the War of 1812, and I captured Mexico City in the Mexican War.
2) I was, however, defeated for the presidency of the U.S. in 1852 by Franklin Pierce.
3) From 1841 to 1861 I was the general in chief of the U.S. Army. I was nicknamed the "Hero of Chippewa," "Hero of Lundy's Lane," and "Old Fuss and Feathers."

Answer: Winfield Scott.

11) BONUS. 20 points. 5 points each.

Name the 3 main islands of the U.S. Virgin Islands, and then name the capital.

Answer: St. Croix, St. Thomas, and St. John (listed in order of area and population from largest to smallest) / Charlotte Amalie.

12) TOSS-UP. 10 points.

Upon what group of people did the Dawes Act of 1887 confer U.S. Citizenship?

Answer: Indians (in return for giving up their tribal lands and accepting individual land grants).

12) BONUS. 20 points. 10 points each.

Name the American author of the following lines and the book of the Bible quoted in the message: "Life is real! Life is earnest! / And the grave is not its goal; / Dust thou are, to dust returnest, / Was not spoken of the soul."

Answer: Henry Wadsworth Longfellow ("A Psalm of Life") / Genesis (3:19).

13) TOSS-UP. 10 points.

Name the American economist who wrote *The Theory of the Leisure Class* (1899).

Answer: Thorstein Bunde Veblen.

13) BONUS. 20 points. 5 points each.

Of which city did each of the following blacks serve as mayor?
1) Andrew Young
2) W. Wilson Goode
3) Coleman A. Young
4) Tom Bradley

Answer: 1) Atlanta (Georgia)
2) Philadelphia (Pennsylvania)
3) Detroit (Michigan)
4) Los Angeles (California).

14) TOSS-UP. 10 points.

Which governor of Massachusetts, later President of the U.S., in reply to a request by Samuel Gompers that the Boston Police Commissioner be removed for asking for state troops to break the Boston Police Strike in 1919 said, "There is no right to strike against the public peace (safety) by anybody, anywhere, any time"?

Answer: Calvin Coolidge.

14) BONUS. 30 points. 10 points each.

Identify the author of each of the following novels and give his nationality. All or nothing for each one.
1) *La Peste* (*The Plague*)
2) *One Day in the Life of Ivan Denisovich*
3) *Sons and Lovers*

Answer: 1) Albert Camus—French
2) Alexander Solzhenitsyn—Russian
3) D.H. Lawrence—English.

15) TOSS-UP. 10 points.

Name the nine-branched candelabrum used during the Jewish festival of Hanukkah (Chanukah).

Answer: Menorah.

15) BONUS. 20 points. 10 points each.

Name the only 2 biblical animals that talk.

Answer: The serpent in the Garden of Eden and Balaam's ass.

16) TOSS-UP. 30 points after the first clue. 20 after the second. 10 after the third.

What is my name?
1) I was born in St. Petersburg (now Leningrad) in 1881, and I became the most famous ballet dancer of my generation.
2) I joined the Imperial Ballet Company in 1899 and became its prima ballerina in 1906. I formed my own company, Ivy House, in London after leaving Russia in 1913.
3) I am famous for "The Dying Swan," a three-minute solo that I frequently performed.

Answer: Anna Pavlova.

16) BONUS. 20 points. 10 points each.

The word *Duumvirate* is the Latin term for 2 officers united in the administration of one public office. Name the U.S. President and his assistant referred to as *Duumvirs* because of the responsibilities they shared during WWI. The assistant made many secret missions to Europe during the war, served on the American commission at the Versailles Peace Conference, and was known as "Colonel."

Answer: Woodrow Wilson and (Colonel) Edward Mandell House.

17) TOSS-UP. 10 points.

D-Day means "the unspecified day on which a military operation is to take place," but on which day does the War Department order active mobilization for war?

Answer: M-Day (Mobilization Day).

17) BONUS. 20 points. 10 points each.

Monument Valley is a vast scenic area within the Navajo Indian reservation. In which 2 U.S. states is this valley located?

Answer: Arizona and Utah.

18) TOSS-UP. 20 points after the first clue. 10 after the second.

Who am I?
1) I shared the Nobel Peace Prize in 1931 with Nicholas Murray Butler.
2) In 1889 Ellen Gates Starr and I founded Hull House in Chicago in order to improve conditions in the city slums.

Answer: Jane Addams.

18) BONUS. 30 points. 10 points each.

Complete the title of each of the following stories by Edgar Allan Poe.
1) "The Mystery of Marie _____"
2) "The Masque of the Red _____"
3) "The Pit and the _____"

Answer: 1) Rogêt
2) Death
3) Pendulum.

19) TOSS-UP. 10 points.

What word has 3 *y*'s, 1 *s*, 1 *z*, and a *g*, etymologically means "yoked together," and is defined in astronomy as "either of two opposing points in the orbit of a celestial body, specifically of the moon, when the moon lies in a straight line with the sun and the earth"?

Answer: Syzygy.

19) BONUS. 20 points. 5 points each.

Identify the name given to any 3 of the following 4 hypothetical geographic sites.
1) The single giant land mass or super continent that many scientists believe once covered the earth from about 300 to about 200 million years ago, a theory advanced by German meteorologist Alfred Wegener
2) The 2 land masses that the supercontinent divided into
3) The world's single ocean which some believe surrounded this supercontinent.

Answer: 1) Pangaea (Pangea)
2) Gondwanaland (Gondwana) and Laurasia
3) Panthalassa.

20) TOSS-UP. 10 points.

Identify the musical instrument and the geometric figure which have the same name.

Answer: Triangle.

20) BONUS. 30 points. 15 points each.

Identify each of the following involving the U.S. Supreme Court.
1) The U.S. President who appointed the only person ever to resign from the Supreme Court under the threat of impeachment (1969)
2) The only Supreme Court justice to resign under the threat of impeachment for his allegedly unethical conduct

Answer: 1) Lyndon Johnson
2) Abe Fortas.

21) TOSS-UP. 30 points after the first clue. 20 after the second. 10 after the third.

What is my name?
1) My sister was a poet, and I was one of the leaders of the Pre-Raphaelites, an art movement founded in 1848.
2) My paintings include *The Girlhood of Mary Virgin* (1849) and *Ecce Ancilla Domini* (1850).
3) I am perhaps better known for burying my manuscript of poems in my wife's coffin, later exhuming and publishing them in a collection entitled *Poems*.

Answer: Dante Gabriel Rossetti.

21) BONUS. 20 points. 10 points each.

Name these 2 "generals": the founder and first superior general of the Jesuit order (1538) and the founder and first general of the Salvation Army (1865).

Answer: St. Ignatius of Loyola / William Booth.

22) TOSS-UP. 10 points.

Name the earliest known inhabitants of Anatolia (now Turkey). These inhabitants, who were one of the first peoples to smelt iron successfully, ruled from the mid-18th through the 13th century B.C., reaching the height of their power between 1400 and 1200 B.C. under such rulers as Suppiluliumas I and Hattusilis III.

Answer: Hittites.

22) BONUS. 30 points. 10 points each.

Give all of the possible parts of speech of each of the following: hunger, hungrily, and hungry.

Answer: Noun and verb (hunger), adverb (hungrily), and adjective (hungry).

23) TOSS-UP. 10 points.

Name the English economist whose belief that population increases more rapidly than food supplies significantly influenced both Charles Darwin and Alfred Russel Wallace.

Answer: Thomas Robert Malthus.

23) BONUS. 20 points. 5 points each.

Identify each of the following.
1) The smooth-shelled, sweet nut, edible when cooked, which comes from trees of the beech family, and whose name today means "an old, stale joke; anything lacking freshness or originality, as a repeated tale or story or piece of music"
2) The phrase from the fable of the monkey and the cat which means "to extricate someone from a predicament; to do a distasteful or dangerous chore for another; to be duped into performing a dangerous or unpleasant task for another"
3) The phrase from the fable of the monkey and the cat which alludes to the monkey's trick of getting the cat to use an append- age to obtain roasted nuts from a fire, and which means "(to be) a person duped into doing a dangerous or unpleasant task; (to be) a dupe"
4) The proper name used to designate "a stale joke," a name derived from a book, _____'s *Jest Book* (1739) by John Mottley containing the jokes of a deceased comedian

Answer: 1) Chestnut
2) To pull one's chestnuts out of the fire
3) (to be made) a cat's paw (of)
4) A Joe Miller.

24) TOSS-UP. 10 points.

What French expression designates *paramnesia*, or "the illusion of having already experienced something actually being experienced for the first time," 2 words translated as "already seen"?

Answer: *Déjà vu.*

24) BONUS. 20 points. 10 points each.

Name both the coach and the college team, nicknamed the "Bruins," that won the NCAA basketball championship 10 times (including 7 straight) from the years 1964 to 1975.

Answer: John Wooden and UCLA (University of California at Los Angeles).

25) TOSS-UP. 10 points.

Name the public market and meeting place in Boston known as the "Cradle of Liberty" because of the historic meetings that took place there during the American Revolutionary and Civil wars.

Answer: Faneuil Hall.

25) BONUS. 30 points. 10 points each.

Identify the world capitals located on each of the following rivers.
1) Tiber
2) Seine
3) Tagus (Tejo)

Answer: 1) Rome
     2) Paris
     3) Lisbon

CATEGORY TOSS-UP. 100 points. 10 points each. 10 points deducted for an incorrect answer.

Identify each of the following U.S. capitals and their states.
1) The state capital, located on the Severn River, which was named in honor of Princess (later Queen) Anne in 1694, and whose state capitol is the oldest one still being used regularly by a legislature
2) The state capital located on the Salt River and named after a mythological bird which arose from its own ashes
3) The state capital named after the legendary home of the Greek gods.
4) The state capital named after its river, which according to some was named after the French word for "middle" as it was the largest river between the Missouri and the Mississippi

5) The state capital located on the Alabama River and named after a Brigadier General who was a Revolutionary War hero killed in 1775 during an attack on Quebec

6) The state capital located on the east bank of the Missouri River and named after a French fur trapper whose last name was Chouteau

7) The state capital settled on the single afternoon of April 22, 1889, when 10,000 land seekers invaded the area during the Great Land Run (or Run of '89) and established a tent city near the Santa Fe railroad tracks

8) The state capital that was founded in 1610 and is today the oldest seat of government in the U.S.

9) The state capital located on both banks of the Mississippi River and formerly known as Pig's Eye

10) The state capital originally named Terminus, later Marthasville, which served as a depot for Confederate arms during the Civil War

Answer: 1) Annapolis, Maryland
2) Phoenix, Arizona
3) Olympia, Washington
4) Des Moines, Iowa
5) Montgomery, Alabama
6) Pierre, South Dakota
7) Oklahoma City, Oklahoma
8) Santa Fe, New Mexico
9) St. Paul, Minnesota
10) Atlanta, Georgia.

ROUND SIXTEEN

1040 points

1) TOSS-UP. 10 points.

In which foreign city would you be if you were crossing the Galata Bridge over the Golden Horn with the Hagia Sophia off to the left?

Answer: Istanbul.

1) BONUS. 20 points. All or nothing.

What are the 3 kinds of rock which make up the Earth's crust?

Answer: Igneous, sedimentary, and metamorphic.

2) TOSS-UP. 10 points.

Whose troops during the Civil War were known as the "Foot Cavalry" since they engaged in many long marches and were noted for their endurance and speed?

Answer: Thomas "Stonewall" Jackson's.

2) BONUS. 20 points. 10 points each.

Name the mythical home of the gods in Greek mythology and the sacred place of the gods in Japanese mythology, the highest mountain in Japan.

Answer: Mount Olympus and Mount Fuji (Fujiyama in Japanese).

3) TOSS-UP. 30 points after the first clue. 20 after the second. 10 after the third.

Who am I?
1) I was the American newspaperman and commentator who made the gossip column a regular feature.
2) I began my broadcasts with "Good evening, Mr. and Mrs. America and all the ships at sea" (or "Good Evening, Mr. and Mrs. North and South America and all the ships and clippers at sea, let's go to press—FLASH!").

3) I coined such unusual and colorful words and phrases as "lohengrined" and "middle-aisled," and I narrated the popular TV series *The Untouchables* (1959-1963).

Answer: Walter Winchell.

3) BONUS. 30 points. 10 points each.

Give the full meaning of each of the following abbreviations as used in pharmacology, science, or biochemistry.
1) LSD
2) TNT
3) DNA

Answer: 1) Lysergic acid diethylamide
2) Trinitrotoluene (or trinitrotoluol)
3) Deoxyribonucleic acid (or desoxyribonucleic acid).

4) TOSS-UP. 10 points.

Name the papyrus-reed boat Thor Heyerdahl built in 1970 and sailed across the Atlantic from Morocco to the West Indies proving that the Egyptians could have done the same thing. The name of the boat is the same as that of a sun god of ancient Egypt.

Answer: Ra.

4) BONUS. 20 points. 10 points each.

Name Elvis Presley's mansion in East Memphis, Tennessee, and the mansion in which the mayor of New York resides.

Answer: Graceland and Gracie Mansion.

5) TOSS-UP. 10 points.

Which term is used to describe gases that are extremely reluctant to combine chemically with other elements? These gases are helium (2), neon (10), argon (18), krypton (36), xenon (54), and radon (86).

Answer: Noble gases or inert gases (also rare gases, helium group gases, Group O elements, or Group VIII A).

5) BONUS. 30 points. 10 points each.

Identify each of the following writers from the given pseudonym.
1) Boz

2) Voltaire
3) Anatole France

Answer: 1) Charles Dickens
          2) François Marie Arouet
          3) Jacques Anatole François Thibault.

6) TOSS-UP. 10 points.

Which word coined in the city of London is defined as "foul, vulgar, abusive talk or language"? This word is derived from the name of a fish market near a city gate where fishwives and their fishmongering husbands engaged in foul and abusive talk.

Answer: Billingsgate.

6) BONUS. 20 points. 10 points each.

Name the monk who heads, or is the superior in, an abbey and the woman who heads, or is the female superior in, a convent of nuns.

Answer: Abbot and abbess.

7) TOSS-UP. 10 points.

Name the historical region of southwestern France, roughly between the Pyrenées and the Garonne River, from which Eleanor, the queen of Louis VII of France, and later Henry II of England came, or give the missing word in Robert Ludlum's novel *The _____ Progression.*

Answer: Aquitaine.

7) BONUS. 25 points. 5 points each.

Name the last 5 territories to become states of the United States.

Answer: Hawaii (8/21/59); Alaska (1/3/59), Arizona (2/14/12), New Mexico (1/6/12).; and Oklahoma (11/16/07).

8) TOSS-UP. 10 points.

About which Russian author, who created the character Raskolnikov, did Joseph Frank write *The Seeds of Revolt, 1821-1849* and *The Years of Ordeal, 1850-1859?*

Answer: Fyodor Mikhailovich Dostoevsky.

194 CAMPBELL'S POTPOURRI II

8) BONUS. 20 points. 10 points each.

Identify the American author of the following lines and the symbolic meaning of the word *Ship*: "Thou, too, sail on, O Ship of State! / Sail on, O UNION, strong and great! / Humanity with all its fears, / With all the hopes of future years, / Is hanging breathless in thy fate!

Answer: Henry Wadsworth Longfellow ("The Building of the Ship") / *Ship* **is the symbol of the U.S.**

9) TOSS-UP. 20 points after the first clue. 10 after the second.

What is my name?
1) I became a major general in the Union army during the Civil War and I either fired the first Union shot in defense of Fort Sumter on April 12, 1861, or commanded the troops there that returned the first shots.
2) A baseball field at Cooperstown, New York, bears my name, and I was at one time credited with inventing the game of baseball.

Answer: Abner Doubleday.

9) BONUS. 30 points. 5 points each.

Identify each of the following concerning a U.S. purchase of land in the 19th century.
1) The name of the purchase made by President Franklin Pierce's minister to Mexico of a strip of land for a southern railroad route to the Pacific Coast
2) The name of the Mexican president with whom the U.S. minister transacted the purchase
3) The name of the 2 present U.S. states formed from territory acquired by this purchase
4) The year in which the treaty of sale was signed or the year in which it was ratified
5) The amount the U.S. paid for the purchase of 29,640 square miles (76,770 square kilometers)

Answer: 1) Gadsden Purchase (made by James Gadsden)
2) Antonio López de Santa Anna
3) Arizona and New Mexico
4) 1853 (December 30) or 1854
5) $10 million.

10) TOSS-UP. 10 points.

Of the following numbers, which 2 are prime numbers: 1, 3, 4,

6, 7, and 8?

Answer: 3 and 7.

10) BONUS. 20 points. 10 points each.

Name the English essayist and his sister who collaborated on writing 3 books for children, the most famous of which is *Tales from Shakespeare* (1807), and tell what vicious crime the sister committed in 1796 during a fit of temporary insanity.

Answer: Charles and Mary Lamb / Fatally stabbed their mother with a knife.

11) TOSS-UP. 10 points.

Name the 19-year-old Southern belle, later an actress, who informed Stonewall Jackson about Union troop maneuvers, enabling him to easily defeat the enemy at Front Royal in May, 1862. In her "career" as a Confederate spy, she was jailed twice but freed for lack of evidence.

Answer: Belle Boyd.

11) BONUS. 30 points. 10 points each.

Identify the American athlete who accomplished each of the following in Olympic Games competition.
1) The swimmer who won 5 gold medals in swimming in 1924 and 1928 combined
2) The track and field star who won 4 gold medals in 1936.
3) The discus thrower who won gold medals in the 1956, 1960, 1964, and 1968 games

Answer: 1) Johnny Weissmuller
2) Jesse Owens
3) Al Oerter.

12) TOSS-UP. 10 points.

Name the ship on which Henry Hudson sailed in search of the Northwest Passage in 1610. A ship in Captain James Cook's expedition to the Hawaiian Islands in 1778 and a U.S. space shuttle bear the same name.

Answer: *Discovery*.

12) BONUS. 30 points. 10 points each.

As of 1990, 8 actresses have won an Oscar for Best Actress on at least 2 occasions. Name the 3 who won awards for the following pairs of films.
1) *Guess Who's Coming to Dinner* (1967) and *The Lion in Winter* (1968)
2) *Dangerous* (1935) and *Jezebel* (1938)
3) *Klute* (1971) and *Coming Home* (1978)

Answer: 1) Katharine Hepburn
        2) Bette Davis
        3) Jane Fonda.

13) TOSS-UP. 10 points.

According to Geoffrey Chaucer, how many pilgrims were gathered at the Tabard Inn?

Answer: 29 (not counting Chaucer).

13) BONUS. 20 points. 5 points each.

Of the 12 signs of the Zodiac, 7 are represented by animals. Give the animal that represents each of the following.
1) Aries
2) Pisces
3) Capricorn
4) Scorpio

Answer: 1) Ram
        2) Fishes
        3) Goat
        4) Scorpion.

14) TOSS-UP. 20 points after the first clue. 10 after the second.

Which word am I?
1) I am "a brilliant or dazzling display, as of eloquence, wit, or rhetoric, or of virtuosity in the performing arts."
2) I am the art of making and using fireworks, or I am a fireworks display.

Answer: Pyrotechnics.

14) BONUS. 30 points. 10 points each.

Identify the author of each of the following novels and give his

nationality. All or nothing for each one.
1) *The Picture of Dorian Gray*
2) *The Tin Drum*
3) *La Arcadia*

Answer: 1) **Oscar Wilde—Irish**
  2) **Günter Grass—German**
  3) **Lope de Vega—Spanish.**

15) TOSS-UP. 30 points after the first clue. 20 after the second. 10 after the third.

What world capital am I?
1) I was called *Ciudad de los Reyes*, or "City of the Kings," when I was founded in 1535 during the season of the Epiphany.
2) The ruins of Pachacamac, an ancient Indian city, are nearby.
3) Francisco Pizarro, a Spanish adventurer, founded me two years after he conquered most of Peru.

Answer: **Lima.**

15) BONUS. 20 points. 5 points each.

Name the only 4 recipients of Nobel Prizes who have twice won the honor.
1) The French scientist (born in Poland) who shared the Nobel Prize for physics in 1903 with Pierre Curie and Antoine Henri Becquerel, and who won the Nobel Prize for chemistry in 1911
2) The American chemist who won the Nobel Prize in chemistry in 1954 and the Nobel Prize for peace in 1962
3) The American physicist who was the first to win a Nobel Prize twice for work in the same field, sharing the Nobel Prize in physics in 1956 and 1972
4) The British chemist who won the 1958 Nobel Prize in chemistry and who shared the 1980 prize with Paul Berg and Walter Gilbert

Answer: 1) **Marie Curie**
  2) **Linus Pauling**
  3) **John Bardeen**
  4) **Frederick Sanger.**

16) TOSS-UP. 10 points.

Name the parasitic worm acquired from eating raw or improperly cooked pork containing encysted larvae.

Answer: Trichina (or *Trichinella spiralis*; these are the causes of trichinosis or trichiniasis).

16) **BONUS. 30 points. 10 points each.**

Name the 3 Canadian provinces known as the "Maritime Provinces."

Answer: New Brunswick, Nova Scotia, and Prince Edward Island.

17) **TOSS-UP. 10 points.**

Name the legendary giant king of Britain in Celtic mythology who was decapitated on his own orders and whose head was buried in London facing the continent as a magical talisman against invasion, or name "the broken outer hull of any cereal grain separated from the flour or meal by sifting or bolting."

Answer: Bran.

17) **BONUS. 30 points. 15 points each.**

Identify the Duke of Marlborough and his wife featured in Virginia Cowles' *The Great Marlborough and His Duchess*. This Duke (1650-1722), a very successful English general in the War of the Spanish Succession, eventually lost his influence and retired from public life. The Duchess was the confidante of Princess (later) Queen Anne.

Answer: John Churchill and Sarah Jennings.

18) **TOSS-UP. 30 points after the first clue. 20 after the second. 10 after the third.**

Which U.S. Army Air Force general am I?
1) I was a cigar-chomping general, the youngest general in the Air Force at 37, and I directed the 21st B-29 Bomber Command in making low level fire bomb runs against Japan late in WWII to destroy weapons factories.
2) I organized and directed the postwar Berlin airlift during the Russian blockade in 1948-1949, commanded the Strategic Air Command of the U.S. Air Force from 1949 to 1957, and became Air Force Chief of Staff in 1961.
3) In 1968, I was the American Independent candidate for Vice President of the U.S. as George Wallace's running mate.

Answer: Curtis Emerson LeMay.

18) BONUS. 30 points. 10 points each.

Complete the title of each of the following stories by Edgar Allan Poe.
1) "The Purloined _____"
2) "The Devil in the _____"
3) "The Cask of _____"

Answer: 1) Letter
2) Belfry
3) Amontillado.

19) TOSS-UP. 10 points.

What is the largest Christian denomination in the world?

Answer: Roman Catholic Church.

19) BONUS. 20 points. 10 points each.

Name the armed revolt of economically depressed farmers demanding relief during 1786-1787, and the state in which this rebellion took place. This rebellion involved an attack on the federal arsenal at Springfield and spurred the drive for a strong national government.

Answer: Shays' Rebellion / Massachusetts.

20) TOSS-UP. 10 points.

Which river rises from Changpai Shan, or Long White Mountains, forms most of the boundary between North Korea and Manchuria (China), and flows into the Yellow Sea?

Answer: Yalu River.

20) BONUS. 20 points. 5 points each.

Identify each of the following concerning the resignation of Supreme Court Justice Abe Fortas.
1) The South Carolina judge rejected by the Senate 55-45 on November 21, 1969, following his nomination as a replacement for Fortas
2) The Florida judge rejected by the Senate 51-45 on April 8, 1970, following his nomination as a replacement for Fortas
3) The Minnesota judge unanimously approved by the Senate on May 12, 1970, following his nomination as a replacement for Fortas
4) The U.S. President whose 2 nominations in 1969 and 1970 were rejected before his 3rd was accepted by the Senate

Answer: 1) **Clement F. Haynsworth**
2) **G. Harrold Carswell**
3) **Harry A. Blackmun**
4) **Richard Nixon.**

21) TOSS-UP. 10 points.

Which of the 9 planets has a chemical atmospheric makeup of approximately 78% nitrogen, 21% oxygen, and 1% argon with small amounts of other gases?

Answer: Earth.

21) BONUS. 20 points. 10 points each.

Name the comedy team that awarded the Fickle Finger of Fate Award, and the U.S. senator from Wisconsin who awarded the Golden Fleece Award for government projects that were especially wasteful of taxpayers' money.

Answer: Rowan and Martin / William Proxmire.

22) TOSS-UP. 10 points.

What does the *plein-air* manner of some schools of French impressionist painting of the late 19th century have in common with an *al fresco* (*alfresco*) dinner?

Answer: Engaged in outdoors, or in the open air.

22) BONUS. 20 points. All or nothing.

Name the 3 types of subordinate clauses.

Answer: Noun clauses, adjective clauses, and adverb clauses.

23) TOSS-UP. 10 points.

What country's poetic name is Albion (meaning "mountain land" or "white land")?

Answer: England.

23) BONUS. 30 points. 10 points each.

The French word *chapeau* is derived from the Latin *cappa*, meaning "head covering." Identify each of the following *chapeaux*, or hats.
1) A tight-fitting Scottish cap with a wide, round, flat top, sometimes having a center pompon or tassel

2) A stiff felt hat with a round crown and a curved brim, worn chiefly by men
3) A brimless, felt hat in a conical shape, usually red with a long, black tassel hanging from a flat crown, formerly the national headdress of the Turks, and named after a town in Morocco

Answer: 1) Tam o'Shanter
2) Derby (or bowler)
3) Fez.

24) TOSS-UP. 10 points.

Name the person in the Bible who was commanded by God to go into battle with just 300 followers (32,000 volunteered), each armed with a sword, a trumpet, and an empty jar with a torch in it. After routing the Midianites by attacking suddenly at night, this leader of Israel became a judge of his people for the remaining 40 years of life, refusing the kingship because of his belief that God was Israel's only king. His story is in Judges 6-8.

Answer: Gideon (or Gedeon, Jerubbaal, or Jerubbesheth).

24) BONUS. 20 points. 10 points each.

What English bard was born in Stratford-upon-Avon, Warwickshire, on April 23, 1564, and whom did he marry?

Answer: William Shakespeare and Anne Hathaway.

25) TOSS-UP. 10 points.

Identify the politician, known for the umbrella he carried, who said, "For the second time in our history, a British Prime Minister has returned from Germany bringing peace with honor. I believe it is peace for our time." He made this statement on September 30, 1938, after returning from Munich.

Answer: Neville Chamberlain.

25) BONUS. 30 points. 10 points each.

Identify the world capitals located on each of the following rivers.
1) Aare
2) Rhine
3) Vistula

Answer: 1) Bern
       2) Bonn
       3) Warsaw.

CATEGORY TOSS-UP. 100 points. 10 points each. 10 points deducted for an incorrect answer.

What is the American equivalent for each of the following British words?
1) Draughts
2) Lift
3) Plimsolls
4) (Black) treacle
5) Torch
6) Flat
7) Sultanas
8) Bonnet
9) Lorry
10) Spanner

Answer: 1) Checkers
       2) Elevator
       3) Sneakers
       4) Molasses
       5) Flashlight
       6) Apartment
       7) Raisins (small and seedless)
       8) Hood (of a car)
       9) Truck
      10) Monkey wrench.

ROUND SEVENTEEN

1025 points

1) TOSS-UP. 30 points after the first clue. 20 after the second. 10 after the third.

Which element am I?
1) My atomic number is 76, and I was discovered in 1804 by Smithson Tennant.
2) I am used in fountain-pen points, phonograph needles, and instrument bearings.
3) I have the greatest density of all known elements, and my chemical symbol is Os.

Answer: Osmium.

1) BONUS. 25 points. 5 points each.

Name from west to east the 5 Arab countries that all touch on the Mediterranean Sea and constitute the northern part of Africa.

Answer: Morocco, Algeria, Tunisia, Libya, and Egypt.

2) TOSS-UP. 10 points.

Name the 2 presidential candidates, who took part in the first TV campaign debate. They both later became U.S. Presidents.

Answer: John F. Kennedy and Richard M. Nixon.

2) BONUS. 20 points. 10 points each.

Name the French colonist who served as governor of French Louisiana, and identify the Michigan city he founded in 1701. An American car is named after him.

Answer: Cadillac (Antoine Laumet de la Mothe Cadillac) / Detroit.

3) TOSS-UP. 20 points after the first clue. 10 after the second.

What is my name?
1) I received the Spingarn Medal in 1923, the Roosevelt Medal in

1939, and the Thomas A. Edison Foundation Award in 1942 for my scientific contributions, and a national monument was established in my behalf in 1951 near Diamond Grove, Missouri.

2) I was an American black who revolutionized Southern agriculture by making more than 300 by-products from sweet potatoes, peanuts, and pecans.

Answer: George Washington Carver.

3) BONUS. 30 points. 10 points each.

Give the full meaning of each of the following abbreviations as used in pharmacology, science, or biochemistry.
1) RNA
2) MSG
3) DDT

Answer: 1) Ribonucleic acid (or ribose nucleic acid)
2) Monosodium glutamate
3) Dichloro-diphenyl-trichlorethane.

4) TOSS-UP. 10 points.

Name both the city and the state where the Chisholm Trail ended, where "Wild Bill" Hickok became a "two-gun" marshal" (c. 1870), and where the Boyhood Home and Museum of Dwight D. Eisenhower are located.

Answer: Abilene, Kansas.

4) BONUS. 20 points. 10 points each.

The suffix -*morphic* means "pertaining to form (shape)." Give the word for "having the form (shape) of an animal," used to describe the Egyptian gods who are characterized as animals, and the word for "having the form (shape) of a man," used to describe the Greek gods with human characteristics.

Answer: Theriomorphic (theriomorphous) or anthropomorphic (anthropomorphous).

5) TOSS-UP. 10 points.

Name the movie actor known as a frustrated, rebellious young man because of the roles he played in *East of Eden* (1955), *Rebel Without a Cause* (1955), and *Giant* (1956). He was killed in an automobile accident in 1955 when he was 24.

Answer: James Dean.

5) BONUS. 30 points. 10 points each.

Identify each of the following writers from the given pseudonym.
1) Elia
2) Saki
3) Stendhal

Answer: 1) **Charles Lamb**
2) **Hector Hugh Munro**
3) **Marie Henri Beyle.**

6) TOSS-UP. 10 points.

To which French king is attributed the expression, "*L'État, c'est moi*" (or "I am the state")?

Answer: **Louis XIV.**

6) BONUS. 25 points. All or nothing.

Give the list that is the source of the mnemonic device ROY G. BIV.

Answer: **Red, Orange, Yellow, Green, Blue, Indigo, and Violet (7 colors of the spectrum).**

7) TOSS-UP. 10 points.

Which name derived from the Greek for "dawn stone," is used in anthropology to designate any of the artifacts once considered to be the first stone tools?

Answer: **Eolith (Eos *lithos*).**

7) BONUS. 20 points. 10 points each.

Name the 2 great English portrait artists, who painted *The Blue Boy* (1770), *Samuel Johnson* (1770's), *Nelly O'Brien* (1760's), and *Commodore Augustus Keppel* (1753-1754).

Answer: **Thomas Gainsborough and Sir Joshua Reynolds.**

8) TOSS-UP. 10 points.

What vegetable of the morning glory family of plants is called a yam or, informally, an ocarina?

Answer: **Sweet potato.**

8) BONUS. 20 points. 10 points each.

Name the South American country and the river, both named for the word "silver", one from the Latin and the other from the Spanish. The river is the country's major estuary.

Answer: Argentina (Latin, *argentum*) and Río de la Plata (Spanish, *plata*).

9) TOSS-UP. 10 points.

Name the private liberal arts college that was the 9th and last colonial institution of higher learning founded by royal decree (1769). It is located in Hanover, New Hampshire, and is nicknamed the "Big Green."

Answer: Dartmouth.

9) BONUS. 20 points. 5 points each.

With which city is each of the following department stores most closely identified?
1) I. Magnin
2) Macy's
3) Marshall Field
4) Nieman-Marcus

Answer: 1) San Francisco
2) New York
3) Chicago
4) Dallas.

10) TOSS-UP. 10 points.

Identify the phrase which completes the passage from Psalm 69: "I sink in deep mire, where there is no standing: I am come into _____, where the floods overflow me." Today the phrase is used to mean "in trouble" or "difficulty."

Answer: Deep water or "deep waters."

10) BONUS. 20 points. 5 points each.

Identify each of the following.
1) The most northern U.S. capital
2) The most southern U.S. capital
3) The most eastern U.S. capital
4) The most western U.S. capital

Answer: 1) **Juneau, Alaska**
2) **Honolulu, Hawaii**
3) **Augusta, Maine**
4) **Honolulu, Hawaii.**

11) TOSS-UP. 10 points.

His birthday is celebrated on June 7, and his name today means "an excessively well-dressed person; any dandy or fop." Name this 19th century English gentleman noted for his fashionable dress and manners.

Answer: (George Bryan) Beau Brummell.

11) BONUS. 30 points. 10 points each.

Identify the American athlete who accomplished each of the following in Olympic Games competition.
1) The swimmer who won 7 gold medals in 1972
2) The speed-skater who won 5 gold medals in 1980
3) The track and field star who won 4 gold medals in 1984.

Answer: 1) **Mark Spitz**
2) **Eric Heiden**
3) **Carl Lewis.**

12) TOSS-UP. 10 points.

What word did George Orwell coin in 1948 in his book *1984* to designate "deliberately contrary thinking that reverses the truth to render it more acceptable" or "the belief in two contradictory points of view at the same time"?

Answer: Double-think (doublethink).

12) BONUS. 30 points. 10 points each.

Of the 8 two-time winners of Best Actress Oscars as of 1990, name the 3 who won awards for the following pairs of films.
1) *Gaslight* (1944) and *Anastasia* (1956)
2) *Women in Love* (1970) and *A Touch of Class* (1973)
3) *Butterfield 8* (1960) and *Who's Afraid of Virginia Woolf?* (1966)

Answer: 1) **Ingrid Bergman**
2) **Glenda Jackson**
3) **Elizabeth Taylor.**

13) TOSS-UP. 10 points.

Name the brittle, flat unleavened bread eaten by Jews during Passover.

Answer: Matzo (or matsah, or matzah).

13) BONUS. 30 points. 10 points each.

Identify the animal that represents each of the following signs of the Zodiac.
1) Leo
2) Cancer
3) Taurus

Answer: 1) Lion
          2) Crab
          3) Bull.

14) TOSS-UP. 10 points.

To the first graduating class, he said, "The good Lord gave me my money, and how could I withhold it from the University of Chicago." Name this philanthropist who gave a $35 million endowment to the University during his lifetime and after whom the Memorial Chapel on campus is named.

Answer: John Davison Rockefeller.

14) BONUS. 30 points. 10 points each.

Identify each of the following abnormal psychological traits.
1) An uncontrollable outburst of emotion or fear, often characterized by irrationality, weeping, etc.; unmanageable fear or emotional excess
2) A persistent false belief resistant to reason with regard to actual things or objective evidence
3) A false perception of reality arising from some mental or physical disorder or in response to drugs; delusion

Answer: 1) Hysteria
          2) Delusion
          3) Hallucination.

15) TOSS-UP. 10 points.

Which famous obelisques bear the names of 2 Egyptian kings, Thutmose III and Ramses II? These obelisques were originally located before the Temple of the Sun in Heliopolis in the 15th century B.C., but today one is located in New York's Central Park and the other on the Thames River's Victoria Embankment in London. These stone pillars have no relationship to the Egyptian queen whose name they bear.

Answer: Cleopatra's Needles (called at one time "Pharaoh's great needles").

15) **BONUS. 20 points. 5 points each.**

Identify the Civil War general who rode each of the following horses.
1) Traveller (originally called Jeff Davis and later Greenbrier)
2) Little Sorrel (Old Sorrel)
3) Cincinnatus (Cincinnati)
4) Lexington and Sam

Answer: 1) Robert E. Lee
2) Thomas Jonathan "Stonewall" Jackson
3) Ulysses S. Grant
4) William Tecumseh Sherman.

16) **TOSS-UP. 10 points.**

In Athens, Aristotle founded his Lyceum, a school so named from its proximity to the temple of Apollon Lykeios (Apollo, the Wolf-God). This school was also called the "peripatetic school." Why was it so called, or define the word *peripatetic*?

Answer: Aristotle occasionally lectured to students while walking about in the school's grove (a Peripatetic was "a follower of Aristotle") / peripatetic means "moving from place to place; walking about"; as a noun it is "a person who walks from place to place."

16) **BONUS. 20 points. 10 points each.**

In an alphabetical list of independent countries, what are the first and last named countries?

Answer: Afghanistan and Zimbabwe.

17) **TOSS-UP. 10 points.**

Name the Belgian Roman Catholic priest and missionary who aided the patients at the leper colony on the Hawaiian island of Molokai from 1873 until his death from leprosy in 1888.

Answer: Father Damien (Father Joseph Damien de Veuster).

17) BONUS. 30 points. 10 points each.

Identify each of the following concerning a famous Victorian couple, the Brownings.
1) The first names of each of them
2) The complete title of her work *Sonnets from the* _____, or the nickname by which her husband called her
3) The name of either her pet and sole companion before she married, or the type of injury she incurred that made her an invalid

Answer: 1) Elizabeth (Barrett) and Robert
2) Portuguese, or "My Little Portuguese"
3) Flush, her dog, or spinal injury from falling off a horse (accept a severe respiratory and a general tubercular condition).

18) TOSS-UP. 10 points.

Name the Hindu love manual written between the 1st-4th centuries A.D. and attributed to Vatsyayana, also known as Mallanaga. Its name in Sanskrit means "love aphorisms."

Answer: *Kamasutra (Kama Sutra)*.

18) BONUS. 20 points. 10 points each.

Six professional baseball players, all in the Hall of Fame, have won the Most Valuable Player Award 3 times. Two of the players played in the National League and four in the American. Name the 2 in the National League.

Answer: Roy Campanella and Stan Musial.

19) TOSS-UP. 30 points after the first clue. 20 after the second. 10 after the third.

What's my name?
1) I wrote, "In spite of everything I still believe that people are really good at heart."
2) I wrote *Tales from the Secret Annex.*
3) I was a German-Jewish girl who hid for two years in a secret attic in the Netherlands during WWII to escape Nazi persecution, but I was discovered and incarcerated in the Bergen-Belsen death

camp, where I died in 1945 at 15.

Answer: Anne Frank (the quote is from *Anne Frank: The Diary of a Young Girl*).

19) BONUS. 20 points. 10 points each.

Name the largest bay in North America and the country in which it is located.

Answer: Hudson Bay / Canada.

20) TOSS-UP. 10 points.

Name the 2 zones of concentric doughnut-shaped regions of electrically charged particles that surround the earth within the magnetosphere and are named for the man who discovered them in 1958.

Answer: Van Allen belts.

20) BONUS. 25 points. 5 points each.

Give the native country of each of the following secretaries-general of the United Nations.
1) Trygve Lie
2) Dag Hammarskjold
3) U Thant
4) Kurt Waldheim
5) Javier Perez de Cuellar

Answer: 1) Norway
2) Sweden
3) Burma
4) Austria
5) Peru.

21) TOSS-UP. 10 points.

In baseball, what 2 players comprise the *battery*?

Answer: Pitcher and catcher.

21) BONUS. 30 points. 10 points each.

Identify each of the following English rulers.
1) The English king (1820-1830) known as "The First Gentleman of Europe"
2) The English king (1760-1820) known as "Farmer George"

3) The English king (1413-1422) known as "Prince Hal"

Answer: 1) George IV
2) George III
3) Henry V.

22) TOSS-UP. 30 points after the first clue. 20 after the second. 10 after the third.

What's my name?
1) I was born in New York in 1819, traveled to Liverpool, wrote *Redburn*, and signed on the whaling ship *Acushnet* for a Pacific Ocean trip.
2) I wrote *Typee* and *Omoo*.
3) I also wrote "Benito Cereno" and "Bartleby the Scrivener."

Answer: Herman Melville.

22) BONUS. 20 points. 10 points each.

Name the ocean that links the Atlantic and Pacific oceans in the north and the passage that links the same bodies of water in the south.

Answer: Arctic Ocean and the Drake Passage.

23) TOSS-UP. 10 points.

What is the sine of pi divided by two?

Answer: One (or positive one).

23) BONUS. 30 points. 10 points each.

Identify each of the following hats.
1) A felt hat with a high crown and wide brim worn by Western cowboys
2) A flat, round visorless felt or cloth cap, worn originally by male Basques
3) A Scottish woolen cap worn by males, creased lengthwise across the top and often having short ribbons at the back, and named after a valley in Scotland

Answer: 1) Stetson
2) Beret
3) Glengarry.

24) TOSS-UP. 10 points.

Name the French painter whose unconventional life is the subject of W. Somerset Maugham's *The Moon and Sixpence* (1919).

Answer: Paul Gauguin.

24) BONUS. 20 points. 10 points each.

The American belief in limited government stems in part from centuries of British experience dating from what famous document of British constitutional history signed in 1215 and from what fundamental instrument of constitutional law of 1689?

Answer: Magna Carta (or Magna Charta) and the Bill of Rights.

25) TOSS-UP. 10 points.

This newspaper, founded by Henry J. Raymond in 1851 and taken over by Adolph S. Ochs in 1896, has the motto "All the news that's fit to print." Name it.

Answer: *New York Times*.

25) BONUS. 20 points. 10 points each.

Name the *locker* which means "the ocean's bottom, especially as the grave of all those who perish at sea," and name "the paradise to which the souls of good sailors are thought to go after death."

Answer: Davy Jones' Locker / Fiddler's Green.

CATEGORY TOSS-UP. 100 points. 10 points each. 10 points deducted for an incorrect answer.

Identify each of the following concerned with the abolitionist movement in the United States.
1) The newspaper publisher of *The Liberator* (1831), who in his newspaper demanded immediate emancipation
2) The newspaper editor of the *Alton Observer* (Alton, Illinois) who in 1837 became a martyr to the antislavery movement after he was killed by a mob wrecking his presses to stop his antislavery editorials
3) The woman who helped organize the American Anti-Slavery Society (1833), the Philadelphia Female Anti-Slavery Society, and in 1837 the Anti-Slavery Convention of American Women

4) The leading black abolitionist who founded in 1847 in Rochester, New York, his antislavery newspaper the *North Star*

5) The leading black woman orator, born Isabella Baumfree, who was among the first black women to speak out against slavery, if not the first

6) The first political party with an exclusive antislavery platform whose candidate was James G. Birney in the presidential elections of 1840 and 1844

7) The founder of the antislavery newspaper *True American* in 1845 in Lexington, Kentucky (called the *Examiner* when he moved to Louisville)

8) The organizer, in 1815, of the Abolitionist Union Humane Society, in St. Clairsville, Ohio, and in 1821 the publisher of *The Genius of Universal Emancipation*

9) The Quaker writer known as the "Abolitionist Poet" and the author of the abolitionist pamphlet *Justice and Expediency* (1833)

10) The poet whose *Biglow Papers* in the 1840's voiced his attack on the Mexican War as an attempt to expand slavery

Answer: 1) **William Lloyd Garrison**
                 2) **Elijah Parish Lovejoy**
                 3) **Lucretia Coffin Mott**
                 4) **Frederick Douglass**
                 5) **Sojourner Truth**
                 6) **Liberty Party**
                 7) **Cassius Marcellus Clay**
                 8) **Benjamin Lundy**
                 9) **John Greenleaf Whittier**
               10) **James Russell Lowell.**

ROUND EIGHTEEN

1065 points

1) TOSS-UP. 30 points after the first clue. 20 after the second. 10 after the third.

What's my name?
1) I was born in Cadiz, Ohio, in 1901, and worked as a laborer in a tire factory, as a callboy in an Akron theatre, and as a lumberjack before I became an actor.
2) I won the 1934 Academy Award for best actor for *It Happened One Night*.
3) I am also remembered for saying "Frankly, my dear, I don't give a damn" in the role of Rhett Butler in *Gone With the Wind*.

Answer: Clark Gable.

1) BONUS. 20 points. 10 points each.

In which novel by which author is there a ship named the *Patna*, which is carrying Muslim pilgrims to Mecca; a white man named Marlow; and a British sailor named Jim?

Answer: *Lord Jim* by Joseph Conrad (Józef Teodor Konrad Korzeniowski).

2) TOSS-UP. 10 points.

Name the Biblical Minor Prophet whose writings are considered by some modern scholars to be the earliest of the prophets' and who was commanded by God to marry a wanton woman.

Answer: Hosea.

2) BONUS. 20 points. 10 points each.

Name both the 7' 1" former National Basketball Association player and the former body builder and muscleman who co-star in *Conan: King of Thieves*, or *Conan II*.

Answer: Wilt Chamberlain and Arnold Schwarzeneger.

3) TOSS-UP. 10 points.

Which wife of Henry VIII was the mother of Queen Elizabeth the First?

Answer: Anne Boleyn.

3) BONUS. 20 points. 10 points each.

How were Clementine Hozier and Jennie Jerome related to Winston Churchill?

Answer: Clementine was his wife and Jennie Jerome was his mother.

4) TOSS-UP. 10 points.

Name the suffocating gas found in coal mines that is a mixture of carbon dioxide and nitrogen and is incapable of supporting life or flame.

Answer: Blackdamp (or chokedamp).

4) BONUS. 20 points. 10 points each.

What is the general name for the Bishop of Rome, and what is the name of the church in which he fulfills his duties in this role?

Answer: The Pope of the Roman Catholic Church / St. John Lateran (San Giovanni in Laterno).

5) TOSS-UP. 10 points.

Name the American industrialist whose large bequest completed the construction of the Peace Palace in the Hague (1903).

Answer: Andrew Carnegie.

5) BONUS. 20 points. 10 points each.

Identify each of the following Japanese dance dramas.
1) One literally means "ability or capacity" and was developed mainly in the 14th century with choral music and dancing, using set themes, elaborately dressed actors, and stylized acting.
2) The other literally means "music and dancing spirit" and was developed mainly in the 17th century with singing and dancing performed in a highly stylized manner and with elaborately costumed men playing female roles.

Answer: 1) **No (or Noh, Nogaku)**
            2) **Kabuki.**

6) TOSS-UP. 10 points.

According to Ralph Waldo Emerson in his 1870 essay "Civilization," to what should you "hitch your wagon"?

Answer: To a star.

6) BONUS. 20 points. 5 points each.

There are 4 U.S. state capitals that begin with the same letter as their state. Name them.

Answer: Dover, Delaware; Honolulu, Hawaii; Indianapolis, Indiana; and Oklahoma City, Oklahoma.

7) TOSS-UP. 10 points.

In the nursery rhyme, what does Little Jack Horner say after pulling a plum out of his Christmas pie?

Answer: "What a good boy am I!"

7) BONUS. 20 points. 5 points each.

Name the 4 major candidates in the presidential election of 1860.

Answer: Abraham Lincoln (Republican Party); John C. Breckinridge (Southern Democrats); John Bell (Constitutional Union Party); and Stephen A. Douglas (Democratic Party).

8) TOSS-UP. 10 points.

Which scientist's reactions to the quantum theory were expressed in these words, "I shall never believe that God plays dice with the world" and "God may be subtle, but He is not malicious"?

Answer: Albert Einstein's.

8) BONUS. 20 points. 10 points each.

The book *Landscape Turned Red* by Stephen W. Sears is an account of a bloody Civil War battle fought between George B. McClellan and Robert E. Lee in which General A.P. Hill's arrival at the 11th hour saved the day for the South and enabled Lee to retreat to Virginia after heavy losses. Give the 2 names for this battle which took place on September 17, 1862.

Answer: Antietam and Sharpsburg.

9) TOSS-UP. 30 points after the first clue. 20 after the second. 10 after the third.

Who am I?
1) I joined George Washington's army as a volunteer, fought with distinction at the Battle of Brandywine, and was made a brigadier general by the Continental Congress.
2) I died on October 11, 1779, after being wounded two days earlier at the siege of Savannah. October 11 is by presidential proclamation my memorial day in the U.S., and a fort near Savannah is named for me.
3) Born to wealth in Poland, I inherited the title of Count, but later became known as the "Father of the American Cavalry."

Answer: Casimir (Kazimierz) Pulaski.

9) BONUS. 20 points. 10 points each.

Name the English countess who, according to legend, rode naked through the town of Coventry in order to persuade her husband to lighten the tax load on the townspeople, and then give the phrase which includes the name of the tailor who allegedly was struck blind when he saw her and today means a person who obtains (sexual) gratification by watching others from a hiding place. Her birthday is celebrated in England on May 25.

Answer: Lady Godiva / Peeping Tom.

10) TOSS-UP. 10 points.

He was finally defeated and killed in battle at Lucania in 71 B.C. by forces under Marcus Licinius Crassus, but this Roman gladiator won fame as the leader of the great slave uprising in Italy that threatened the Roman Republic in 73 B.C. Name him.

Answer: Spartacus.

10) BONUS. 30 points. 10 points each.

By what common name is the graph of each of the following known?
1) y equals three
2) y equals x squared plus one

3) y squared plus x squared equals one

Answer: 1) A straight line
       2) Parabola
       3) Circle.

11) TOSS-UP. 20 points after the first clue. 10 after the second.

1) I am the term for the mistlike substance believed by mediums to emanate from them to produce communication with the spirits of the dead.
2) In biology, I am the outer layer of the cytoplasm of a cell.

Answer: Ectoplasm.

11) BONUS. 30 points. 10 points each.

Identify each of the following plays from the description.
1) The Thornton Wilder play featuring the meddlesome Dolly Levi, a play on which the musical *Hello, Dolly!* is based
2) The Dore Schary play concerning Franklin Roosevelt's battle with infantile paralysis
3) The Jerome Lawrence and Robert E. Lee play that dramatizes the Scopes trial

Answer: 1) *The Matchmaker*
       2) *Sunrise at Campobello*
       3) *Inherit the Wind.*

12) TOSS-UP. 10 points.

What punctuation is used between figures indicating the chapter and verse of a Biblical reference?

Answer: The colon.

12) BONUS. 30 points. 10 points each.

Name the highest navigable lake in the world and the 2 South American countries between which it is located.

Answer: Lake Titicaca / Peru and Bolivia.

13) TOSS-UP. 10 points.

Identify the Methodist-affiliated Daytona Beach, Florida, college established in 1923 and partly named for its first president, who was also the founder of the National Council of Negro Women.

Answer: Bethune-Cookman College.

13) BONUS. 20 points. 10 points each.

Identify both of the following fictional characters from Charles Dickens' *David Copperfield*.

1) A sneaky and malignant sycophant; a sanctimonious hypocrite who is always wringing his hands and proclaiming how 'umble he is while trying to ruin his employer, Mr. Wickfield, and marry his daughter Agnes

2) A person who is persistently optimistic, despite constant adversity, about a change in his fortune, and who is eventually relieved of his debts

Answer: 1) Uriah Heep
2) Micawber (Wilkins Micawber).

14) TOSS-UP. 10 points.

Aboard the *Josephine Ford* in 1926 and the *Floyd Bennett* in 1929, who was the first to fly over the North Pole and the South Pole respectively?

Answer: Richard Evelyn Byrd.

14) BONUS. 30 points. 10 points each.

Identify each of the following abnormal psychological traits.

1) Any of the various mental or emotional functional disorders without the obvious physical lesion or change

2) Any major, severe form of mental disorder (such as paranoia) or disease characterized by deterioration of normal social functioning or by lost contact with reality

3) A specific major mental disorder marked by loss of contact with reality with accompanying behavorial and intellectual disturbances or deterioration

Answer: 1) Neurosis (or psychoneurosis)
2) Psychosis (or insanity)
3) Schizophrenia (or dementia praecox).

15) TOSS-UP. 30 points after the first clue. 20 after the second. 10 after the third.

What's my name?

1) The smallest of the 4 Galilean satellites of Jupiter is named after me.

2) I was the daughter of Agenor, king of Phoenicia, in Greek mythology, and I became the Queen of Crete.

3) A continent is also named after me.

Answer: Europa.

15) BONUS. 30 points. 10 points each.

Give the year in which the St. Lawrence Seaway was officially opened, and name the U.S. President and the representative from Great Britain present at the opening ceremonies.

Answer: 1959 (first used on April 25 and officially opened on June 26) / Dwight D. Eisenhower and Queen Elizabeth.

16) TOSS-UP. 10 points.

What name is given to "a highly cultured, educated person who has acquired a skilled level of many, if not all, of the arts and sciences," a term which refers to the 14th through 16th centuries when it was possible to know almost everything about a great variety of given subjects?

Answer: Renaissance man.

16) BONUS. 30 points. 10 points each.

Identify the author of each of the following pairs of works.

1) *Coming of Age in Samoa* and *Growing Up in New Guinea*
2) *The Interpretation of Dreams* and *The Ego and The Id*
3) *Under the Sea* and *The Sea Around Us*

Answer: 1) Margaret Mead
2) Sigmund Freud
3) Rachel Louise Carson.

17) TOSS-UP. 10 points.

Name either the French inventor and painter or the photographic process he invented in 1839 by which an original image picture was made on a light-sensitive silver-coated copper plate and developed with mercury vapor.

Answer: Louis Jacques Mandé Daguerre or Daguerreotype.

17) BONUS. 30 points. 10 points each.

Identify each of the following concerning a famous Victorian couple, the Brownings.
1) The city in Italy where they lived permanently after secretly marrying and fleeing England
2) The completion of the line "How do I love thee" in the 43rd sonnet
3) The title of her autobiography

Answer: 1) **Florence**
2) **"Let me count the ways"**
3) *Let Me Count the Ways.*

18) TOSS-UP. 10 points.

In which city are the Pushkin Museum of Fine Arts, Gorki (Gorky) Park, and the Bolshoi Theatre located?

Answer: Moscow (USSR).

18) BONUS. 20 points. 5 points each.

Six professional baseball players, all in the Hall of Fame, have won the Most Valuable Player Award 3 times. Two of the players played in the National League and 4 in the American. Name the 4 in the American League.

Answer: Yogi Berra, Joe DiMaggio, Jimmie Foxx, and Mickey Mantle.

19) TOSS-UP. 10 points.

He said, "I not only 'don't choose to run' (for President) but I don't even want to leave a loophole in case I am drafted, so I won't 'choose.' I will say 'won't run' no matter how bad the country will need a comedian by that time." What well-known Oklahoma political comedian made this statement in 1931?

Answer: Will Rogers.

19) BONUS. 30 points. 10 points each.

Identify each of the following U.S. women.
1) The first woman elected to Congress (1916)
2) The first woman senator (1922)
3) The first woman governor (1925)

Answer: 1) **Jeanette Rankin (Montana)**

2) **Rebecca Latimer Felton (Georgia)**
3) **Nellie T. Ross, Wyoming (Miriam A. Ferguson, Texas, was sworn in 15 days later than Ross).**

20) TOSS-UP. 10 points.

To what tune is the "Battle Hymn of the Republic" sung?

Answer: "John Brown's Body."

20) BONUS. 20 points. 10 points each.

Name any 2 volumes in Isaac Asimov's *Foundation* trilogy.

Answer: *Foundation* **(1951),***Foundation and Empire* **(1952), and** *Second Foundation* **(1953).**

21) TOSS-UP. 10 points.

Which figurative expression meaning "to change one's opinion, to make new plans, or to change leaders during an activity or crisis" did Abraham Lincoln use on June 9, 1864, in response to the National Union League's congratulations on his renomination?

Answer: "to swap horses when crossing streams" (or in the middle of a stream, or when crossing the river, or in midstream).

21) BONUS. 30 points. 10 points each.

Identify each of the following English rulers.
1) The English king (1509-1547) known as "Bluff King Hal"
2) The English queen (1558-1603) known as "Gloriana" or Good Queen Bess"
3) The English Lord Protector of the Commonwealth (1653-1658) known as "Ironsides"

Answer: 1) Henry VIII
           2) Elizabeth I
           3) Oliver Cromwell.

22) TOSS-UP. 10 points.

Which word refers to 2 separate collections of Old Norse poems, one called the *Elder or Poetic* _____, assembled by the beginning of the 13th century, and the other the *Younger, or Prose* _____, compiled in the first quarter of the 13th century?

Answer: Edda.

22) BONUS. 25 points. 5 points each.

Name the 5 largest islands in the world.

Answer: Greenland, New Guinea, Borneo, Madagascar, and Baffin.

23) TOSS-UP. 10 points.

About 2500 B.C. it was called Thuban; about A.D. 1 it was called Kochab; about A.D. 4000 it will be called Alderaimin; and about A.D. 14,000 it will be the first magnitude star called Vega. By what name is this star known today?

Answer: Polaris (or Pole star).

23) BONUS. 20 points after the first clue. 5 points each.

Identify the author and title of each of the following.
1) The 1877 so-called *"Uncle Tom's Cabin* of animal stories," an autobiography of a horse who is mistreated by a groom and eventually rescued by a kind woman
2) The 1945 autobiography by a black U.S. novelist and social critic whose works include *Uncle Tom's Children* (1938) and *Eight Men* (1960).

Answer: 1) Anna Sewall's *Black Beauty* (1877).
2) Richard Wright's *Black Boy*.

24) TOSS-UP. 10 points.

Which sport originated with Ellis according to this inscription: "This stone commemorates the exploits of William Webb Ellis, who with fine disregard for the rules of football as played in his time, first took the ball in his arms and ran with it, thus originating the distinctive feature of the _____ game"?

Answer: Rugby (1823 at the Rugby School, Rugby, England).

24) BONUS. 30 points. 10 points each.

Identify each of the following ballets by Peter Ilich Tchaikovsky from the following events, places, and characters.
1) 16th birthday; Princess Aurora; the wicked fairy, Carabosse; Lilac Fairy; Prince Florimund
2) Christmas Party; Clara; toy soldiers; Kingdom of Sweets; Sugar Plum Fairy

3) 21st birthday; Prince Siegfried; Odette; Rothbart the evil magician; Odile; Lake of Tears

Answer: 1) *Sleeping Beauty* **(1890)**
2) *The Nutcracker* **(1892)**
3) *Swan Lake* **(1895).**

25) TOSS-UP. 30 points after the first clue. 20 after the second. 10 after the third.

Identify the American author of the following novels.
1) *Burning Bright* (1950) and *In Dubious Battle* (1936)
2) *Tortilla Flat* (1935) and *Cup of Gold* (1929)
3) *Travels with Charley* (1962) and *East of Eden* (1952)

Answer: John Steinbeck.

25) BONUS. 20 points. 10 points each.

From which 2 countries do Tyroleans come?

Answer: Austria and Italy.

CATEGORY TOSS-UP. 100 points. 10 points each. 10 points deducted for an incorrect answer.

For each of the following secret identities, give the real name of the fictional character.
1) Spiderman
2) The Phantom
3) Batman
4) Aquaman
5) Hawkman
6) The Hulk
7) Wonder Woman
8) Batgirl
9) The Green Hornet
10) The Shadow

Answer: 1) Peter Parker
2) Kit Walker
3) Bruce Wayne
4) Arthur Curry
5) Carter Hall

6) **David Banner (accept Bruce Banner)**
7) **Diana Prince**
8) **Babs Gordon**
9) **Britt Reid**
10) **Lamont Cranston.**

ROUND NINETEEN

1080 points

1) TOSS-UP. 10 points.

What "secretary" is the director of the world's largest office building?

Answer: Secretary of Defense heads the Pentagon.

1) BONUS. 30 points. 10 points each.

Identify the U.S. states from the following information.
1) The state whose name means "snowy" or "snow-covered" in Spanish
2) The state named after a river and a bay named after the first governor of Virginia
3) The state named for Queen Henrietta Maria, wife of King Charles I of England

Answer: 1) Nevada
       2) Delaware
       3) Maryland.

2) TOSS-UP. 10 points.

Which American artist late in her career painted mothers and children in family situations? Famous in both the U.S. and France, she was the only American artist ever to exhibit with the Impressionists, and she is known for *The Bath* (1891-1892) and *After the Bath* (1901).

Answer: Mary Cassatt.

2) BONUS. 20 points. 5 points each.

Identify each of the following triangles.
1) My name means "with equal legs."
2) My name means "uneven" or "unequal."
3) My name means "equal sides."
4) My name means "blunted" or "not acute."

Answer: 1) Isosceles

2) **Scalene**
3) **Equilateral**
4) **Obtuse.**

3) TOSS-UP. 30 points after the first clue. 20 after the second. 10 after the third.

What's my name?
1) My popular lecture to children published as *The Chemical History of A Candle* has become a classic.
2) A unit of electrical capacitance is named after me.
3) I was the English chemist and physicist who discovered the principle of electromagnetic induction in 1831.

Answer: Michael Faraday.

3) BONUS. 20 points. 10 points each.

Identify the pen name of the Cape May Point, New Jersey, writer named Mary O'Hara Alsop and the title of the book she wrote in 1941 about a boy and his colt.

Answer: Mary O'Hara and *My Friend Flicka*.

4) TOSS-UP. 10 points.

Which phrase from Daniel 2:31-45 is used to designate "a surprising character defect in a greatly admired or respected person"? This phrase refers to Nebuchadnezzar's dream of a great metallic image with one weak part which Daniel interpreted as a symbol of man's potential for destruction.

Answer: Feet of clay.

4) BONUS. 30 points. 10 points each.

Identify the American credited with each of the following citations.
1) "Our country! In her intercourse with foreign nations may she always be in the right, and always successful, right or wrong" (sometimes quoted as "May she always be in the right; but our country, right or wrong.")
2) "I am in earnest—I will not equivocate—I will not excuse—I will not retreat a single inch—AND I WILL HE HEARD!"
3) "I will not accept if nominated and will not serve if elected."

Answer: 1) Stephen Decatur
         2) William Lloyd Garrison
         3) William Tecumseh Sherman.

5) TOSS-UP. 10 points.

Name the 7th century B.C. Athenian statesman and lawgiver who introduced the first written code of law about 621 B.C., a code so severe that it was said to be written in blood. The adjective form of his name means "rigorous; severe; or cruel."

Answer: Draco (adjective form is draconian).

5) BONUS. 30 points. 10 points each.

Listed below are the names of 3 women taken from literature. Give the title and the author of the literary work in which each appears.
1) Emma Bovary
2) Mildred Rogers
3) Wendy Darling

Answer: 1) *Madame Bovary* **by Gustave Flaubert**
2) *Of Human Bondage* **by W. S. Maugham**
3) *Peter Pan* **by Sir James Barrie.**

6) TOSS-UP. 10 points.

What name is given to the group of seven 16th century French Renaissance poets, or the 7 tragic poets of ancient Alexandria, or the 7 nymphs who were the 7 daughters of Atlas and Cleione, or the 7 stars in a cluster in the constellation Taurus (also called the Seven Sisters)?

Answer: Pleiad (*La Pléiade* or the Pleiades).

6) BONUS. 30 points after the first clue. 20 after the second. 10 after the third.

Who am I?
1) I enlisted in World War I as a private and was killed as a sergeant in the Royal Fusiliers at Beaumont-Hamel in France.
2) I was a British writer born in Burma in 1870 and took my pen name from the cupbearer in the *Rubáiyát of Omar Khayyám*.
3) I wrote *Beasts and Super-Beasts* (1914), *Reginald* (1904), *The Unbearable Bassington* (1912), and *The Square Egg* (published posthumously in 1924).

Answer: Hector Hugh Munro or Saki.

7) TOSS-UP. 10 points.

Name the lawyer, later a U.S. President, whose sense of justice obligated him to defend Captain Thomas Preston and the British soldiers charged with murder in the Boston Massacre of March 5, 1770.

Answer: John Adams (with the assistance of Josiah Quincy and Robert Auchmutz).

7) **BONUS. 30 points after the first clue. 20 after the second. 10 after the third.**

What's my name?
1) My reputation was severely damaged by the "Diamond Necklace Affair" of 1785-1786, for people believed I sold myself to Cardinal de Rohan for a piece of jewelry.
2) I was known as "Madame Deficit" because of the bankruptcy of the crown and the country's severe economic straits.
3) I was forced to move from Versailles to the Tuileries Palace, was captured in Varennes, and was "imprisoned" in Paris. I became "the widow Capet" after my husband was executed on January 21, 1793, and I was subject to the same fate for treason on October 16, 1793.

Answer: Marie Antoinette.

8) **TOSS-UP. 10 points.**

Which ancient Greek or Roman name for "a public place for training or exercise in wrestling or athletics" is today the name for a Philadelphia gymnasium?

Answer: Palestra (spelled Palaestra in Greek or Latin).

8) **BONUS. 20 points. 10 points each.**

What are the last names of the famed murderers and bank robbers Bonnie and Clyde?

Answer: Bonnie Parker and Clyde Barrow.

9) **TOSS-UP. 20 points after the first clue. 10 after the second.**

Who am I?
1) I said, "*J'estime mieux que autrement, que c'est la terre que Dieu donna à Caïn*" ("I am rather inclined to believe that this is the land God gave to Cain").
2) I made this statement in 1534 upon seeing the dismal banks of the Gulf of St. Lawrence and am considered the French

discoverer of Prince Edward Island and the St. Lawrence River as far as Québec and Montréal.

Answer: Jacques Cartier.

9) BONUS. 20 points. 5 points each.

Which 4 major golf tournaments constitute the Grand Slam of golf?

Answer: Masters (April), U.S. Open (June), British Open (July), and the PGA (Professional Golfers Association) Championship (August).

10) TOSS-UP. 10 points.

Dear Bess is part of a title of a collection of letters edited by Robert H. Ferrell and sent between 1910 and 1959 from whom to whom?

Answer: Harry S Truman to Bess Truman.

10) BONUS. 30 points. 10 points each.

By what common name is the graph of each of the following known?
1) y squared minus x squared equals four
2) x squared plus two y squared equals one
3) x squared plus y squared is less than or equal to zero

Answer: 1) Hyperbola
        2) Ellipse
        3) A point (or a point circle).

11) TOSS-UP. 10 points.

He said, "Here I stand; I can do no other. God help me. Amen." He made this speech at the Diet of Worms on April 18, 1521. Name him.

Answer: Martin Luther.

11) BONUS. 30 points. 10 points each.

Identify each of the following plays from the description.
1) The play about a milkman named Tevye, his family, and the village of Anatevka and its traditions, a play based on stories by Sholom Aleichem
2) The Oscar Wilde play, subtitled "a trivial comedy for serious people," about Jack Worthing and his invented brother, Ernest, and Algy Moncrief's invented friend, Bunbury
3) The play in which Anna Leonowens comes to Siam with her son,

to teach English to the King's children, a play based on Margaret Landon's *Anna and the King of Siam*

Answer: 1) *Fiddler on the Roof*
         2) *The Importance of Being Earnest*
         3) *The King and I.*

12) TOSS-UP. 10 points.

Name the British leader of the 19th century utilitarian movement who wrote *A System of Logic* (1843), *The Principles of Political Economy* (2 volumes; 1848), and *On Liberty* (1859).

Answer: John Stuart Mill.

12) BONUS. 20 points. 5 points each.

1) Which U.S. state is listed first and which state last in an alphabetical order?
2) Which U.S. state is listed first and which state last chronologically in order of admission to the Union?

Answer: 1) Alabama and Wyoming
         2) Delaware and Hawaii.

13) TOSS-UP. 10 points.

I was called the "Admiral of the Sea of India," for I became the first explorer to reach India from Europe by way of the Cape of Good Hope. I did so on May 22, 1498. Identify me.

Answer: Vasco da Gama.

13) BONUS. 30 points. 10 points each. All or nothing on each one.

Complete the title of each of the following American novels or short stories with the correct color, and identify the author.
1) *The _____ Badge of Courage*
2) *_____ Hills of Africa*
3) *Riders of the _____ Sage*

Answer: 1) Red—by Stephen Crane
         2) Green—Ernest Hemingway
         3) Purple—Zane Grey.

14) TOSS-UP. 10 points.

Name the crystalline carbohydrate found in abnormally low levels in the blood in a condition called *hypoglycemia*.

Answer: Glucose (or sugar).

14) **BONUS. 20 points. 10 points each.**

Name both the New York-born doctor who developed the first effective inoculated vaccine to prevent polio and the Russian-born doctor who developed an oral vaccine that has eliminated polio as a major threat to human health.

Answer: Jonas Edward Salk and Albert Bruce Sabin.

15) **TOSS-UP. 30 points after the first clue. 20 after the second. 10 after the third.**

Who am I?
1) In the Civil War, during which I was wounded three times, I reputedly said: "Get down, you fool" to a civilian exposed to fire, only to discover later that this civilian was Abraham Lincoln.
2) I was a coeditor of the *American Law Review*, and I wrote *The Common Law* in 1881.
3) I was appointed an associate justice of the Supreme Court by Theodore Roosevelt in 1902 and served for nearly thirty years. I was named for my famous father, the author of many well-known poems and *The Autocrat of the Breakfast Table*.

Answer: Oliver Wendell Holmes, Jr.

15) **BONUS. 20 points. 10 points each.**

Name the Roman author and his masterpiece which begins with *Arma virumque cano*, "Of arms and the man I sing" (or "I sing of arms and the man").

Answer: Virgil (Publius Vergilius Maro) and *The Aeneid*.

16) **TOSS-UP. 10 points.**

What are you asking someone if you say *Wie geht es Ihnen* or *Wie geht's*?

Answer: How are you?

16) **BONUS. 30 points. 10 points each.**

Identify the author of each of the following pairs of works.
1) *The Idea of Freedom* and *How to Read a Book*
2) *How to Win Friends and Influence People* and *How to Stop*

Worrying and Start Living
3) *North to the Orient* and *Gift from the Sea*

Answer: 1) Mortimer Jerome Adler
           2) Dale Carnegie
           3) Anne Morrow Lindbergh.

17) TOSS-UP. 10 points.

Name the English Romantic poet who composed the lines: "Thou wast not born for death, immortal Bird! / No hungry generations tread thee down." The ode from which these lines come is addressed to a nightingale.

Answer: John Keats.

17) BONUS. 30 points. 10 points each.

Identify any 3 of the following concerning a 19th century European battle incident.
1) The translation of the phrase *"La garde meurt, et ne se rend pas jamais"* as the reply to a request for surrender
2) The person who supposedly made this statement
3) The commander-in-chief of the guard mentioned in the statement
4) The event or location which occasioned this statement when this guard made its last charge for the French
5) The year the statement was made

Answer: 1) "The guard dies and never surrenders" (The actual statement may have begun with the word "Merde!" This word is frequently called *le mot de Cambronne*—"the word of Cambronne"—or *les cinq lettres*—the five letters)
           2) General Pierre-Jacques-Étienne Cambronne
           3) Napoleon (his Imperial Guard or Old Guard)
           4) Waterloo (Battle of)
           5) 1815.

18) TOSS-UP. 10 points.

Name the U.S. state that completes the following citation: "I come from _____, the home of more first-rate second-class men than any state in the Union." This statement was made by Thomas Riley Marshall, Vice President to Woodrow Wilson.

Answer: Indiana.

18) BONUS. 20 points. 10 points each.

Name the 2 Canadian provinces without any sea coastline.

Answer: Saskatchewan and Alberta.

19) TOSS-UP. 30 points after the first clue. 20 after the second. 10 after the third.

What statue am I?
1) My name means "a mysterious person who is difficult to know or understand, especially one given to enigmatic questions or answers."
2) In Egyptian mythology, I have the body of a lion and the head of a man, ram, or hawk.
3) In Greek mythology, I am a winged monster with a lion's body and a woman's head and bust. I allegedly sat on a rock near Thebes posing riddles to travellers and killing them when they answered incorrectly.

Answer: Sphinx.

19) BONUS. 30 points. 10 points each.

Identify each of the following U.S. women.
1) The first woman to serve in both Houses of Congress (she won a special election in 1940 to fill a House seat vacated by the death of her husband and was reelected four times; she was also elected to the Senate in 1948 and reelected three times.)
2) The first black woman elected to Congress (1968)
3) The first woman Supreme Court justice (1981)

Answer: 1) Margaret Chase Smith (Maine)
2) Shirley Chisholm (New York)
3) Sandra Day O'Connor.

20) TOSS-UP. 10 points.

From 1378 to 1417 after a controversy over papal succession split the Roman Catholic Church, there were two, and sometimes three, claimants to the papal office. By what name is this division in the church known?

Answer: Great Schism (or Schism of the West or Western Schism).

20) BONUS. 30 points. 10 points each.

Give both the English and Latin names of the 3 movable little bones of the middle ear.

Answer: Hammer and *malleus*, anvil and *incus*, and stirrup and *stapes*.

21) TOSS-UP. 10 points.

Name the first woman to hold a cabinet post in the U.S. She did so as the Secretary of Labor (1933-1945) under Franklin D. Roosevelt.

Answer: Frances Perkins.

21) BONUS. 20 points. 5 points each.

Following WWII, a world leader made this statement: "From Stettin on the Baltic to Trieste on the Adriatic, an _____ has descended across the continent." Answer the following questions based on the above.
1) Who spoke those words on March 5, 1946?
2) At which U.S. college did he make his address?
3) In which city or state is this college located?
4) What words are missing from the above citation?

Answer: 1) Sir Winston Churchill
           2) Westminster College
           3) Fulton, Missouri
           4) "iron curtain."

22) TOSS-UP. 10 points.

Which word is the name of an animal, the nickname of a state, and a verb meaning "to harass persistently; to nag at; to tease; to pester"? The animal was named for the mark, usually white, on its head.

Answer: Badger (the mark on the animal is called a "badge"; the nickname for Wisconsin is the "Badger State").

22) BONUS. 20 points. 10 points each.

Give the international distress telegraph signal from a ship at sea, a call for help which has no literal meaning and consists of 3 dots, 3 dashes, and 3 dots. Then give the international distress telegraph signal first used by Marconi and used until 1911.

Answer: SOS (not Save Our Ship or Save Our Souls) and

CQD (for "come-quick-danger (distress)" according to some; CQ is a general company call to alert others that a message is coming).

23) TOSS-UP. 30 points after the first clue. 20 after the second. 10 after the third.

Which rebellion am I?
1) I took place in Virginia in 1676.
2) I was a movement against Governor William Berkeley's colonial policies and the Indians on the frontier during which Jamestown was burned.
3) I was led by a wealthy planter named Nathaniel who died of swamp fever in the same year.

Answer: Bacon's Rebellion.

23) BONUS. 30 points. 5 points each.

Eight films have won 8 or more Oscars. Name at least 6.

Answer: *Ben Hur* (1959; 11), *Gone With the Wind* (1939; 10), *West Side Story* (1961; 10), *Gigi* (1958; 9), *From Here to Eternity* (1953; 8), *On the Waterfront* (1954; 8), *Cabaret* (1972; 8), and *Gandhi* (1982; 8).

24) TOSS-UP. 10 points.

What is the name for "a knitted helmet or woolen cap that covers the head, neck, and tops of the shoulders with an opening for the nose and eyes, worn for protection against wind and extreme cold"? This garment was named after a U.S.S.R. port in the Black Sea which was the site of the battle in the Crimean War celebrated in Alfred, Lord Tennyson's poem *The Charge of the Light Brigade*.

Answer: Balaclava (after Balaklava).

24) BONUS. 30 points. 10 points each.

Identify the American credited with each of the following citations.
1) "Lafayette, we are here."
2) "What is good for the country is good for General Motors, and what's good for General Motors is good for the country."
3) "The energy crisis has not yet overwhelmed us, but it will if we do not act quickly...(This is) the greatest challenge that our country will face in our lifetimes...It is the moral equivalent of war."

Answer: 1) **Charles E. Stanton**
2) **Charles Erwin Wilson**
3) **Jimmy Carter.**

25) TOSS-UP. 10 points.

Name the strong, bitter, yellowish-green liqueur that is 68% alcohol and is prepared from wormwood, anise, and other herbs.

Answer: Absinthe (absinth).

25) BONUS. 30 points. 10 points each.

Identify the U.S. states from the following information.
1) The state named from the words which mean "green mountain" in French
2) The state whose name means "reddish-brown" in Spanish, a name first applied to the river
3) The state whose name probably came from the Dutch word for "red" although it may have come from an island in the Mediterranean Sea

Answer: 1) **Vermont**
2) **Colorado**
3) **Rhode Island.**

CATEGORY TOSS-UP. 100 points. 10 points each. 10 points deducted for an incorrect answer.

"The Big Apple" phrase originated among black jazz musicians in New Orleans by way of the Spanish word *manzana*, which means both "apple" and "city block." To play in the "Big Apple" meant to play in the big city, or New York. Identify each of the following New York City locations.
1) The haven for songwriters and publishers of popular music
2) The Bohemian district, a center for arts and crafts
3) The area for saloons, cheap hotels, and derelicts
4) The heart of the advertising district
5) The haven for artists, students, and writers
6) The wealthy residential area, a symbol of luxury, fashion, and high society
7) The theatre district
8) The fashion center
9) The financial district
10) The shopping district

Answer: 1) Tin Pan Alley
2) SoHo (*South of Houston* Street)
3) the Bowery
4) Madison Avenue
5) Greenwich Village
6) Park Avenue
7) Broadway
8) Seventh Avenue
9) Wall Street
10) Fifth Avenue.

ROUND TWENTY

1010 points

1) TOSS-UP. 10 points.

Whose life is featured in James Boswell's famous 1791 biography of an English poet, critic, essayist, and lexicographer?

Answer: Samuel Johnson's.

1) BONUS. 20 points. 5 points each.

Name the 4 U.S. states that touch the same point at a location known as "Four Corners."

Answer: Arizona, Colorado, New Mexico, and Utah.

2) TOSS-UP. 10 points.

Name the largest heavenly body orbiting the Earth.

Answer: The Moon.

2) BONUS. 20 points. 5 points each.

Give the nickname or acronym for "Young Urban Professionals" and the one for "Young Upwardly Mobile Professionals."

Answer: Yuppies and Yumpies.

3) TOSS-UP. 10 points.

Which word designates "a person who makes or repairs barrels, wooden tubs, and casks" or is the last name of the pseudonym of the successful skyjacker of Northwest Flight 727 from Portland to Seattle on November 24, 1971?

Answer: Cooper (D. B. Cooper with $200,000).

3) BONUS. 20 points. 5 points each.

Give the Latin names of each of the following constellations.
1) The Chained Lady
2) The Lady in the Chair, or the Queen

3) The Monarch, or the King
4) The Swan

Answer: 1) Andromeda
2) Cassiopeia
3) Cepheus
4) Cygnus.

4) TOSS-UP. 10 points.

Identify the system developed in the 1920's for making written records of choreography and named after its inventor, Rudolf von Laban.

Answer: Labanotation (or Laban system).

4) BONUS. 20 points. 10 points each.

Which 2 states have earned the nickname "Mother of Presidents"? One southern state is identified with 8 U.S. Presidents, including three in a row—Jefferson, Madison, and Monroe—and the other, a midwestern state, with 7, including three in a row—Grant, Hayes, and Garfield?

Answer: Virginia and Ohio.

5) TOSS-UP. 10 points.

Name the country whose flag is a white field with an outline map of the island in gold above crossed green olive branches. This country is an island in the Mediterranean where Greek, Turkish, and English are the principal languages. Its capital is Nicosia.

Answer: Cyprus.

5) BONUS. 30 points. 10 points each.

Listed below are the names of 3 women taken from literature. Give the title and the author of the literary work in which each appears.
1) Eustacia Vye
2) Eppie Cass
3) Wife of Bath

Answer: 1) *The Return of the Native* **by Thomas Hardy**
2) *Silas Marner* **by George Eliot**
3) *Canterbury Tales* **by Geoffrey Chaucer.**

6) TOSS-UP. 10 points.

What Civil War battle of November 24, 1863, was fought over a mountain occupied by Confederate forces? Union forces under Major General Joseph Hooker scaled the mountain and won the battle. Because the crest of the mountain was enshrouded in heavy fog during the action, the fight became popularly known as the "Battle Above the Clouds."

Answer: Battle of Lookout Mountain.

6) BONUS. 20 points. 5 points each.

Identify each of the following.
1) The Swiss psychiatrist and psychologist who believed that the members of every race share a level of unconsciousness called the *collective unconscious*
2) The Austrian physician-neurologist who divided the mind into three parts: the *id*, the *ego*, and the *superego*
3) The Austrian physician and psychologist-psychiatrist who believed that an inferiority complex is the driving force of all human activity, a theory he called *individual psychology*
4) The American psychiatrist who developed the *interpersonal theory* of personality which stresses the influence of personal relationships and deemphasizes biology and sexuality

Answer: 1) Carl Gustav Jung
2) Sigmund Freud
3) Alfred Adler
4) Harry Stack Sullivan.

7) TOSS-UP. 10 points.

What word from Matthew 6:24 or Luke 16:9,11,13 means "riches, material wealth, and avarice personified as a false god; riches regarded as an object of worship or an evil influence"?

Answer: Mammon (or mammon).

7) BONUS. 30 points. 10 points each.

Name the 3 cities that have twice hosted the summer Olympic Games.

Answer: Paris (1900 and 1924), London (1908 and 1948), and Los Angeles (1932 and 1984). Stockholm hosted the 1912 Games and the equestrian events in 1956.

8) TOSS-UP. 10 points.

Name the only U.S. President ever re-elected after having been defeated.

Answer: Grover Cleveland.

8) BONUS. 20 points. 5 points each.

Name the 4 plays by William Shakespeare which had their major source in Plutarch's *Parallel Lives*.

Answer: *Antony and Cleopatra, Julius Caesar, Coriolanus,* or *Timon of Athens.*

9) TOSS-UP. 10 points.

What is the name for a full-grown male deer, or for a man who attends a social gathering without being accompanied by a woman, or the adjective describing a social gathering or party for men only?

Answer: Stag.

9) BONUS. 20 points. All or nothing.

Give the 3 requirements a person must fulfill to become President of the U.S. according to Article II, Section 1 of the Constitution.

Answer: A natural-born citizen, at least 35 years of age, and a resident of the U.S. for at least 14 years.

10) TOSS-UP. 10 points.

What am I if in Spanish *tengo sed*?

Answer: You are thirsty.

10) BONUS. 30 points. 10 points each.

Identify each of the following phrases, all of which have the word *white* in the answer.
1) The name for the theatre district along Broadway, near Times Square in New York City
2) The name given by the American Indians to the President of the U.S.
3) The name by which the disease tuberculosis, especially pulmonary tuberculosis, is known

Answer: 1) **Great White Way**
    2) **Great White Father**
    3) **White Plague.**

11) TOSS-UP. 10 points.

Approximately three-fourths of what world events take place in the Pacific-area belt popularly called the *Ring of Fire*?

Answer: Earthquakes, or volcanic eruptions.

11) BONUS. 20 points. All or nothing.

Name the 3 colleges in Massachusetts, New Jersey, and Connecticut called "The Big Three."

Answer: Harvard, Princeton, and Yale.

12) TOSS-UP. 10 points.

Name the American atheist whose legal action suit against the city of Baltimore in 1963 resulted in the Supreme Court decision outlawing prayer recitation and Bible reading in public schools. This woman later became the head of the American Atheist Center in Texas.

Answer: Madalyn (Mays) Murray O'Hair.

12) BONUS. 20 points. 10 points each.

Name the Norse god who made thunder and lightning by throwing a hammer (Mjolnir) at his enemies and the Greek god who used a bolt of lightning as a weapon.

Answer: Thor and Zeus.

13) TOSS-UP. 10 points.

What is the former name of the African country now called Burkina ("ancestral home") Faso ("those who are dignified")?

Answer: Upper Volta.

13) BONUS. 30 points. 10 points each.

Complete the title of each of the following American novels or short stories with the correct color, and identify the author. All or nothing on each one.
1) "The Stolen _____ Elephant"

2) *Hans Brinker, or, The* _____ *Skates*
3) *The* _____ *Pony*

Answer: 1) White—Mark Twain (Samuel Clemens)
           2) Silver—Mary Elizabeth Mapes Dodge
           3) Red—John Steinbeck.

14) TOSS-UP. 30 points after the first clue. 20 after the second. 10 after the third.

Who am I?
1) I was born in Glasgow, Scotland, in 1819, and moved to the U.S. in 1842, later becoming a deputy sheriff of Kane County and Cook County in Illinois.
2) I became Chicago's first detective in 1853, and I wrote *Thirty Years a Detective* in 1884.
3) I was nicknamed "The Eye" for using innovative methods in my own detective agency which I established in 1850.

Answer: Allan Pinkerton.

14) BONUS. 30 points. 10 points each.

Identify the artist of each of the following paintings.
1) *Olympia* (1863)
2) *The Venus of Urbino* (1538)
3) *Mona Lisa* (1503-1506)

Answer: 1) Édouard Manet
           2) Titian
           3) Leonardo da Vinci.

15) TOSS-UP. 10 points.

Name the only country in South America that touches the Caribbean Sea, the Pacific Ocean, and Panama.

Answer: Colombia.

15) BONUS. 30 points. 10 points each.

Identify the author of each of the following.
1) *The Lady of the Lake*
2) "Ulysses" (the poem)
3) "My Last Duchess"

Answer: 1) Sir Walter Scott

2) **Alfred, Lord Tennyson**
3) **Robert Browning.**

16) TOSS-UP. 10 points.

Name the ram's horn blown in ancient times as a wind instrument to communicate in battle and still blown today in synagogues on Rosh Hashanah and at the end of Yom Kippur.

Answer: Shofar.

16) BONUS. 20 points. 10 points each.

Give the contrasting words that mean "beautiful handwriting" and "bad, ugly handwriting."

Answer: Calligraphy and cacography.

17) TOSS-UP. 10 points.

According to mythology, Cadmus introduced the alphabet and the art of writing into Greece. Which Cherokee Indian was called the "Cadmus of America" because of his development of a syllabary of 86 symbols for the Cherokee language in 1812 after 12 years of work?

Answer: Sequoya (or Sequoyah).

17) BONUS. 30 points. 10 points each.

Answer the following concerning the U.S. prison known as "America's Devil's Island" and "The Rock": the official name of this prison, the meaning of the prison's name in Spanish, and the bay in which the prison is located.

Answer: Alcatraz / Pelicans / San Francisco Bay.

18) TOSS-UP. 10 points.

Which French phrase means "a group, as of writers and artists, that develops ultramodern or experimental concepts," and is literally translated as "fore-guard"?

Answer: Avant-garde.

18) BONUS. 30 points. 10 points each.

With which Broadway musical is each of the following songs associated?
1) "I Cain't Say No"

2) "How Are Things in Glocca Morra?"
3) "Climb Every Mountain"

Answer: 1) *Oklahoma*
    2) *Finian's Rainbow*
    3) *The Sound of Music.*

19) TOSS-UP. 20 points after the first clue. 10 after the second.

What U.S. city am I?
1) I am called the "City That Turned Back Time."
2) I was the second capital (1699-1780) of Virginia.

Answer: Williamsburg.

19) BONUS. 20 points. 10 points each.

Name the train on which he traveled and the American railroad engineer who on April 30, 1900, died in a collision trying to deliver the 8-hour-late southbound mail on time. This engineer kept his hand on the brake lever, thus minimizing the impact and saving lives.

Answer: *The Cannonball Express* / (John Luther) Casey Jones.

20) TOSS-UP. 10 points.

Which U.S. President proclaimed, "If it takes the entire army and navy of the United States to deliver a postal card in Chicago, that card will be delivered"? His statement was made during the Pullman strike in Chicago in 1894.

Answer: Grover Cleveland.

20) BONUS. 20 points. 5 points each.

Give the middle names of each of the following writers.
1) William Bryant
2) Samuel Coleridge
3) James Lowell
4) George Shaw

Answer: 1) Cullen
    2) Taylor
    3) Russell
    4) Bernard.

21) TOSS-UP. 10 points.

Name the deformed dwarf in German folklore who agrees to spin gold from flax in exchange for a young bride's first born, unless she can guess his name. She does and the dwarf disappears (he kills himself).

Answer: Rumpelstiltskin (or Rumpelstilzchen).

21) BONUS. 20 points. 5 points each.

Identify each of the following associated with an 11th century religious confrontation.
1) The phrase that alludes to a place of penitence and means "to admit one's faults; to apologize; to submit oneself to humiliation"
2) The country in which the village in the phrase is located
3) The Holy Roman Emperor who after defying the Pope in 1075 traveled to this village in 1077 to do penance while barefoot and bareheaded in the snow for three days before being given absolution by the Pope
4) The Pope who excommunicated and then gave absolution to this emperor

Answer: 1) To go (journey) to Canossa
        2) Italy
        3) Henry IV
        4) Pope Gregory VII.

22) TOSS-UP. 10 points.

Name the machine used to scrape the ice from a rink and to squeegee the water from astro-turf ball fields.

Answer: Zamboni machine (invented by Frank Zamboni).

22) BONUS. 30 points. 10 points each.

Name any of the 3 colleges in Massachusetts and Connecticut known as "The Little Three." The students in these colleges are nicknamed the "Lord Jeffs," the "Cardinals," and the "Ephmen."

Answer: Amherst, Wesleyan, and Williams.

23) TOSS-UP. 10 points.

Name the fictional mysterious racketeer of the Twenties who entertains lavishly on Long Island and whose attempt to revive an old romance ends in disaster. Nick Carraway tells of this racketeer's affection for Daisy and his death at the hands of George Wilson.

Answer: Jay Gatsby (in *The Great Gatsby* by F. Scott Fitzgerald).

23) **BONUS. 30 points after the first clue. 20 after the second. 10 after the third.**

What is my name?
1) I have been called the "Poet of Black Africa," and I was the first African to hold a seat in the French Cabinet.
2) I am sometimes called the "Philosopher of Négritude," because I was one of the originators of the black literary and philosophical movement Négritude, which is an assertion of pride in African history and culture.
3) I had the honor in 1964 of shaking the hand of the author of this book at a reception I hosted for Peace Corps Volunteers at my presidential palace in Dakar, Senegal, during my presidency (1960-1981).

Answer: Léopold-Sédar Senghor.

24) **TOSS-UP. 10 points.**

What is the probability of rolling a sum of 7 with a pair of dice?

Answer: 1 out of 6 (6 out of 36).

24) **BONUS. 20 points. All or nothing.**

Name the world's 3 largest bodies of water in order from the largest to the smallest.

Answer: Pacific, Atlantic, and Indian oceans.

25) **TOSS-UP. 30 points after the first clue. 20 after the second. 10 after the third.**

What am I?
1) I am a *Mandoura* in Crete, a *Zampogna* in Italy, a *Dudlesack* in Germany, a *cornemuse* in France, and I am similar to a *gaita* in Spain and a *musette* in France.
2) I am made up of 5 wooden pipes: the blowpipe, the chanter, and the drone pipes.
3) I am considered to be the national musical instrument of Scotland.

Answer: Bagpipe.

25) **BONUS. 30 points. 5 points each. Point total stops at the first mistake.**

Arrange each of the following Soviet leaders in the chronological order in which they held office: Anton Chernenko, Vladimir Lenin, Joseph Stalin, Yuri Andropov, Leonid Brezhnev, and Nikita Khrushchev.

Answer: Lenin, Stalin, Khrushchev, Brezhnev, Andropov, and Chernenko.

CATEGORY TOSS-UP. 100 points. 10 points each. 10 points deducted for an incorrect answer.

Identify each of the following Latin phrases from the definition.
1) "in place of the parent; acting as guardian"
2) "(by) my fault; I am to blame; admission of guilt"
3) "something for something; something given in return for something received"
4) "without which not; an indispensable condition; an absolute prerequisite"
5) "for this specific purpose; for the present situation; temporary"
6) "from what is done afterwards; after the fact; retrospectively"
7) "by the very fact itself; intrinsically; by the very nature of the deed
8) "by the day; a daily allowance, as for expenses"
9) "for whose good?; to what purpose?; for whose benefit?"
10) "it does not follow; a conclusion or inference which does not follow from the premises"

Answer: 1) *In loco parentis*
        2) *Mea culpa*
        3) *Quid pro quo*
        4) *Sine qua non*
        5) *Ad hoc*
        6) *Ex post facto*
        7) *Ipso facto*
        8) *Per diem*
        9) *Cui bono*
       10) *Non sequitur.*

ROUND TWENTY-ONE

1) TOSS-UP. 10 points.

Name the river in China called "China's Sorrow" because of its frequent floods that ruin crops and bring famine.

Answer: Hwang Ho (Huang Ho) River (or Yellow River).

1) BONUS. 30 points after the first clue. 20 after the second. 10 after the third.

Identify the case.
1) This was an important civil rights case in the 1930's, a *cause célèbre* concerning the rights of blacks in the South.
2) The convictions in the case in Alabama courts were reversed by the Supreme Court in *Powell v. Alabama* (1932) and *Norris v. Alabama* (1935); however, Alabama persisted in prosecuting the case and achieved convictions and long prison sentences for 4 of the 9 defendants in 1936 and 1937.
3) The case involved 9 Negroes falsely accused of raping two white girls in 1931 in a railroad freight car.

Answer: Scottsboro Case.

2) TOSS-UP. 10 points.

Which word means "giving an account from the same point of view" and is used to describe the gospels of Matthew, Mark, and Luke as parallel accounts of the life of Jesus?

Answer: Synoptic.

2) BONUS. 20 points. 10 points each.

Because of his adulterous love for a queen, Lancelot could see the Holy Grail only in a dream. Name the queen he loved, and then name his son whose purity enabled him to obtain the Holy Grail.

Answer: Guinevere and Galahad.

3) TOSS-UP. 10 points.

He was the third son of Henry II of England and Eleanor of Aquitaine, and his courage in battle earned him the honor of being called *Coeur de Lion*. Who was he?

Answer: Richard I (the "Lion-Hearted").

3) BONUS. 20 points. 5 points each.

In which body of water is each of the following islands located?
1) St. Helena
2) Seychelles
3) Fiji
4) New Guinea

Answer: 1) Atlantic Ocean
2) Indian Ocean
3) Pacific Ocean
4) Pacific Ocean.

4) TOSS-UP. 10 points.

In physics I am used to designate "the ratio of the mass of an object to its volume," and in general I mean "thickness; dullness; stupidity." I also mean "the number of inhabitants per unit geographical region." Which word am I?

Answer: Density.

4) BONUS. 20 points. 10 points each.

Identify the Biblical source for and the missing words of the following verse from the King James Version: "_____; I shall not want. / He maketh me to lie down in green pastures: / He leadeth me beside the still waters. / He restoreth my soul: / He leadeth me in the paths of righteousness for his name's sake."

Answer: Psalm 23(1-3) / "The Lord is my shepherd."

5) TOSS-UP. 10 points.

Which Italian, born in Genoa, Italy, and nicknamed "The Great Admiral," skirted the New World for Henry VII of England in 1497-1498, probably landing on Cape Breton Island or Newfoundland?

Answer: John Cabot (Giovanni Caboto).

5) BONUS. 25 points. 5 points each.

Name the 5 Bolivaran countries that Simón Bolívar liberated from Spanish authority even though he never accomplished the unification of South America into one nation as he had wanted.

Answer: Venezuela, Columbia, Ecuador, Peru, and Bolivia.

6) TOSS-UP. 10 points.

Identify the African mammal whose name in Dutch means *earth pig*. This animal has a long piglike snout and eats ants and termites.

Answer: Aardvark.

6) BONUS. 30 points. 10 points each.

Give the Latin names of each of the following constellations.
1) The Winged Horse
2) The Rescuer, or the Champion
3) The Hunter

Answer: 1) Pegasus
2) Perseus
3) Orion.

7) TOSS-UP. 10 points.

Which amendment to the Constitution deals with U.S. citizenship?

Answer: 14th Amendment.

7) BONUS. 20 points after the first clue. 10 after the second.

What is my name and whose animal was I?
1) I was a milk-white horse with the wings of an eagle, a human face with horses' cheeks, and a pace equal to the farthest range of human sight.
2) My name in Arabic means "the lightning," and I was ridden from the earth to the seventh heaven.

Answer: Al-Borak was ridden by Mohammed (Mahomet).

8) TOSS-UP. 10 points.

If you were "laying down," what exactly would you be doing?

Answer: Spreading *down*, that is, fine, soft feathers, as on young birds, on a surface (if you were *lying down*, you would be resting).

8) BONUS. 30 points after the first clue. 20 after the second. 10 after the third.

Identify the author and the short poetic drama.
1) I am set in Asolo, Italy, in the early 19th century.
2) I am a story of a young and innocent silk-mill worker whose singing on New Year's Day brings those who hear her voice to repent and be saved from wrongdoing.
3) One of her songs is: "The year's at the spring / And day's at the morn; / Morning's at seven; / The hillside's dew-pearled; / The lark's on the wing; / The snail's on the thorn: / God's in His heaven— / All's right with the world!"

Answer: Robert Browning / *Pippa Passes* (1841).

9) TOSS-UP. 10 points.

Which French artist had so many works rejected by the critics and the public that Napoleon III established a *Salon des Refusés* (Salon of the Rejects) in order to display his paintings? This artist even built a pavilion at his own expense at the 1867 Universal Exposition in Paris to exhibit his works after they had been rejected by the jury for official display.

Answer: Édouard Manet.

9) BONUS. 20 points. 10 points each.

Which novel by which author treats 5 major families—the Bezuhjovs, the Rostovs, the Bolkonskys, the Kuragins, and the Drubetskois?

Answer: *War and Peace* by Leo Tolstoy.

10) TOSS-UP. 10 points.

What city was ancient Egypt's first capital, founded by Menes, Egypt's first king, about 3150 B.C.? Almost nothing remains of this ancient city which was located near present-day Cairo. A city in Tennessee is named for this ancient Egyptian capital.

Answer: Memphis.

10) BONUS. 30 points. 10 points each.

Identify each of the following phrases, all of which have the word *white* in the answer.
1) The nickname of the building housing the executive branch of the U.S. government

2) The name for "the supposed duty of white peoples to manage the affairs of the underdeveloped colored races" (from the title of a poem by Rudyard Kipling)

3) The name of "any person whose accomplishments are expected to bring fame, glory, and prestige to a group, place, or country" (originally applied to Caucasoid boxers, who might have been able to defeat Jack Johnson, the Negro heavyweight champion about 1910)

Answer: 1) White House
2) White Man's Burden
3) (Great) White Hope.

11) TOSS-UP. 10 points.

Name the "First American Negro Martyr," also known as the "First Hero of the American Revolution," who was killed by the British during the Boston Massacre on March 5, 1770.

Answer: Crispus Attucks.

11) BONUS. 30 points. 10 points each.

Identify the following killed by Theseus in Greek mythology. The first 2 were robbers and killers along the road to Athens whom Theseus destroyed by their own methods.

1) The person who made prisoners kneel and wash his feet and then kicked them down into the sea

2) The highwayman who placed his victims upon an iron bed and either stretched them to fit it if they were too short or cut off parts of their bodies if they were too long

3) The half-man, half-bull monster located in the Labyrinth on Crete who fed on the human flesh of others (Theseus killed him with his fists according to one legend)

Answer: 1) Sciron (Sceiron; Skiron)
2) Procrustes (Damastes or Polypemon was his real name)
3) Minotaur.

12) TOSS-UP. 10 points.

Name the Russian who wrote under the pseudonym Koba, a name meaning "The Indomitable" taken from a legendary Georgian folk hero. This Russian writer's well-known surname means "The Man of Steel."

Answer: Joseph Stalin (Iosif Vissarionovich Dzhugashvili).

12) BONUS. 20 points. 10 points each.

Name the 2 U.S. states with the longest ocean coastlines.

Answer: Alaska and Florida.

13) TOSS-UP. 10 points.

Name the historian who wrote, "History…is indeed little more than the register of the crimes, follies, and misfortunes of mankind." He is well known for his *The History of the Decline and Fall of the Roman Empire* (1766-1788).

Answer: Edward Gibbon.

13) BONUS. 30 points. 10 points each.

Name the 3 Alpine skiing events.

Answer: Downhill, giant slalom, and slalom.

14) TOSS-UP. 10 points.

Which U.S. President had a malignant growth on his upper left jaw removed and was fitted with an artificial jaw of vulcanized rubber in complete secrecy on a private yacht, the *Oneida*, in 1893? He was the 24th U.S. President at the time.

Answer: Grover Cleveland.

14) BONUS. 30 points. 10 points each.

Identify the artist of each of the following paintings.
1) *Marie Arrives at Marseille* (one of a series of paintings 1622-1625 of Marie de Medicis)
2) *Les Demoiselles d'Avignon* (1906-1907)
3) *The Nude Maja* or *The Naked Maja* (1800-1805)

Answer: 1) Peter Paul Rubens
2) Pablo Picasso
3) Francisco Goya.

15) TOSS-UP. 10 points.

Name any 2 of the first 5 popes.

Answer: St Peter (the Apostle), St. Linus, St. Anacletus (Cletus), St. Clement I, or St. Evaristus (listed in chronological order).

15) BONUS. 30 points. 10 points each.

Identify the author of each of the following.
1) *Nana*
2) *Tess of the D'Urbervilles*
3) *Ulysses* (the book)

Answer: 1) Emile Zola
        2) Thomas Hardy
        3) James Joyce.

16) TOSS-UP. 10 points.

Name the national cemetery located in the South where the mast of the battleship *Maine*, the Confederate Monument, and the Tomb of the Unknown Dead of the Civil War are located.

Answer: Arlington National Cemetery (Arlington, Virginia).

16) BONUS. 30 points. 10 points each.

In which U.S. national park is each of the following sites located?
1) Old Faithful
2) General Sherman Tree
3) Jackson Hole, or Jackson Lake

Answer: 1) Yellowstone
        2) Sequoia
        3) Grand Teton.

17) TOSS-UP. 10 points.

In which city is MOMA located? MOMA is an acronym for the Museum of Modern Art.

Answer: New York.

17) BONUS. 30 points. 10 points each.

Name the 3 presidents of France who succeeded Charles De Gaulle after his resignation in April 1969 following the rejection of his reforms by the French people. The first one was elected president in 1969, the second in 1974, and the third in 1981.

Answer: Georges Pompidou, Valéry Giscard d'Estaing, and François Mitterrand.

18) TOSS-UP. 10 points.

What is the English translation of the French phrase originated by Sainte-Beuve in the 19th century to mean "a place of withdrawal from reality; an attitude of disrespect for practical matters"? In French the phrase is *tour d' ivoire*.

Answer: Ivory tower.

18) BONUS. 30 points. 10 points each.

With which Broadway musical is each of the following songs associated?
1) "Don't Rain on My Parade"
2) "The Rain in Spain"
3) "They Call the Wind Maria"

Answer: 1) *Funny Girl*
2) *My Fair Lady*
3) *Paint Your Wagon.*

19) TOSS-UP. 10 points.

Who said, "No one ever went broke underestimating the intelligence of the American people"?

Answer: H(enry) L(ouis) Mencken (at least attributed to him).

19) BONUS. 20 points. 10 points each.

Name the person whose name appeared in the Chicago *Tribune*'s erroneous headline "_____ DEFEATS TRUMAN" following the 1948 presidential election and the person whose name erroneously appeared in the New York newspapers as "THE PRESIDENT-ELECT—CHARLES EVANS _____," as the winner defeating Woodrow Wilson in the 1916 presidential election.

Answer: Dewey / Hughes.

20) TOSS-UP. 10 points.

Which word means "to vote against letting a candidate join an organization; to ostracize," and comes from the practice of placing a certain colored ball in the ballot box?

Answer: Blackball.

20) BONUS. 20 points. 5 points each.

Give the middle names of each of the following writers.
1) William Thackeray
2) Henry Thoreau
3) Harriet Stowe
4) Elizabeth Browning

Answer: 1) Makepeace
2) David
3) Beecher
4) Barrett.

21) TOSS-UP. 10 points.

In which month is the Earth nearest the sun?

Answer: January.

21) BONUS. 30 points. 10 points each.

Identify the author of each of the following novels and give his nationality. All or nothing for each one.
1) *The Return of the Native* (1878)
2) *Vanity Fair* (1847-1848)
3) *All Quiet on the Western Front* (1929)

Answer: 1) Thomas Hardy—English
2) William Makepeace Thackeray—English
3) Erich Maria Remarque—German.

22) TOSS-UP. 10 points.

One sportswriter called Jones's feat the "impregnable quadrilateral," but an Atlanta journalist used a term from the game of bridge to describe Bobby Jones's 4 major tournament victories in 1930. What term did he use that today refers to victory in the 4 major golf tournaments in one year?

Answer: Grand Slam.

22) BONUS. 20 points. 5 points each.

Name 4 of the 6 major organs of the United Nations.

Answer: General Assembly, Security Council, Secretariat, Economic and Social Council, International Court of Justice, and Trusteeship Council.

23) TOSS-UP. 10 points.

What is my name? Born the son of a slave in Dayton, Ohio, in 1892, I became an American novelist and poet and wrote *Lyrics of Lowly Life* (1896) and *The Sport of the Gods* (1902). Many high schools throughout the country, especially basketball powers in Baltimore, Washington D.C., and Fort Worth are named for me.

Answer: Paul Laurence Dunbar.

23) BONUS. 30 points after the first clue. 20 after the second. 10 after the third.

By what names were we possibly better known?
1) Our names were Robert (or George) LeRoy Parker and Harry Longbaugh.
2) Our gang was the Wild Bunch or the Hole-in-the-Wall Gang.
3) We fled the U.S. and went to South America where we continued to rob banks and trains. We took our names from a friend, and from a town in the Wyoming Territory.

Answer: Butch Cassidy and the Sundance Kid.

24) TOSS-UP. 10 points.

200 is what percent of 40?

Answer: 500 percent.

24) BONUS. 20 points. 10 points each.

Name the fort off the southern tip of Florida (68 miles west of Key West) that was used as a military prison during the Civil War, and name the prison superintendent for the Confederate stockade at Andersonville, Georgia, who was convicted of murder by a U.S. Military court and hanged in 1865.

Answer: Fort Jefferson, and Captain Henry Wirz.

25) TOSS-UP. 10 points.

Name France's greatest school of fine arts. It developed out of the *École Académique* founded by Jules Cardinal Mazarin in 1648 and the *École de l'Académie d'Architecture* founded by Jean Baptiste Colbert in 1671.

Answer: École (Naturale Supérieure) Des Beaux-Arts.

25) **BONUS. 20 points. 5 points each.**

Name the 4 attorneys general of the U.S. who were appointed by President Richard Nixon.

Answer: John N. Mitchell, Richard G. Kleindienst, Elliot L. Richardson, and William B. Saxbe.

CATEGORY TOSS-UP. 100 points. 10 points each. 10 points deducted for an incorrect answer.

Identify each of the following concerning the Trojan War in which Greece defeated Troy.
1) The 3 epic poems, two by Homer and one by Virgil, that contain some of the events before and after the Trojan War
2) The length of the Trojan War and the century in which it probably took place
3) The person who carried off the "Face that launched a Thousand Ships," and the name of this Queen of Sparta
4) A King of Sparta, the husband of the woman taken, and his brother who helped organize the Greek expedition
5) The 2 Greek warriors who were reluctant to go to Troy, one who feigned madness because an oracle had told him that he would be 20 years away from home and the other whose mother disguised him in women's clothing because she knew he would have a short but glorious life
6) The 2 Trojan heroes, Priam's oldest son and the son of Anchises and Venus (Aphrodite) who escaped from Troy
7) The bravest Greek warrior's friend who was killed and the Trojan leader who killed him
8) The Queen of the Amazons and the King of the Ethiopians killed by Achilles
9) The Greek hero who was fatally wounded by an arrow which struck him in the right heel and the Trojan who shot the arrow
10) The prophetess and the priest who warned the Trojans not to allow the Trojan horse into the city

Answer: 1) *Iliad* and *Odyssey* by Homer and the *Aeneid* by Virgil

2) **10 years / 1100's or 1200's B.C. (12th or 13th century)**
3) **Paris and Helen**
4) **King Menelaus and Agamemnon**
5) **Odysseus (Ulysses) and Achilles**
6) **Hector and Aeneas**
7) **Patroclus and Hector**
8) **Penthesilea and Memnon**
9) **Achilles and Paris**
10) **Cassandra and Laocoön.**

ROUND TWENTY-TWO

980 points

1) TOSS-UP. 10 points.

On which body of water are the following gulfs located: Hammammet, Lions, Cagliari, Gabès, Valencia, Sidra, and Tunis?

Answer: Mediterranean Sea.

1) BONUS. 30 points. 10 points each.

The Union Jack of the United Kingdom combines the crosses of which 3 saints—the patron saints of England, Scotland, and Ireland?

Answer: St. George, St. Andrew, and St. Patrick.

2) TOSS-UP. 10 points.

Which phrase designates "a country or place where immigrants of different cultures and nationalities are assimilated"?

Answer: Melting pot.

2) BONUS. 30 points. 5 points each.

Identify each of the following concerning a Democratic vice presidential nomination.
1) The only vice-presidential candidate ever nominated by a national convention to resign his candidacy after it was revealed that he had been hospitalized 3 times for emotional exhaustion and depression
2) The state from which this man was a senator
3) The name of the presidential candidate who selected him
4) The state from which this man was a senator
5) The name of the person who replaced him on the ticket for Vice President
6) The year in which this happened

Answer: 1) Thomas Francis Eagleton
            2) Missouri

3) George Stanley McGovern
4) South Dakota
5) R. Sargent Shriver (for whom this author once worked)
6) 1972.

3) TOSS-UP. 10 points.

By what initial are some of Franz Kafka's protagonists known?

Answer: K.

3) BONUS. 20 points. 10 points each.

Name the autonomous and semi-independent coprincipality, 180 square miles in area, located in the Pyrenees Mountains, and name the 2 countries on whose borders it is located. This country was initially under the dual control of the bishop of Urgel and the count of Foix.

Answer: Andorra / France and Spain.

4) TOSS-UP. 10 points.

Which English unit of measurement equals 550 foot-pounds per second or 746 watts?

Answer: One horsepower.

4) BONUS. 20 points. 5 points each.

Thomas Carlyle wrote an extensive study of the life of a king of Prussia. He made special mention of one 11 year period (1745-1756) in this ruler's reign. Identify each of the following related to this ruler and this period of time.
1) The name of this king of Prussia
2) The translation of the chapter title "Sans-Souci," a term which Carlyle used to characterize this period of time
3) The adjective Carlyle used to describe this period, a word derived from the name of a bird thought to calm the seas during its nesting
4) The completion of what Carlyle calls "Montesquieu's aphorism": "Happy the people whose annals are blank in _____ books"

Answer: 1) Frederick the Great
2) "without concern; without worry or care"
3) Halcyon ("Halcyon Period")
4) history.

5) TOSS-UP. 10 points.

Which adjective is used today to mean "hard to read or understand; undecipherable," and pertains to a picture or symbol representing a word, syllable, or sound used by the ancient Egyptians? The word etymologically means "pertaining to sacred writing."

Answer: Hieroglyphic.

5) BONUS. 20 points. 10 points each.

What are the meanings of the business initialisms NYSE and AMEX?

Answer: New York Stock Exchange and American Exchange.

6) TOSS-UP. 10 points.

What's my name? I am sometimes called a *harvestman* or *crane fly*. I am an arachnid of the order *Phalangida* with a rounded body and very long, slender legs.

Answer: Daddy-Longlegs (granddaddy longlegs).

6) BONUS. 20 points. 10 points each.

Name the existentialist French authors of *Le deuxième sexe* (*The Second Sex*; 1949) and *L'Être et le néant* (*Being and Nothingness*; 1943).

Answer: Simone de Beauvoir and Jean-Paul Sartre.

7) TOSS-UP. 10 points.

Name the statue of a woman, probably sculpted about 100 B.C., found by a peasant in the Greek island of Melos in 1820, and often called the "Aphrodite of Melos." This sculpted woman, which Louis XVIII presented to the Louvre in Paris, may have been holding a shield to look at her reflection, but since her arms are missing, this is only conjecture.

Answer: Venus de Milo.

7) BONUS. 30 points. 5 points each. Point total stops at the first mistake.

Name the 6 largest continents in area in order from the largest to the smallest.

Answer: Asia, Africa, North America, South America, Antarctica, and Europe.

8) TOSS-UP. 10 points.

What is the name for "an alphabetical index of the principal words used in a book, showing every passage in which they occur"?

Answer: Concordance.

8) BONUS. 20 points. 10 points each.

Name the 2 longest rivers in Europe.

Answer: The Volga River and the Danube River.

9) TOSS-UP. 10 points.

Which phrase derived from Greek mythology means "to clean up an accumulated mess" or "to get rid of massive corruption"? This phrase comes from one of the 12 labors of Hercules.

Answer: To clean the Augean stables.

9) BONUS. 20 points. 10 points each.

Give the French national motto in French, a motto first used in Revolutionary France, and then give the English translation of these 3 words.

Answer: *Liberté, Egalité, Fraternité* / Liberty, Equality, Fraternity.

10) TOSS-UP. 10 points.

This Spanish poet and dramatist, known as the "Poet of Blood" because of his works and the manner in which he died, is as widely translated as Miguel de Cervantes. He wrote *Llanto por Ignacio Sánchez Mejías* (*Lament for Igancio Sánchez Mejías*; 1935) and *Bodas de sangre* (*Blood Wedding*; 1933) before being killed in the Spanish Civil War by followers of Francisco Franco. Name him.

Answer: Federico García Lorca.

10) BONUS. 20 points. 5 points each.

In which body of water is each of the following located?
1) Madeira Islands
2) Sri Lanka

3) Azores
4) Marshall Islands

Answer: 1) Atlantic Ocean
             2) Indian Ocean
             3) Atlantic Ocean
             4) Pacific Ocean.

11) TOSS-UP. 10 points.

Name the pope's central administrative body in the Vatican that helps him govern the church.

Answer: Roman Curia (*Curia Romana*).

11) BONUS. 30 points. 10 points each.

Identify the state in which each of the following landmarks is located.
1) Mark Twain Cave
2) Walt Whitman House
3) Booker T. Washington National Monument

Answer: 1) Missouri
             2) New Jersey
             3) Virginia.

12) TOSS-UP. 10 points.

Name the American known as the "Father of Economic Determinism" who wrote *An Economic Interpretation of the Constitution of the United States* (1913) and *Economic Origins of Jeffersonian Democracy* (1915). This author maintained that the Founding Fathers who wrote the new Constitution were primarily motivated by their own economic considerations.

Answer: Charles Austin Beard.

12) BONUS. 30 points. 10 points each.

Identify each of the following "Ages."
1) The period which marked the golden age of Latin literature, named after the first Roman emperor (27 B.C.-A.D. 14) who was a patron of the arts and literature
2) The period which marked the intellectual and material preeminence of Athens, Greece, named after an Athenian statesman who ruled from about 460-429 B.C.

3) The period from 1815 to 1848 in Europe, which was dominated by and named after an Austrian diplomat

Answer: 1) Age of Augustus (Augustan Age; after Gaius Julius Caesar Octavianus, or Octavian, or Augustus Caesar)
2) Age of Pericles (Periclean Age)
3) Age of Metternich (Metternichean Age).

13) TOSS-UP. 10 points.

Say the word *something* in Spanish.

Answer: *Alguna cosa.*

13) BONUS. 20 points. 10 points each.

Name the Scandinavian city in which the statue of *The Little Mermaid* is located and the writer for whom this statue is a memorial.

Answer: Copenhagen (Denmark)/Hans Christian Andersen.

14) TOSS-UP. 10 points.

Name David Seville's 3 chipmunks.

Answer: Alvin, Simon, and Theodore.

14) BONUS. 20 points. 5 points each.

Identify each of the following concerning Abraham (originally called Abram), the "Father of Many Nations" and the founder of Judaism.
1) The name of his first wife, his half-sister
2) The name of the handmaid of his wife who bore him a child
3) The name of the child of Abraham and the handmaid
4) The name of the child born to Abraham by his first wife who gave birth in accord with a divine promise, the child whom God later commanded Abraham to sacrifice in the land of Moriah

Answer: 1) Sarah (Sarai)
2) Hagar
3) Ishmael
4) Isaac.

15) TOSS-UP. 10 points.

I published a volume of my portraits called *A Gallery of Illustrious Americans* in 1850, and later became a famous Civil War photographer. What's my name?

Answer: Mathew Brady.

15) **BONUS. 20 points. 10 points each.**

Identify the phrase which means "the female or maternal side of the family," and the phrase which means "the male or paternal side of the family."

Answer: Distaff side / Spear side.

16) **TOSS-UP. 10 points.**

Translate the Latin phrase *ars gratia artis*, the slogan of a group of 19th century artists and writers of a movement also known as *aestheticism*.

Answer: Art for Art's Sake.

16) **BONUS. 30 points. 10 points each.**

In which U.S. national park is each of the following sites located?
1) Mount McKinley
2) Clingmans Dome
3) Bridalveil Fall

Answer: 1) Denali
2) Great Smoky Mountains
3) Yosemite.

17) **TOSS-UP. 10 points.**

Complete the second line in the following stanza: "Fe fi fo fum! / I smell the _____; / Be he alive or be he dead, / I'll grind his bones to make my bread."

Answer: "blood of an Englishman."

17) **BONUS. 30 points after the first clue. 20 after the second. 10 after the third.**

What's my name?
1) I am a tropical, cephalopod mollusk of the Pacific and Indian oceans, the only one in existence with a fully developed shell, and I am a kind of diving bell.
2) I am the name of both Robert Fulton's 1800 submarine and a tempera painting by Andrew Wyeth.

3) I am the name of the world's first nuclear-powered submarine, launched by the U.S. Navy in 1954, and Captain Nemo's submarine in Jules Verne's *20,000 Leagues Under the Sea.*

Answer: Nautilus.

18) TOSS-UP. 10 points.

In his work *On the Revolutions of the Heavenly Spheres* (1543), who postulated that the sun and not the earth was the center of the universe, thus dispelling Ptolemy's theories that had endured for 1,400 years?

Answer: Nicolaus Copernicus.

18) BONUS. 20 points. 5 points each.

Name the 4 "Freedoms" President Franklin Roosevelt promised in a January 6, 1941, message to Congress in which he said, "In the future days, which we seek to make secure, we look forward to a world founded upon four essential human freedoms."

Answer: Freedom of speech and expression [everywhere in the world] / Freedom of [every person to] worship [God in his own way—everywhere in the world] / Freedom from want [everywhere in the world] / Freedom from fear [anywhere in the world].

19) TOSS-UP. 10 points.

She was called the "Queen of the Nets" and was considered by most to be the greatest female tennis player of her time. She won the U.S. Women's Singles Championship 7 times between 1923-1931, Wimbledon Singles 8 times between 1927-1938, French Singles 4 times, and the Wightman Cup Singles 18 times. Name this American tennis star.

Answer: Helen Wills Moody (or Helen Newington Wills; later Mrs. Aidan Roark).

19) BONUS. 20 points. 10 points each.

Identify the author and title of the novel whose principal character is known as the original literary gold digger and social climber. This character marries Rawdon Crawley, has a liaison with Lord Steyne who introduces her to smart London society, becomes an adventuress, cheats Joe Sedley out of his money, and then turns respectable. Her name is Becky Sharp.

Answer: William Makepeace Thackeray's *Vanity Fair*.

20) **TOSS-UP. 10 points.**

The Roosevelt Corollary opposed European intervention in the Americas, but which doctrine "proclaimed the Soviet Union's right to intervene in any 'socialist' country"?

Answer: Brezhnev Doctrine.

20) **BONUS. 20 points. 5 points each.**

Identify each of the following concerning U.S. Presidents.
1) The only father and son presidential pair
2) The only grandfather and grandson presidential pair
3) The Presidents who were 5th cousins
4) The 4th and 12th Presidents who were second cousins

Answer: 1) John Adams and John Quincy Adams
**   2) William Henry Harrison and Benjamin Harrison**
**   3) Theodore Roosevelt and Franklin Roosevelt**
**   4) James Madison and Zachary Taylor.**

21) **TOSS-UP. 10 points.**

What is the length of the hypotenuse of a right triangle whose legs are of lengths 5 and 6?

Answer: The square root of 61.

21) **BONUS. 30 points. 10 points each.**

Identify the author of each of the following novels and give his nationality. All or nothing for each one.
1) *The Swiss Family Robinson* (4 volumes; 1812-1827)
2) *Crime and Punishment* (1866)
3) *Silas Marner* (1861)

Answer: 1) Johann Rudolf Wyss—Swiss
**   2) Feodor (Fyodor) Mikhailovich Dostoevski (Dostoyevsky)—Russian**
**   3) George Eliot (Mary Ann Evans)—English.**

22) TOSS-UP. 10 points.

Name the Italian operatic tenor who, on tour in San Francisco, on April 18, 1906, the day of the famous earthquake, said, "San Francisco will never hear my voice again"—and indeed he never returned to San Francisco. He was born in Naples in 1873, died in 1921, and Arturo Toscanini said of him, "This Neapolitan will make the whole world talk about him."

Answer: Enrico Caruso.

22) BONUS. 30 points. 10 points each.

Give an alternate name for each of the following Civil War battles.
1) Stones River
2) Pittsburg Landing
3) Seven Pines

Answer: 1) Murfreesboro
2) Shiloh
3) Fair Oaks.

23) TOSS-UP. 20 points after the first clue. 10 after the second.

What's my name?
1) I spoke out against the arms race in the late 1960's, and in 1980 I was arrested and exiled to the city of Gorki for having criticized the Soviet invasion of Afghanistan.
2) I won the Nobel Prize for peace in 1975 for my efforts in promoting peace and in opposing violence and brutality.

Answer: Andrei D. Sakharov.

23) BONUS. 30 points. 5 points each.

Identify each of the following.
1) The 4 Horsemen of Calumny named in a Declaration of Conscience Speech made by Senator Margaret Chase Smith in the U.S. Senate on June 1, 1950, in which she said, "But I don't want to see the Republican Party ride to political victory on the Four Horsemen of Calumny—_____, _____, _____, and _____" (5 points each)
2) The Senator toward whom this speech was directed
3) The state Senator Smith represented

Answer: 1) Fear, Ignorance, Bigotry, and Smear
2) Senator Joseph McCarthy
3) Maine.

24) TOSS-UP. 10 points.

What name is given to the 1618 incident when representatives of the Protestant nobility in Bohemia in protest against the Roman Catholic Hapsburg king *threw out of the window* of the Hradcany Castle in Prague three royal councillors, an act which started the Thirty Years' War?

Answer: Defenestration of Prague.

24) BONUS. 30 points. 10 points each.

Identify each of the following concerning Cadmus, the Phoenician prince, in Greek mythology.
1) The name of the sister, kidnapped by Zeus, for whom Cadmus searched
2) The animal which the oracle at Delphi told him would lead him to a good site for the founding of a new kingdom
3) The animal which Cadmus slew at the spring after it had killed all his servants whom he had sent for water

Answer: 1) Europa
         2) (Snow-white) cow
         3) Dragon (sometimes pictured as a serpent).

25) TOSS-UP. 10 points.

Name the "magic mineral" found in metamorphic rocks whose soft grayish, threadlike fibers are used in cement, fireproof clothing, and electrical insulation.

Answer: Asbestos.

25) BONUS. 30 points after the first clue. 20 after the second. 10 after the third.

What is my name?
1) At my birth in Ireland in 1854, I was given the middle names Fingal O'Flahertie Wills.
2) I won the Newdigate poetry prize at Magdalen College, Oxford, in 1878 with *Ravenna*.
3) I wrote *A Woman of No Importance* (1893) and *The Importance of Being Earnest* (1895).

Answer: Oscar Wilde.

CATEGORY TOSS-UP. 100 points. 10 points each. 10 points deducted for an incorrect answer.

Identify each of the following concerning *The Wizard of Oz*. Multiple answers are required on most identifications.
1) The author of this work and the 38 *Oz* sequels
2) The state in which the little girl lives and the type of turbulent wind which blows the house into the Land of Oz
3) The name of the little girl, the actress who plays her in the 1939 musical film, and the name of her little black dog
4) The name of the farmer and the farmer's wife, the little girl's Aunt and Uncle with whom she lives
5) The city in which Oz, the Great Wizard, lives and the color of the brick road that leads to this city
6) The name of the people who live in the countries of the Good Witches of the North and South or the colors which distinguish these two countries
7) The name of the people who live in the countries of the Wicked Witches of the East and West or the colors which distinguish these two countries
8) The characteristic which the Scarecrow desires from the Wizard of Oz and the actor who plays him in the film
9) The characteristic which the Tin Woodsman desires and the actor who plays him in the film
10) The characteristic which the Cowardly Lion wants and the actor who plays him in the film

Answer: 1) **Lyman Frank Baum**
2) **Kansas / Cyclone**
3) **Dorothy (Dorothy Gale in the film) / Judy Garland / Toto**
4) **Uncle Henry and Aunt Em (Emily)**
5) **City of Emeralds / Yellow Brick Road**
6) **Gillikins or purple in the North / Quadlings or red in the South**
7) **Munchkins or blue in the East / Winkies or yellow in the West**
8) **Brains / Ray Bolger**
9) **Heart / Jack Haley**
10) **Courage / Bert Lahr.**

ROUND TWENTY-THREE

885 points

1) TOSS-UP. 10 points.

Name Don Quixote's bony horse in the 1616 Spanish novel *Don Quixote* by Miguel de Cervantes Saaverdra. This name today means "any ancient nag" or "an old, decrepit horse."

Answer: Rocinante (or Rosinante).

1) BONUS. 20 points. All or nothing.

Although the phrase *seven seas* meaning "all the water or oceans of the world" originally had no literal meaning because the phrase preceded an exact knowledge of the world's bodies of water, what are the names of the 7 bodies of water generally considered to be the "Seven Seas"?

Answer: Pacific, Atlantic, Indian, and Arctic oceans, the Mediterranean and Caribbean seas, and the Gulf of Mexico (accept also the Antarctic Ocean).

2) TOSS-UP. 10 points.

Name the southern area extending from Virginia to California which has experienced the greatest population growth in the latter part of the 20th century.

Answer: Sunbelt.

2) BONUS. 25 points. 5 points each.

Identify each of the following concerning a famous gunfight on October 26, 1881.
1) The names of any two of the Earp brothers involved in the fight
2) The last name of the "Doc," deputized for the occasion, who was involved in the fight on the side of the Earps
3) The last name of either set of brothers opposing the Earps
4) The city and state in which this fight took place
5) The specific site whose name is used to designate this fight

Answer: 1) **Morgan, Virgil (the town marshal), or Wyatt**
2) **(John "Doc") Holliday**
3) **McLaury (McLowery or McLowry), or Clanton**
4) **Tombstone, Arizona**
5) **O.K. Corral.**

3) TOSS-UP. 10 points.

Name both the U.S. President and the Vice President who served together without being elected to their respective offices.

Answer: Gerald Ford and Nelson Rockefeller.

3) BONUS. 20 points. 10 points each.

Identify the author who created them and the characters whose names refer today to "a person who is alternately completely good and completely evil." In this story a man of excellent character and reputation discovers a drug by which he becomes a debased and monstrous person, a personality in which he ultimately becomes trapped.

Answer: Robert Louis Stevenson's Dr. Jekyll and Mr. Hyde (in *The Strange Case of Dr. Jekyll and Mr. Hyde* (1886).

4) TOSS-UP. 10 points.

Name the German engineer credited with designing and building (1885) the first automobile powered by an internal-combustion engine. His car had three wheels, an electric ignition, and differential gears.

Answer: Karl F. Benz.

4) BONUS. 20 points. 10 points each.

Name the "tall, pointed hat with peaks in front and back, worn by bishops and other ecclesiastics as a mark of office," and the "staff with a crook or cross at the end, carried by a bishop or archbishop as a symbol of office."

Answer: Miter (or mitre) and crosier (crozier).

5) TOSS-UP. 10 points.

Name the most densely-populated country in Central America.

This country is also the smallest republic in land area on the American mainland.

Answer: El Salvador.

5) BONUS. 25 points. 5 points each.

Identify the anniversary theme by which each of the following is known or the anniversary gift appropriate for each one.
1) 20th
2) 25th
3) 30th
4) 50th
5) 75th

Answer: 1) China (accept platinum or furniture)
2) Silver
3) Pearl (accept diamond)
4) Gold
5) Diamond (accept gold).

6) TOSS-UP. 10 points.

Which 2 animals are used in the description of how the month of March comes in and goes out?

Answer: Lion and lamb ("March comes in like a lion and goes out like a lamb").

6) BONUS. 20 points. 5 points each.

Identify each of the following medical initials.
1) AMA
2) NIH
3) SIDS
4) CDC

Answer: 1) American Medical Association
2) National Institutes of Health
3) Sudden Infant Death Syndrome
4) Centers for Disease Control.

7) TOSS-UP. 10 points.

Name the Akkadian ruler (c. 2334-2279 B.C.), who established the first empire in recorded history. The Akkadians conquered all of Mesopotamia and ruled from Persia to the Mediterranean.

Answer: Sargon the Great (also called Sargon of Akkad; his dynasty was Agade).

7) BONUS. 20 points. 5 points each.

Indicate whether each of the following is a metal or nonmetal.
1) Sodium
2) Calcium
3) Chlorine
4) Sulfur

Answer: 1) Metal
2) Metal
3) Nonmetal
4) Nonmetal.

8) TOSS-UP. 10 points.

What common word is also known as *aeroembolism, nitrogen narcosis, caisson disease,* and *decompression sickness*?

Answer: The bends or air bends (accept also the chokes or the staggers).

8) BONUS. 20 points. 5 points each.

Answer each of the following.
1) Between which 2 rivers was Philadelphia laid out?
2) Between which 2 lakes is Niagara Falls located?

Answer: 1) Delaware and Schuylkill rivers
2) Lake Ontario and Lake Erie.

9) TOSS-UP. 10 points.

Charles de Gaulle said, "Politics are too serious a matter to be left to the politicians"; Winston Churchill said, "Politics are almost as exciting as war, and quite as dangerous. In war you can only be killed once, but in politics many times." Which American humorist and social critic in *The Illiterate Digest* (1924) said, "All politics is apple sauce"?

Answer: Will Rogers.

9) BONUS. 20 points.

What is the sum of the coefficients and the constant term of the polynomial which is the product of x squared minus two x plus three and the polynomial x squared plus three x minus one?

Answer: Six (6).

10) TOSS-UP. 10 points.

In the following sentence, which punctuation mark is needed after *beef* to avoid a description of cannibalism? "PTA mothers eat roast beef children, chicken."

Answer: A semi-colon.

10) BONUS. 20 points after the first clue. 10 after the second.

Which gem am I?
1) The Romans called me "sapphire," the Egyptians used me in their jewelry, and I was the original pigment for ultramarine, a blue pigment used by artists in their paints.
2) I am a beautiful azure-blue mineral composed mainly of lazurite, a name by which I am sometimes called, and I am usually flecked with bright, shining spots of pyrite.

Answer: Lapis lazuli.

11) TOSS-UP. 10 points.

At which college, whose students are nicknamed the "Indians" or "The Tribe," did Phi Beta Kappa originate? Both Thomas Jefferson and James Monroe attended this college, which is the second oldest in the U.S. and is located in Williamsburg, Virginia.

Answer: William & Mary.

11) BONUS. 30 points. 10 points each.

Identify the state in which each of the following landmarks is located.
1) Will Rogers Memorial
2) Wadsworth-Longfellow House and Museum
3) George Rogers Clark Memorial

Answer: 1) Oklahoma
2) Maine
3) Indiana.

12) TOSS-UP. 10 points.

Name the proposal submitted to the United States Senate in 1860 just prior to the Civil War by a Kentucky senator in an attempt to prevent a split between slave and free states. This proposal to prohibit slavery north of the Missouri Compromise line of 36 degrees 30 minutes and to extend federal protection south of that line was rejected.

Answer: Crittenden Compromise.

12) BONUS. 30 points. 10 points each.

Identify each of the following concerning a U.S. spy plane shot down over the Soviet Union in 1960.
1) The American President in office at the time
2) The soviet leader who met with the President in Paris shortly thereafter
3) The month in which it occurred

Answers: 1) Dwight D. Eisenhower
        2) Nikita Khrushchev
        3) May (1).

13) TOSS-UP. 10 points.

Give the full name of the organization known as the KKK.

Answer: Ku Klux Klan.

13) BONUS. 20 points. 5 points each.

Identify the author of each of the following Victorian novels.
1) *Hard Times*
2) *Middlemarch*
3) *Jude the Obscure*
4) *Wuthering Heights*

Answer: 1) Charles Dickens
        2) George Eliot
        3) Thomas Hardy
        4) Emily Brontë.

14) TOSS-UP. 10 points.

Which U.S. state consists of 2 separate land areas, the Upper Peninsula and the Lower Peninsula?

Answer: Michigan.

14) BONUS. 20 points. 5 points each.

Identify each of the following concerning Abraham (originally called Abram), the "Father of Many Nations" and the founder of Judaism.
1) The name of the 2 cities which Abraham pleaded with God to save for the sake of the righteous people living there (all or nothing)
2) The name of Abraham's nephew who escaped from one of the 2 cities with his two daughters
3) The woman Abraham married after his first wife died

Answer: 1) Sodom and Gomorrah
**   2) Lot**
**   3) Keturah.**

15) TOSS-UP. 10 points.

A *trompe l'oeil* is literally "a trick of the eye." This phrase is used to describe a type of painting that creates a strong illusion or visual deception. Is the plural of this phrase *trompe les yeux, trompes l'oeil,* or *trompe l'oeils*?

Answer: *Trompe l'oeils*.

15) BONUS. 20 points. 5 points each.

Verbals are verb forms that do not serve as predicates. Name the 3 verbals, and identify the one which always functions as an adjective.

Answer: Participles, gerunds (accept verbal nouns), and infinitives / participle.

16) TOSS-UP. 10 points.

Which word is used to identify the English grammatical construction in which words are omitted but clearly understood as in the clause, "while waiting for my sister..."?

Answer: Elliptical (clause) or ellipsis.

16) BONUS. 20 points. 5 points each.

Identify these European leaders from their nicknames.
1) "The Iron Lady"
2) "The Florentine"
3) "The Man With the Iron Teeth"
4) *"Der Alte"*

Answer: 1) **Margaret Thatcher (or Gro Harlem Bruntland)**
2) **François Mitterrand**
3) **Mikhail Gorbachev**
4) **Konrad Adenauer.**

17) TOSS-UP. 10 points.

Of which state did Mario Cuomo become governor, or of which large city did Ed Koch became mayor?

Answer: New York.

17) BONUS. 20 points. 5 points each.

Identify each of the following concerning New York.
1) The capital
2) New Netherland's last Dutch governor, also known as "Old Silver Nails"
3) The battle which started on October 7, 1777, and ended on October 18 with the surrender of General John Burgoyne
4) The location of the oldest military college in the U.S.

Answer: 1) **Albany**
2) **Peter Stuyvesant**
3) **Saratoga**
4) **West Point (U.S. Military Academy).**

18) TOSS-UP. 10 points.

Identify the German leader responsible for the start of the Reformation in the 16th century in the town of Wittenberg.

Answer: Martin Luther.

18) BONUS. 20 points. 5 points each.

Identify each of the following.
1) The number of *Theses* Martin Luther posted on the door of the Castle church in Wittenberg
2) The year in which he posted the *Theses*
3) The Pope who excommunicated Martin Luther in 1521
4) The city in which Charles V, emperor of the Holy Roman Empire, ordered Luther to appear before a *diet*, or assembly, of princes and clergymen

Answer: 1) 95
        2) 1517
        3) Pope Leo X
        4) Worms.

19) TOSS-UP. 10 points.

Who is the author of *Little Dorrit?*

Answer: Charles Dickens.

19) BONUS. 20 points. 5 points each.

Identify each of the following.
1) The work featuring Little Nell and the author of this work
2) The work featuring Little Eva, a saintly child whose full name is
Evangeline St. Clair, and the author of this work

Answer: 1) *The Old Curiosity Shop* **by Charles Dickens**
        2) *Uncle Tom's Cabin* **by Harriet Beecher Stowe.**

20) TOSS-UP. 10 points.

Which type of cell contains a nucleus, a plasma membrane, a large
central vacuole, a cell wall, mitochondria, chloroplasts, and cytoplasm?

Answer: Plant cell.

20) BONUS. 15 points. 5 points each.

Give the activity associated with each of these organelles in plant
cells.
1) Chloroplast
2) Mitochondrion
3) Ribosome

Answer: 1) Photosynthesis
        **2) Respiration—energy release (or ATP Produc-
tion)**
        3) Protein synthesis.

21) TOSS-UP. 10 points.

Identify the Italian city known as the "Queen of the Adriatic" or the
"Mistress of the Adriatic."

Answer: Venice.

21) BONUS. 20 points. 5 points each.

Identify each of the following.
1) The Saskatchewan city known as the "Queen City of the Plains"
2) The Canadian province off whose coast are the Queen Charlotte Islands
3) The continent on which Queensland, the second largest state, is located
4) The continent on which the Queen Maud Mountain Range is located south of the Ross Ice Shelf

Answer: 1) Regina
          2) British Columbia
          3) Australia
          4) Antarctica.

22) TOSS-UP. 10 points.

The cube root of the square root of 2 is the same as 2 raised to what power?

Answer: One-sixth (⅙).

22) BONUS. 30 points. 10 points each.

Give an alternate name for each of the following Civil War battles.
1) Sharpsburg
2) (First and Second) Manassas
3) Henrico, King's School House, The Orchards, or French's Field

Answer: 1) Antietam
          2) (First and Second) Bull Run
          3) Oak Grove.

23) TOSS-UP. 10 points.

Which axiom of basic algebra justifies that $2a + 7a = 9a$? Is it associativity, commutativity, or distributivity?

Answer: Distributivity.

23) BONUS. 20 points. 5 points each.

Decode each of the following acronyms or initialisms.
1) COBOL
2) ALGOL
3) BASIC
4) ASCII

Answer: 1) **Common (Ordinary) Business Oriented Language**
2) **Algebraically Oriented Language**
3) **Beginners All-Purpose Symbolic Instruction Code**
4) **American Standard Code for Information Interchange.**

24) TOSS-UP. 10 points.

In which city is the Whitney Museum of American Art located?

Answer: New York City.

24) BONUS. 30 points. 10 points each.

Identify each of the following concerning Cadmus, the Phoenician prince in Greek mythology.
1) The phrase used figuratively to mean "to plant seeds of strife; to stir up trouble, especially by peaceful intent," a phrase coming from the action of Cadmus in following the advice of Athena
2) The name of the city Cadmus founded with the help of the five warriors who remained after the wild fight which developed from Athena's directive
3) The daughter of Aphrodite and Ares whom Zeus gave Cadmus for his queen, or the object Aphrodite gave his bride to keep her young and beautiful which brought disaster in a later generation

Answer: 1) **"Sow dragon's teeth"**
2) **Thebes**
3) **Harmonia, or a (magic) necklace (or robe).**

25) TOSS-UP. 10 points.

What name is given to the political entity ruled by German kings from 962, when King Otto I became Emperor, until 1806 when Francis renounced the title?

Answer: Holy Roman Empire.

25) BONUS. 20 points. 5 points each.

Identify each of the following.
1) The Holy Rood
2) The Holy Father
3) The Holy Wars
4) The Holy See

Answer: 1) **The cross upon which Jesus was crucified**
2) **The Pope**
3) **The Crusades**
4) **The position (accept authority, jurisdiction, or court) of the Pope.**

CATEGORY TOSS-UP. 100 points. 10 points each. 10 points deducted for an incorrect answer.

The Greek prefix *epi-* means "at, on, upon, among, before, after, besides, over." For each of the following definitions, give the English word which contains this Greek prefix.

1) A short poem, often satirical, expressing a single thought with terseness and wit; any witty, clever, or pointed statement tersely expressed
2) A brief poem or statement commemorating a deceased person; an inscription on a tombstone or monument in memory of the person buried there
3) A word or phrase applied to characterize the nature of a person or thing; a descriptive name or title; a word or phrase used disparagingly as a term of abuse or contempt
4) A summary or condensed statement, especially of a book, article, report, etc.; a representative of an entire class or type
5) A song or poem in honor of a bride and bridegroom; a nuptial song or poem
6) A concluding part added to a literary work, as a novel, play, or long poem; a short speech or poem delivered by one of the actors at the end of a play
7) A chronic disease of the nervous system characterized by convulsive attacks, usually with loss of consciousness
8) The outermost layer of the skin
9) A branch of philosophy that investigates the origin, nature, methods, and limits of knowledge
10) The lidlike piece of plastic cartilage at the base of the tongue that prevents food and drink from entering the larynx during swallowing

Answer: 1) **Epigram**
2) **Epitaph**
3) **Epithet**
4) **Epitome**
5) **Epithalmion (or epithalmium)**

6) **Epilogue (or epilog)**
7) **Epilepsy (or epilepsia)**
8) **Epidermis**
9) **Epistemology**
10) **Epiglottis.**

ROUND TWENTY-FOUR

1) TOSS-UP. 10 points.

Which book of the Bible includes the verse, "He that troubleth his own house shall inherit the wind: and the fool shall be servant to the wise of heart"?

Answer: Proverbs (11:29).

1) BONUS. 20 points. 10 points each.

In which roles did Fredric March and Spencer Tracy debate the theory of evolution in Stanley Kramer's 1960 film based on Lawrence and Lee's play *Inherit the Wind*?

Answer: William Jennings Bryan and Clarence Seward Darrow.

2) TOSS-UP. 10 points.

What is the ten-thousandths digit of the decimal expression for one-eleventh?

Answer: 9.

2) BONUS. 20 points. 5 points each.

The International System of Units (SI) was adopted in 1960. What are the base SI units for each of the following?
1) Length
2) Mass
3) Temperature
4) Electric current

Answer: 1) Meters (m)
2) Kilograms (Kg)
3) Kelvin (K) or Celsius (C)
4) Amperes.

3) TOSS-UP. 10 points.

Which words based on Isaiah 2:4 make up the motto of the United Nations?

Answer: "We Shall (Let Us) Beat Our Swords Into Plough-shares."

3) BONUS. 20 points. 5 points each.

Name 4 of the first 5 Secretaries-General of the United Nations.

Answer: Trygve Lie, Dag Hammarskjöld, U Thant, Kurt Waldheim, and Javier Pérez de Cuéllar.

4) TOSS-UP. 10 points.

What name is given to the gigantic statue of Apollo (Helios) set at the entrance to the harbor of Rhodes?

Answer: Colossus (of Rhodes).

4) BONUS. 20 points. 5 points each.

Identify each of the following.
1) The island on which the Statue of Liberty is located in New York Harbor
2) The country in which the statue of the Great Buddha is located at Kamakura
3) The city in which the colossal statue called *Christ the Redeemer* is atop Corcovado Mountain
4) The countries on whose boundary stands the gigantic statue called *Christ of the Andes*

Answer: 1) Liberty Island
2) Japan
3) Rio de Janeiro (Brazil)
4) Chile and Argentina.

5) TOSS-UP. 10 points.

What is the remainder when x cubed plus three x squared minus two x plus 7 is divided by x plus one?

Answer: Eleven (11).

5) BONUS. 15 points. 5 points each.

If f of x equals x cubed minus two x squared plus three x minus one, what is each of the following?
1) f of zero
2) f of one
3) f of minus one

Answer: 1) **Negative one**
2) **One**
3) **Negative seven.**

6) TOSS-UP. 10 points.

Name the first book both written and printed in the English colonies of America. It was printed in the Massachusetts Bay Colony in 1640.

Answer: *The Bay Psalm Book* (accept *The Book of Psalms*).

6) BONUS. 20 points. 5 points each.

Identify each of the following writers.
1) The first American to make a living as a professional writer, the author of *A History of New York by Diedrich Knickerbocker*
2) The American writer who wrote *Wieland: or The Transformation*, considered to be the first American (Gothic) novel
3) The American who wrote the first detective story, "The Murders in the Rue Morgue"
4) The American considered this country's first important naturalistic writer, the author of *The Octopus* and *The Pit*

Answer: 1) **Washington Irving**
2) **Charles Brockden Brown**
3) **Edgar Allan Poe**
4) **Frank Norris.**

7) TOSS-UP. 20 points after the first clue. 10 after the second.

Which disease am I?
1) I am a disease genetically transmitted through females, although I usually affect only males, and I am called the "King's Disease."
2) I am a disorder in which poor clotting ability of the blood results in excessive bleeding.

Answer: **Hemophilia.**

7) BONUS. 20 points. 5 points each.

Spell the words *hemophilia, hemoglobin, hemorrhage,* and *hemorrhoids.*

Answer: H-E-M-O-P-H-I-L-I-A / H-E-M-O-G-L-O-B-I-N / H-E-M-O-R-R-H-A-G-E / H-E-M-O-R-R-H-O-I-D-S.

8) TOSS-UP. 10 points.

Of which country was Kurt Waldheim elected president in 1986?

Answer: Austria.

8) BONUS. 20 points. 5 points each.

Identify the following, each of which begins with the letter *E.*
1) The day in April set aside to dramatize the need for pollution control
2) The French phrase for "water of Cologne"
3) The Old Testament book supposedly written by Solomon
4) The small Alpine plant whose name in German means "noble white"

Answer: 1) Earth Day
    2) *Eau de Cologne*
    3) Ecclesiastes
    4) Edelweiss.

9) TOSS-UP. 10 points.

In which square were hundreds, possibly thousands, killed as troops retook the center of Beijing (or Peking) from pro-democracy demonstrators on June 4, 1989?

Answer: Tiananmen Square.

9) BONUS. 20 points. 5 points each.

Identify each of the following.
1) The leader whose body lies in state inside a crystal sarcophagus in Beijing
2) The name given to the 6,000-mile, year-long march on which this leader led the Communists in 1934
3) The name of this leader's 1958 low-budget modernization crash program that failed
4) The name of this leader's wife from 1939 to 1976

Answer: 1) Mao Tse-tung
       2) The Long March
       3) The Great Leap Forward
       4) Jiang Qing (Chiang Ch'ing).

10) TOSS-UP. 10 points.

Which Southern state, the home of Mammoth Springs and the world-famous health center at Hot Springs, is known as the "Land of Opportunity"?

Answer: Arkansas.

10) BONUS. 20 points. 5 points each.

Identify each of the following concerning Arkansas.
1) The capital
2) The English translation of the state motto *Regnat Populus*
3) The building after which the state capital building is modeled
4) The park in the state capital which honors the commander of Allied forces in the Southwest Pacific during WWII

Answer: 1) Little Rock
       2) "The People Rule"
       3) The U.S. Capitol in Washington, D.C.
       4) MacArthur Park.

11) TOSS-UP. 10 points.

Identify the famous indoor sports and entertainment arena completed in 1968 and located at 4 Pennsylvania Plaza in New York City.

Answer: Madison Square Garden.

11) BONUS. 20 points. 5 points each.

Identify each of the following concerning New York City.
1) The names of its 2 major league baseball teams
2) The names of the 2 NFL teams with New York in their names
3) The names of its 2 NHL teams
4) The name of its 1 NBA team

Answer: 1) Yankees (AL) and Mets (NL)
       2) Jets (AC) and Giants (NC)
       3) Islanders and Rangers
       4) Knickerbockers (Knicks).

12) TOSS-UP. 10 points.

Which character in which Shakespearean play says, "Out, damned spot! out, I say!"

Answer: Lady Macbeth in *Macbeth*.

12) BONUS. 20 points. 10 points each.

Name the character whose ghost appears to Macbeth, and then name the aged king of Scotland murdered by Macbeth.

Answer: Banquo / Duncan.

13) TOSS-UP. 10 points.

In 1950 he proposed that comets originate in a vast cloud of material orbiting the sun in a huge asteroid belt at about a light year away. Is this Dutch astronomer named Van Gogh, De Hooch, Oort, or Delft?

Answer: (Jan Hendrik) Oort.

13) BONUS. 20 points. 5 points each.

Identify each of the following.
1) The U.S.'s first reusable spacecraft
2) The shuttle that made its maiden flight in October 1985
3) The rocket used by the European Space Agency
4) The country in which the European Space Operations Center is located

Answer: 1) *Columbia*
2) *Atlantis*
3) *Ariane*
4) Germany (in Darmstadt).

14) TOSS-UP. 10 points.

Identify the Saskatchewan city whose original name, Pile o' Bones, was changed in 1882 to honor Queen Victoria of England.

Answer: Regina.

14) BONUS. 20 points. 5 points each.

Identify each of the following.
1) The Canadian province whose capital is Victoria
2) The British Crown Colony whose capital is Victoria

3) The African country that consists of about 100 islands in the Indian Ocean and whose capital is Victoria

4) The country in which Victoria is the smallest mainland state in area

Answer: 1) British Columbia
2) Hong Kong
3) Seychelles
4) Australia.

15) TOSS-UP. 10 points.

What is the geometric term for the set of points at a given distance from a given point in a plane?

Answer: Circle.

15) BONUS. 25 points. 5 points each.

Give the mathematical term beginning with the letter C for each of the following.
1) A rectangular solid with square faces
2) A number or letter placed before an algebraic expression to show that the expression is to be multiplied by that factor
3) The relationship meaning "and" in symbolic logic
4) A segment joining 2 points on a circle
5) A drawing made with only a compass and a straightedge

Answer: 1) Cube
2) Coefficient
3) Conjunction
4) Chord
5) Construction.

16) TOSS-UP. 10 points.

Identify the New York museum that is the world's largest natural history museum.

Answer: American Museum of Natural History.

16) BONUS. 20 points. 5 points each.

Identify each of the following concerning New York City.
1) The unusual circular museum designed by Frank Lloyd Wright

2) The branch of the Metropolitan Museum devoted to art of the Middle Ages and designed like a medieval monastery
3) The museum on W. 53rd Street featuring contemporary art
4) The museum on Madison Avenue at 75th Street featuring 20th-century American artists

Answer: 1) Guggenheim Museum
         2) The Cloisters
         3) Museum of Modern Art
         4) Whitney Museum.

17) TOSS-UP. 10 points.

What name is given to the belief that monarchs are responsible not to their subjects but to God alone?

Answer: Divine right of kings.

17) BONUS. 20 points. 5 points each.

Identify the royal family to which each of the following belongs.
1) Henry VIII (1509-1547)
2) Anne (1702-1714)
3) Victoria (1837-1901)
4) George V (1917-1936)

Answer: 1) Tudor
         2) Stuart
         3) Hanover
         4) Windsor.

18) TOSS-UP. 10 points.

Who is known as the spiritual ruler of the Roman Catholic Church?

Answer: The Pope (accept Bishop of Rome).

18) BONUS. 20 points. 5 points each.

Identify each of the following.
1) The palace in which the Pope lives
2) The independent state in which the Pope lives
3) The Pope's personal bodyguard
4) The treaty that established the sovereignty of the independent state in 1929

Answer: 1) Vatican Palace

2) **Vatican City**
3) **Swiss Guard**
4) **Lateran Treaty.**

19) TOSS-UP. 10 points.

Which U.S. state's plains near Yucca Flat have served as a testing ground for nuclear devices?

Answer: Nevada's.

19) BONUS. 15 points. 5 points each.

Name the 3 parts of the U.S. nuclear triad.

Answer: Land-based ICBM's, airborne bombers, and submarine-based missiles.

20) TOSS-UP. 10 points.

By which name is the Minnesota Mining and Manufacturing Corporation better known?

Answer: 3M.

20) BONUS. 20 points. 5 points each.

Give the letter which identifies each of the following.
1) Hester Prynne's scarlet letter
2) The letter that stands for 500 in Roman numerals
3) The letter for an absolute temperature scale with the zero point comparable to –273.16 Celsius
4) The title of the 1969 Oscar-winner for Best Foreign Film, a movie based on a real political assassination

Answer: 1) A
        2) D
        3) K (for Kelvin) or R (for Rankine)
        4) Z.

21) TOSS-UP. 10 points.

Which term is used to designate a male horse whose reproductive organs have been removed, thus prohibiting it from breeding?

Answer: Gelding.

21) BONUS. 20 points. 5 points each.

Give the country of origin of each of the following horses or ponies.
1) Appaloosa
2) Clydesdale
3) Welsh Pony
4) Percheron

Answer: 1) United States
          2) Scotland
          3) Wales
          4) France.

22) TOSS-UP. 10 points.

Which state, 6th in size among all states and 3rd in size among southwestern states, has the 3rd largest Indian population in the U.S.? Only California and Oklahoma have more Indians.

Answer: Arizona.

22) BONUS. 20 points. 5 points each.

Identify each of the following concerning Arizona.
1) The capital
2) The postal abbreviation
3) The largest Indian tribe in Arizona
4) The 2nd largest city in population

Answer: 1) Phoenix
          2) AZ
          3) Navajo
          4) Tucson.

23) TOSS-UP. 10 points.

In thermodynamics, another name for heat content is enthalpy. What symbol is used to show a change in enthalpy?

Answer: Delta H (Δ H).

23) BONUS. 20 points. 5 points each.

Identify the following, each of which begins with the letter D.
1) The German word for Germany
2) The figurative phrase for a burial at sea

3) The record of a survey of English lands made by order of William the Conqueror in 1086

4) The name for a discus thrower in ancient Greece or Rome, or the name for the statue of a discus thrower by Myron in the 400's B.C.

Answer: 1) *Deutschland*
2) **Deep six**
3) **Domesday Book**
4) **Discobolus.**

24) TOSS-UP. 10 points.

Which element in the Inert or Noble Gas family violates the octet rule?

Answer: Helium.

24) BONUS. 20 points.

What is the density of a liquid if 30 milliliters has a mass of 20 grams?

Answer: 0.66 grams per milliliter (or .667 or 2 / 3 grams per milliliter).

25) TOSS-UP. 10 points.

In which Scandinavian country does its parliament, the *Folketing*, hold sessions in the Christiansborg Palace?

Answer: Denmark.

25) BONUS. 20 points. 5 points each.

Identify each of the following concerning Denmark.
1) The capital
2) The official language
3) The basic monetary unit
4) The famous amusement park located in the capital

Answer: 1) **Copenhagen**
2) **Danish**
3) **Krone**
4) **Tivoli Gardens.**

CATEGORY TOSS-UP. 100 points. 10 points each. 10 points deducted for an incorrect answer.

Identify each of the following concerning the biblical account of the crucifixion.
1) The full name of the disciple who betrayed Jesus (Matthew 26:14, 28)
2) The garden in which he betrayed Jesus (Matthew 26:36)
3) The manner in which he identified Jesus to the soldiers, an action which led ultimately to Jesus' death by crucifixion
4) The phrase associated with this incident which means "a sign of betrayal or duplicity; an act which appears friendly, but is one of insincerity"
5) The amount of money he received for his actions, money which he returned to the chief priests of Jerusalem
6) The "burial ground for paupers or strangers" located in the Valley of Hinnom and bought by the chief priests with the money that the "traitor" returned to them (Matthew 27:7)
7) The name for "any place of great carnage and bloodshed" from the Aramaic for "field of blood," a name also given to the "burial ground for paupers or strangers" outside Jerusalem (Acts 1:18, 19)
8) The tree from which, according to legend, the "traitor" hanged himself
9) The full name for "a peephole or small window, as in the door of a prison cell"
10) The exclamation of exasperation or disgust which today uses this "traitor's" name, an exclamation which is a euphemism for Jesus Christ

Answer: 1) **Judas Iscariot**
2) **Garden of Gethsemane**
3) **A kiss**
4) **Judas kiss**
5) **30 pieces of silver**
6) **Potter's field**
7) **Aceldama (Akeldama)**
8) **Judas tree (*Cercis siliquastrum*, or *Cercis canadensis*, the American Judas tree)**
9) **Judas window (or hole or slits)**
10) **Judas Priest.**

ROUND TWENTY-FIVE

1) TOSS-UP. 10 points.

In which novel by which author does Tom forget his former love, Amy Lawrence, when he sees the "lovely little blue-eyed creature with yellow hair" named Becky Thatcher?

Answer: *The Adventures of Tom Sawyer* by Mark Twain (Samuel Langhorne Clemens).

1) BONUS. 30 points. 10 points each.

Identify each of the following Toms.
1) The Thomas who wrote *The Imitation of Christ*
2) The Thomas who was brutally murdered in the Canterbury cathedral in 1170
3) The Thomas who wrote *The Black Rose* and *The Silver Chalice*

Answer: 1) Thomas à Kempis
2) St. Thomas à Becket
3) Thomas Costain.

2) TOSS-UP. 10 points.

Name the only non-metallic element that is a liquid at room temperature under ordinary conditions.

Answer: Bromine.

2) BONUS. 20 points. 5 points each.

Does the last electron in each of the following go into an $s, p, d,$ or f orbital?
1) Boron
2) Sodium
3) Iron
4) Silicon

Answer: 1) p
2) s
3) d
4) p.

3) TOSS-UP. 10 points.

In which country did French armies establish the Helvetic Republic in 1798 during the French Revolution?

Answer: Switzerland.

3) BONUS. 15 points. 5 points each.

Identify the country in which each of the following took place.
1) The Boxer Rebellion in 1899-1900
2) The Sepoy Rebellion or Sepoy Mutiny in 1857-1858
3) The Rebellion of 1837-1838, an attempt to limit harsh British rule

Answer: 1) China
2) India (also called the Indian Mutiny)
3) Canada.

4) TOSS-UP. 10 points.

Which U.S. state is known as the "Old Dominion," so named by King Charles II because it remained loyal to the crown during the English Civil War of the 17th century?

Answer: Virginia.

4) BONUS. 20 points. 5 points each.

Identify each of the following U.S. states from the nickname.
1) Old Line State
2) Old Man of the Mountain State
3) Old North State
4) Old Colony State

Answer: 1) Maryland
2) New Hampshire
3) North Carolina
4) Massachusetts.

5) TOSS-UP. 10 points.

What is the area of a trapezoid with a height of 4 units and bases of lengths 6 units and 8 units?

Answer: 28 square units.

5) BONUS. 20 points. 5 points each.

In each of the following pairs, select the geometric figure with the greater area.
1) A square of side 2 cm or an equilateral triangle of side 2 cm
2) A square of side 2 cm or a circle of radius 2 cm
3) A regular hexagon of side 2 cm or a right triangle with legs of 4 cm and 5 cm
4) A circle inscribed in a square of side 2 cm or a circle circumscribed about a square of side 2 cm

Answer: 1) Square of side 2 cm
2) Circle of radius 2 cm
3) Regular hexagon of side 2 cm
4) Circle circumscribed about the square of side 2 cm.

6) TOSS-UP. 10 points.

Identify the ancient Roman poet who wrote *Metamorphoses*, a collection of tales about mythological, legendary, and historical figures.

Answer: Ovid.

6) BONUS. 20 points. 10 points each.

Identify each of the following concerning Ovid.
1) Ovid's most famous work, *Art of* _____
2) The translation of the title *Metamorphoses*

Answer: 1) *Love*
2) *Transformations*.

7) TOSS-UP. 10 points.

What color is called *cyan*?

Answer: (Greenish) blue.

7) BONUS. 15 points. 5 points each.

Identify each of the following.
1) The bluish coloration of the skin, caused by a lack of oxygen in the blood
2) The color of magenta
3) The country in which Magenta, site of an 1859 battle, is located

Answer: 1) **Cyanosis**
2) **(Purplish-)red**
3) **Italy.**

8) TOSS-UP. 10 points.

Name the judicial organ of the United Nations.

Answer: International Court of Justice, or the World Court.

8) BONUS. 20 points. 5 points each.

Identify each of the following concerning the World Court.
1) The city and country in which it is located
2) The number of judges and the length of the term to which they are elected by the General Assembly and the Security Council

Answer: 1) **The Hague in the Netherlands**
2) **15 judges elected to 9-year terms.**

9) TOSS-UP. 15 points.

Which prison in which city was stormed by a revolutionary mob on July 14, 1789? This prison stood as a hated symbol of the oppression of the people of the country.

Answer: Bastille in Paris.

9) BONUS. 15 points. 5 points each.

Identify each of the following.
1) The country in which the Soviet Union used military force to put down a revolt and restore "socialist order" in 1956
2) The country in which the Soviet Union used military force to put down a revolt and restore "socialist order" in 1968
3) The German city in which the Beer Hall Putsch was unsuccessful on November 8, 1923

Answer: 1) **Hungary**
2) **Czechoslovakia**
3) **Munich.**

10) TOSS-UP. 10 points.

Which civil rights organization is known by the initials NAACP?

Answer: National Association for the Advancement of Colored People.

10) BONUS. 20 points. 5 points each.

Identify each of the following.
1) The consumer organization whose initials are BBB
2) The civil rights organization whose initials are NOW
3) The college organization whose initials are NCAA
4) The sports organization known as the AAU

Answer: 1) Better Business Bureau
2) National Organization for Women
3) National Collegiate Athletic Association
4) Amateur Athletic Union.

11) TOSS-UP. 10 points.

In which city were the 1988 Summer Olympic Games held on the Han River?

Answer: Seoul (South Korea).

11) BONUS. 20 points. 5 points each.

Identify the New York boroughs in which the following are located.
1) La Guardia Field and John F. Kennedy Airport
2) St. George and the Ferry Terminal
3) Central Park
4) Bedford-Stuyvesant

Answer: 1) Queens
2) Staten Island
3) Manhattan
4) Brooklyn.

12) TOSS-UP. 10 points.

Who is known as the "Father of English History"? He is the author of *Ecclesiastical History of the English Nation.*

Answer: The Venerable Bede.

12) BONUS. 30 points. 10 points each.

Identify each of the following "fathers."
1) The "Father of English Poetry" and author of the *Canterbury Tales*
2) The "Father of Angling" and author of *The Compleat Angler*
3) The "Father of History" and author of 9 books on the Persian Empire

Answer: 1) Geoffrey Chaucer
2) Izaak Walton
3) Herodotus.

13) TOSS-UP. 20 points after the first clue. 10 after the second.

What's my name?
1) I am both a New York city on the Hudson and the site of a famous war in an ancient Phrygian city in Asia Minor, present day Turkey.
2) I am a system of weights used for gold, silver, and precious gems.

Answer: Troy.

13) BONUS. 20 points. 5 points each.

Identify each of the following.
1) The number of ounces in 16 drams
2) The number of pounds in 32 ounces
3) The number of hundredweights in 300 pounds
4) The number of tons in 8,000 pounds

Answer: 1) 2 ounces
2) 2 pounds
3) 3 hundredweights
4) 4 tons.

14) TOSS-UP. 10 points.

Identify the African country called the Gold Coast until Britain gave it independence in 1957.

Answer: Ghana.

14) BONUS. 20 points. 10 points each.

Of which African "Coast" is Abidjan the capital, and which "Coast" was an African region noted for piracy?

Answer: Ivory Coast / Barbary Coast.

15) TOSS-UP. 10 points.

Identify the popular Gilbert & Sullivan musical from which this quotation is derived: "I'm very well acquainted too with matters mathematical, / I understand equations, both simple and quad-

ratical, / About binomial theorem I'm teeming with a lot of news—
/ With many cheerful facts about the square of the hypotenuse."

Answer: *The Pirates of Penzance.*

15) BONUS. 20 points. 5 points each.

Work or identify each of the following.
1) Solve the "simple" equation $x + 4 = 6$.
2) Solve the quadratic equation x squared $= 4$.
3) Name the triangle frequently used as an aid in determining the coefficients of the terms in a binomial expansion.
4) Name the father of this theorem: The square of the hypotenuse of a right triangle equals the sum of the squares of the other 2 sides.

Answer: 1) $x = 2$
           2) $x = 2$ and -2
           3) **Pascal's Triangle**
           4) **Pythagoras.**

16) TOSS-UP. 10 points.

Which building houses the New York Philharmonic and the Metropolitan Opera?

Answer: Lincoln Center for the Performing Arts.

16) BONUS. 20 points. 5 points each.

Identify each of the following concerning New York City.
1) Either one of the 2 major railroad stations
2) The famous concert hall near Central Park
3) The largest museum
4) The world's largest cathedral

Answer: 1) **Grand Central Station or Pennsylvania Station**
           2) **Carnegie Hall**
           3) **Metropolitan Museum of Art**
           4) **Episcopal Cathedral of Saint John the Divine.**

17) TOSS-UP. 10 points.

What is the role of a Queen if she is called the *queen regnant*?

Answer: She is ruling in her own right (not to be confused with *queen regent*, who rules in behalf of another).

17) BONUS. 20 points. 5 points each.

Identify the specific title for each of the following.
1) The wife of a reigning king
2) The widow of a king
3) The mother of a ruling monarch
4) The husband of a reigning queen

Answer: 1) Queen consort
2) Queen dowager
3) Queen mother
4) Prince consort.

18) TOSS-UP. 10 points.

Whom was Jesus describing in Matthew 16:18 when He said, "and upon this rock I will build my church"?

Answer: Peter.

18) BONUS. 30 points. 10 points each.

Identify each of the following concerning the Pope.
1) The word defined as "incapable of error in defining doctrines of faith and morals," used to describe the nature of the Pope's authority
2) The Latin phrase for "from a position of authority," used to describe the Pope's authority in matters concerning faith and morals
3) The council called by the Pope to consider the worldwide Christian church, especially in regard to unity

Answer: 1) Infallible
2) *Ex cathedra*
3) Ecumenical council (accept Vatican council).

19) TOSS-UP. 10 points.

Fans of which fictional detective are known as the "Baker Street Irregulars"?

Answer: Sherlock Holmes.

19) BONUS. 15 points. 5 points each.

Identify each of the following.
1) Fans of which operetta creators are known as "Savoyards"?

2) Fans of which professional golfer are known as "Lee's Fleas"?

3) Fans of which professional golfer are known as "Arnie's Army"?

Answer: 1) Gilbert and Sullivan
2) Lee Trevino
3) Arnold Palmer.

20) TOSS-UP. 10 points.

In which novel by which author does Tom, an adopted baby boy, grow up to pursue his true love, Sophia Western?

Answer: *Tom Jones (The History of Tom Jones, a Foundling)* **by Henry Fielding.**

20) BONUS. 20 points. 5 points each.

Identify each of the following Toms.

1) The nursery rhyme Tom who "sings for his supper"

2) Thomas Hughes' fictional Tom who attended Rugby

3) The tiny knight in an old legend who lived in a gold palace, drove a coach drawn by 6 white mice, and was killed while fighting a spider

4) The nickname given to the Biblical person who wouldn't believe in Christ's resurrection until he saw the wounds from the crucifixion

Answer: 1) Little Tommy Tucker
2) Tom Brown (*Tom Brown's Schooldays*)
3) Tom Thumb
4) Doubting Thomas (also called Didymus).

21) TOSS-UP. 10 points.

What number is not in the domain of the function y equals one divided by x?

Answer: Zero (0).

21) BONUS. 20 points. 5 points each.

How many real number solutions does each of the following equations have?

1) x cubed minus x equals zero.

2) x squared plus two x plus ten equals zero.

3) five plus three equals four x.

4) two plus x equals x minus three.

Answer: 1) 3
           2) 0 (none)
           3) 1
           4) 0 (none).

22) TOSS-UP. 10 points.

What name is given to the year 46 B.C., the year to which Julius Caesar assigned 445 days in order to realign the calendar with the seasons?

Answer: The (Last) Year of Confusion (450 days according to some sources).

22) BONUS. 20 points. 5 points each.

Give the Latin words for 7th, 8th, 9th, and 10th.

Answer: *Septem, octo, novem,* and *decem* (as in SEPTEMber, OCTOber, NOVEMber, and DECEMber).

23) TOSS-UP. 10 points.

What name is given to the interest rate that large commercial banks charge their very best customers for commercial and industrial loans?

Answer: Prime rate.

23) BONUS. 20 points. 5 points each.

Identify the following, each of which contains the word *green*.
1) The legal-tender note issued by the U.S. government
2) The inflated price paid by a company for the corporate raider's stock in order to avoid a takeover by the raider
3) The dramatic increase in production of food grains due to the introduction of high-yielding varieties
4) The British word for a retailer of fresh vegetables and fruit

**Answer: 1) Greenback
           2) Greenmail
           3) Green revolution
           4) Greengrocer.**

24) TOSS-UP. 10 points.

Which New England state did George Washington refer to as the "Provision State" because of the large quantities of supplies it provided to the Colonial Army during the Revolutionary War?

Answer: Connecticut.

24) **BONUS. 15 points. 5 points each.**

Identify each of the following concerning Connecticut.
1) The capital
2) The state song
3) The name for the public park in the center of many towns in the state

Answer: 1) Hartford
2) "Yankee Doodle"
3) Green.

25) **TOSS-UP. 10 points.**

Give the meaning of the acronym AIDS.

Answer: Acquired Immune Deficiency Syndrome.

25) **BONUS. 20 points. 5 points each.**

Identify the following, each of which begins with the letter *A*.
1) The older brother of Moses and the first high priest of the Israelites
2) The French phrase for "down with" as "down with the king"
3) A slaughterhouse
4) The monastery where monks live a religious life under an abbot's rule

Answer: 1) Aaron
2) *A bas* (*à bas le roi*)
3) Abattoir
4) Abbey.

CATEGORY TOSS-UP. 100 points. 10 points each. 10 points deducted for an incorrect answer.

Identify each of the following baseball greats.
1) The "Georgia Peach" with a .367 lifetime batting average and 4,191 hits
2) The "Gray Eagle" who threw out a record 35 runners from center field
3) The "Yankee Clipper" who hit safely in a record 56 successive games

4) The "Big Train" who struck out 3,508 and had 110 shutouts
5) The "Ol' Perfessor" who led the Yankees to 7 world championships in 12 years
6) The "Tall Tactician" who managed the A's for 50 years
7) The "Big Poison" with a .333 career batting average
8) The "Flying Dutchman" who won 8 batting titles and had a .327 career average
9) The "Fordham Flash" who managed the St. Louis Gashouse Gang
10) The "Big Six" who had three successive 30-game victory seasons (1903-1905)

Answer: 1) Ty Cobb
        2) Tris Speaker
        3) Joe DiMaggio
        4) Walter Johnson
        5) Casey Stengel
        6) Connie Mack
        7) Paul Waner
        8) Honus Wagner
        9) Frankie Frisch
        10) Christy Mathewson.

INDEX

Pascal, Blaise, 26, 150
Passion Sunday, 100
Passover, 208
Paton, Alan Stewart, 108
Patton, George S., 109
Pauley Pavilion, 2
Pauling, Linus, 120, 197
Pavlov, Ivan Petrovich, 25
Pavlova, Anna, 109, 185
Peace Corps, 250
Peace Palace, 8, 216
Peace and Freedom Party, 169
Peach melba, 125
Pearl Harbor, 20
Pebble Beach Golf Links, 92
Pebble Beach, California, 92
Peck, 63
Peking Convention, 143
Peking Man, 112
Peking, China, 52
Pelican, 247
Península Valdés, 133
Pennsylvania Station, 309
Pentagon Papers, 43
Pentagon, The, 227
Pentateuch, 44
Pepys, Samuel, 59
Percheron, 300
Periodic table, 143
Perkins, Frances, 236
Perrault, Charles, 160
Perry, Commodore, 100
Persia, 279-280
Persian Gulf, 30, 35, 30
Persians, 146
Pertussis, 162
Peru, 142, 219, 255
Peruggia, Vicenzo, 110
Pétain, Henri Philippe, 131, 175
Peter I (the Great), 21
Peter Principle, 61-62
Peter the Hermit, 164-165
Peters Projection, 71
Peters, Arno, 71
Petersburg, Virginia, 72
Petty, Richard, 94
Pheidippides, 146
Phi Beta Kappa, 281
Philadelphia, Pennsylvania, 2-3, 84-85, 161, 175, 184, 280
Philip Augustus, 164-165
Philip VI, 85
Philippine Insurrection, 52
Philippines, 52
Phlegm, 161
Phoenix, Arizona, 189-190, 300
Photograph, 221
Phrases
    Accidental Presidents, 19
    Albatross around the neck, 34
    At the eleventh hour, 63-64
    Between a rock and a hard place, 119-120
    Black power, 61-62
    Building the World of Tomorrow, 69

Caesar's wife must be above suspicion, 141
Clean the Augean stables, 268
Davy Jones' Locker, 213
Dead Man's Hand, 93
Dead reckoning, 81
Deep six, 300-301
Distaff side, 271
Energy Turns the World, 69
Every Man a King, 9
Feet of clay, 228
Fourth Estate, 84
Fiddler's Green, 213
Green revolution, 312
Halcyon Period, 266
In God We Trust, 80
In deep water, 206
Ivory tower, 260
Joe Miller, A, 188
Journey to Canossa, 249
Judas kiss, 302
Judas Priest, 302
Liberty, Equality, Fraternity, 268
Like a cat on a hot tin roof, 34
Lone wolf, 38
Love conquers all, 135
Man in the Space Age, 69
Melting pot, 265
Not Quite Our Sort, 160
Peace Through Understanding, 69
Pecking order, 136
Peeping Tom, 218
Quaker guns, 170
Renaissance man, 221
Salt of the earth, 116
Sealed With A Kiss, 160
Share the Wealth, 9
Spear side, 271
Swap horses when crossing streams, 223
To be made a cat's paw of, 188
To bell the cat, 34
To pay the piper, 34
To pull one's chestnuts out of the fire, 188
Too Tacky For Words, 160
White Man's Burden, 257
Work Conquers All, 135
World of Rivers—Fresh Water as a Source of Life, The, 69
Young, Adaptable, Verbal, Intelligent and Successful, 160
Physicians Oath, 107
Picasso, Pablo, 111-112, 258
Pierce, Franklin, 183, 194
Pierre, South Dakota, 190
Piltdown Man, 131
Pinehurst Country Club, 92
Pinehurst, North Carolina, 92
Pinkerton, Allan, 246
Pitti Palace, 9
Pittsburgh, Pennsylvania, 153
Pizzaro, Francisco, 197
Planets
    Earth, 71, 173, 200
    Jupiter, 71, 126, 173, 220-221
    Mars, 71, 140